The Church, the People of God, with Ch[rist] in its midst, is pilgrimaging to the promi[sed] land, the parousia when sin and sor[row] will be no more and our total incorporation with our Risen Lord will find its fulfill- ment. As it journeys homeward, the Com- munity of Christ is sustained by the Eu- charist: the sacrament of salvation, the pasch of the Church.

This book sets out to give us a more inte- grated and total appreciation of the Eu- charist. Avoiding technical terminology as far as possible, it clarifies the biblical notions of salvation and the Church as a community. From this vantage point it proceeds to dwell on the transforming ef- fects of the Eucharist in the life of the Church. It probes the Scriptures and brings out their rich nuances; it sifts the extraordinary insights of the Eastern and Western Fathers; it brings the living tradi- tion of the Church into theological perspec- tive — and the modern reader is enabled to view the sacrament of salvation in a fresh and vital light.

The Church, journeying with and to the Lord, is ever deepening its consciousness of its mystery, reality and mission. At the very heart of all its activities stands the Bread of Life: everything flows from it, all life surges to it. For its perceptive and integrated vision of the Eucharist, this work of living theology merits attention. It de- serves to stand beside and complement Abbot Vonier's *Key to the Eucharist.*

AUTHOR

the Second Vatican Council d as editor of the Commen- ree *Perfectae Caritatis* (ed. collaborator on the Interna- ntary on the Constitution es, J.-M. R. Tillard, O.P. is several books, among them *Nous a Aimés, En Alliance Sacrement - Événement de Pastorale Mise en Question.* his Ph.D. in Rome and theological studies at Le r Tillard has held positions dogmatic and kerygmatic Dominican faculty of theo- logy and at the *Institut Sedes Sapientiae* in O'Harva and at the *Institut de Catéchèse* in Quebec. His work appears regularly in the *Nouvelle Revue Théologique de Lou- vain, La Vie Spirituelle* and the *Review for Religious.*

THE
EUCHARIST

alba house ▪ DIVISION OF THE SOCIETY OF ST. PAUL
STATEN ISLAND, N. Y. 10314

THE EUCHARIST

Pasch of God's People

J.M. R. Tillard, O.P.

Translated by Dennis L. Wienk

Original title: *L'Eucharistie, Pâue de l'Église*

published by Les Editions du Cerf

Nihil Obstat:

Myles M. Bourke, S.T.L. — Censor Librorum

Imprimatur:

✝ Terence J. Cooke, D.D., V.G.

New York, N.Y. — July 20, 1966

Library of Congress Catalog Number: 66-17219

Designed, printed and bound in the U.S.A. by the Pauline Fathers and Brothers of the Society of St. Paul at Staten Island, New York as a part of their communications apostolate.

CONTENTS

Contents 7

THE MOST FREQUENT
ABBREVIATIONS AND INITIALS

A.A.S. *Acta Apostolicae Sedis*, Rome, 1909.

AN *The Ante-Nicene Fathers*, eds. Alexander Roberts and James Donaldson, New York, 1926.

Anaphorae syriacae *Anaphorae syriacae quotquot adhuc repertae sunt cura Jnstituti Studiorum Orientalium editae et latine versae*, Pontificium Institutum Orientalium Studiorum, Roma, 1939.

Brightman F. Brightman, *Liturgies Eastern and Western, Being the Texts, Original or Translated, of the Principal Liturgies of the Church*, vol. I, *Eastern Liturgies*, Oxford, 1896.

B.T. *Bulletin Thomiste*, Le Saulchoir, Etiolles (S.-et-O.).

C.J.C. *Codex Juris Canonici Pii X Pontificis Maximi jussu digestus, Benedicti Papae XV auctoritate promulgatus*, Citta del Vaticano, 1917.

Coll. Mechl. *Collectanea Mechlinensia*, Malines.

C.S.C.O. *Corpus Scriptorum Christianorum Orientalium*, Louvain, 1903.

C.S.E.L. *Corpus Scriptorum Ecclesiasticorum Latinorum*, Vienne, 1866.

Denz. H. Denzinger, C. Bannwart, J. B. Umberg, C. Rahner, *Enchiridion Symbolorum definitionum et declarationum de rebus fidei et morum*, edit. 29, Freiburg im Breisgau, 1953.

Ephem. Theol. Lov. *Ephemerides Theologicae Lovaniensis*, Louvain.

FC   The Fathers of the Church, ed. Roy Joseph Deferrari, Washington, 1963.

G.C.S.   Die Griechischen Christlichen Schriftsteller der ersten drei Jahrhunderte, Berlin, 1897.

Greek Orth. Theol. Rev.   The Greek Orthodox Theological Review, New York.

Greg.   Gregorianum, Rome.

Harvey   W. W. Harvey, Sancti Jrenaei episcopi Lugdunensis libros quinque Adversus Haereses, 2 vol., Cambridge, 1857.

Journal of Bibl. Lit.   Journal of Biblical Literature, New Haven and Boston.

Journal of Theol. Stud.   Journal of Theological Studies, London and Oxford.

Kittel   See T.W.N.T.

Lum. et Vie   Lumière et Vie, Saint-Alban-Leysse, Lyon.

M.D.   La Maison-Dieu, Paris.

Mercenier-Paris   E. Mercenier et F. Paris, La prière des Eglises de rite byzantin, Chevetogne, 1937.

Mercier   B.-Ch. Mercier, La Liturgie de Saint-Jacques, édition critique du texte grec avec traduction latine, Patrologia orientalis, t. 26, Paris, 1950.

NPN   A Select Library of the Nicene and Post-Nicene Fathers of the Christian Church (1st series), ed. Philip Schaff, New York, 1886.
.... (2nd series), ed. Philip Schaff and Henry Wace, New York, 1892.

N. R. Théol.   Nouvelle Revue Théologique, Louvain.

Petit Paroissien   Petit Paroissien des Liturgies orientales, Harissa, 1941.

P.G.   Migne, Patrologia, series graeca.

P.L.   Migne, Patrologia, series latina.

P.O.   Patrologia Orientalis, ed. R. Graffin and F. Nau, Paris, 1907.

Q.L.P.   Les Questions Liturgiques et Paroissiales, Louvain.

Quasten J. Quasten, *Monumenta eucharistica et liturgica vetustissima*, Bonn, 1935. (*Florilegium patristicum*, 7)

R.B. *Revue Biblique*, Paris.

Rech. de Sc. Rel. *Recherches de Science Religieuse*, Paris.

Rev. de Théol. et de Philos. *Revue de Théologie et de Philosophie*, Lausanne.

Rev. d'Hist. Ecclés. *Revue d'Histoire Ecclésiastique*, Louvain.

Rev. Etud. Byzant. *Revue des Etudes Byzantines*, Paris.

Rev. Lit. et Monast. *Revue Liturgique et Monastique*, Maredsous.

R.S.P.T. *Revue des Sciences philosophiques et théologiques*, Paris.

R.T. *Revue Thomiste*, Paris.

R.T.A.M. *Recherches de Théologie ancienne et médiévale*, Louvain.

Sources chrét. *Sources chrétiennes*, sous la direction de H. de Lubac et J. Danielou, Paris.

Suppl. Dict. de la Bible *Dictionnaire de la Bible, Supplement*, Paris, 1920.

Texte und Unters. *Texte und Untersuchungen*, Leipzig and Berlin, 1882.

The Cath. Bibl. Quart. *The Catholic Biblical Quarterly*, Washington.

Theol. Quartalschr. *Theologische Quartalschrift*, Tubingen and Stuttgart.

Theol. Stud. *Theological Studies*, Woodstock.

T.W.N.T. *Theologisches Wörterbuch zum Neuen Testament*, hrsg. von G. Kittel, Stuttgart, 1933.

Tonneau-Devreesse R. Tonneau in collaboration with R. Devreesse, *Les Homélies Catéchetiques de Théodore de Mopsueste*, Citta del Vaticano, 1949 (*studi e Testi*, 145).

Vie Spir. *La Vie Spirituelle*, Paris.

Zeitsch. für die Neutest. *Zeitschrift für die neutestamentliche Wissenschaft und die Kunde der alteren Kirche*, Giessen.

Zeitsch. für Kathol. Theol. *Zeitschrift für Katholische Theologie*, Innsbruck.

The asterisk after a word refers to the brief lexicon of principal technical terms placed in the appendix.

We cite the *Summa Theologica* of Saint Thomas Aquinas in the following manner: the first number (in Roman numerals) refers to the *Pars*, the second to the *Quaestio*, the third to the *Articulus*, the fourth, preceded by *ad*, to the *Responsio ad argumentum*. Thus, I, 2, 3, ad 1 should be read: *Prima Pars, quaestio 2, articulus 3, ad 1 um argumentum*.

INTRODUCTION

Our purpose in writing this book is simply to underscore the roots of traditional truth in ecclesiology and sacramental theology: *"The Eucharist makes the Church."*

Investigation undertaken since the time of our theological studies at Saulchoir has gradually led us to realize that the usual explanation of this truth was somewhat lacking with respect to the richness of revelation and, in particular, in showing how the diverse effects of the Sacrament of the Body of Christ unite directly in the edification of the ecclesial Body of the Lord. It is our aim to show this unification.

To do this, we shall let Scripture speak, and we shall listen to the commentaries of the Fathers on the revealed texts. Restating, but often modifying, articles which we have already published in the *Nouvelle Revue Theologique* of Louvain, we shall try to show how living Tradition has understood this relationship between the Eucharist and the Church. Our method is not that of a simple cataloguing of testimonies. Instead, we want to plunge these documents into their theological climate in order to grasp how they meet the very life of the most typical Christian communities. After reviewing the Christian notion of Salvation in the Lord Jesus, we shall show especially how the affirmations of these documents are rooted in the universal certainty that the Sacrament of the Lord's Table effects the Pasch of the Church on the way to the Eschatological Kingdom.

It is obvious that we cannot say or cite everything on this important point. For the convenience of the reader (who will often feel the need to plunge these testimonies into their full context), we have confined ourselves, in all possible measure, to texts drawn from patristic works which have been translated and are generally accessible. This explains certain omissions. For the same reason we have also limited our medieval investigation to Thomas Aquinas. However, an attentive study of the medieval commentaries on the Mass, such as the treatises De Sacramentis or De sacramento altaris, would often have given us marvelous explanations. These would have tired the reader in the long run and only added to the weight of a book already full of testimonies. By the same token it would have been necessary for us to pursue investigation and see how the Churches of the Reformation, in their own theology of the Sacrament of the Eucharist, have preserved the traditional deposit, how they live by it today, and how the problem poses itself squarely in the face of ecumenical concern. But that would have lengthened our work unduly and perhaps would have destroyed its unity. We would rather save this investigation for a later work.

We could not avoid using a certain technical vocabulary, and consequently it was reduced to a minimum. To remedy this, we have, as an appendix, first a brief lexicon of the principal technical terms (to which we refer by an asterisk in the text), then an index of the principal theological notions involved in our research.

We hope that, in spite of all this, the book will be able to supply contemporary ecclesiology a certain theological support. In fact, it is on sacramental reality, inseparable from faith in the Word (if the sacraments are really sacraments of the faith), that rests above all the mystery of the Church, the Body of Christ, reunited mysteriously but truly, however, into the person of the Lord Jesus.

The whole redeemed city, that is to say, the congregation or community of the saints, is offered to God as our sacrifice through the great High Priest, who offered Himself to God in His passion for us, that we might be members of this glorious head, according to the form of a servant. For it was this form He offered, in this He was offered, because it is according to it He is Mediator, in this He is our Priest, in this the Sacrifice.... As we have many members in one body, and all members have not the same office, so we, being many, are one body in Christ, and every one members one of another, having gifts differing according to the grace that is given to us. This is the sacrifice of Christians: we, being many, are one body in Christ. And this also is the sacrifice which the Church continually celebrates in the sacrament of the altar, known to the faithful, in which she teaches that she herself is offered in the offering she makes to God.

Saint Augustine, *De Civitate Dei*,
lib. 10, cap. 6.

CHAPTER I

THE COMMUNION OF LIFE
IN JESUS LORD AND SAVIOR

Exactly why was the Son sent out among men? The natural response of each Christian is that of the Nicene Creed: "For us men and for our salvation,* he came down from heaven and was incarnate." [1] Even if it is lacking in several creeds, notably in the Roman Credo and the group of Latin credos,[2] this little sentence answers perfectly, nonetheless, all that Scripture and living Tradition teach us. Jesus is awaited as Savior.

The first chapters of the Gospel by Luke are typical on this point. "Blessed be the Lord, the God of Israel; he has visited his people, and wrought their redemption. He has raised up a sceptre of salvation for us among the posterity of his servant David, according to the promise which he made by the lips of holy men that have been his prophets from the beginning; salvation from our enemies, and from the hand of all those who hate us. So he would carry out his merciful design towards our fathers, by remembering his holy covenant. He had sworn an oath to our father Abraham, that he would enable us to live without fear in his service, delivered from the hand of our enemies, passing all our days in holiness, and approved in his

---

1. The term used is *sôteria*, stemming from the translation of the LXX in the fertile ground of the Biblical theology of Salvation. The asterisk refers to the lexicon at the end.

2. We find it in the creeds of Cesarea and of Mopsuestia. Others have equivalent formulae: "who came down *for us*" (Antioch), "who died *for us*" (Apostolic Constitutions), "who, *in order to destroy sin,* dwelt in the flesh" (Egyptian Credo, supposedly of St. Macarus.)

sight. And thou, my child, wilt be known for a prophet of the most High, going before the Lord, to clear his way for him; thou wilt make known to his people the salvation that is to release them from their sins. Such is the merciful kindness of our God, which has bidden him come to us, like a dawning from on high, to give light to those who live in darkness, in the shadow of death, and to guide our feet into the way of peace" (Luke 1, 68-79), prophecies Zachary at the circumcision of John the Baptist. "This day, in the city of David, a Savior has been born for you, the Lord Christ himself" (2, 11), announces the angel of the Lord to the shepherds of Bethlehem. "For my own eyes have seen that saving power of thine which thou hast prepared in the sight of all nations. This is the light which shall give revelation to the Gentiles, this is the glory of thy people Israel" (2, 30-32), says the aged Simeon receiving Jesus in his arms. The vocabulary, the mystique, of the *anawim* (poor *) springs out too much here for us not to affirm the close bond between this waiting for a *Soter* (Savior *) and the mysterious figure of the Suffering Servant.* [3] Of himself Jesus will affirm that "this is what the Son of Man has come for, to search out and to save what was lost" (Luke 19, 10), and John puts this declaration on his lips: "When God sent his Son into the world, it was not to reject (or judge) the world, but so that the world might find salvation through him" (John 3, 17; see 4, 42; I John 4, 14). Furthermore, is not the whole Gospel

---

3. The great connection between these first chapters of Luke and the "spirituality of the poor of Yahweh" has been clarified by A. Gelin, *Les pauvres de Yahvé*, Paris, 1953, pp. 121-132; R. Laurentin, *Structure et théologie de Luc I-II*, Paris, 1957, especially pp. 101-104. The "Messias of the Poor," such as given us in the Songs of the Servant (Is. 42, 1-9; 49, 1-6; 50, 4-11; 52, 13-53, 12) and in Psalm 22, is essentially a Savior who saves by atoning mysteriously, through his own sufferings, for the sins of others "thus giving peace" to them. See A. Brunot, *Le poème du Serviteur et ses problèms*, in *R.T.*, 1961, pp. 5-24; "a fourth aspect in this composite portrait which Deutero-Isaias draws for us of the Servant of Yahweh is his soteriological character: the Servant is a Savior. Here we are at the summit of the sacerdotal tradition . . . . We see uniting and harmonizing in the death of the Servant the sacerdotal idea of the sacrifice of expiation by substitution

the *Good News of Salvation* (Eph. 1, 13; see Rom. 1, 16)? [4]

We need not be astonished then to see the Fathers and the Liturgies put this fact of Salvation in the foreground.[5] To remove from the Christian mystery its dimension of Salvation would amount to removing its very substance. The experience of Salvation is not situated on the periphery of Christian experience, but at its heart, more intensely even than the experience of the exodus for the *Qahal* (People*) of the Old Covenant. Indeed, the Acts of the Apostles can characterize the converts of the first Christian generation by the expression, those "that

---

and the prophetic idea of intercessory prayer. These two elements joined make of this offering something absolutely unique" (pp. 20-21). If we insist on this aspect, it is because of the problem raised by the fact that the title *Soter* is rarely applied to Jesus in the most ancient Christian writings. See O. Cullmann, *Christologie du Nouveau Testament*, Neuchâtel-Paris, 1958, pp. 206-212. This title seems really to be in close connection with the Old Testament, more precisely with the theology of purification and of pardon of sins: God is the *Soter* because he delivers his People, especially from their sins. If the title is relativey late, the reality which it expresses belongs to the most primitive Christian conviction. O. Cullmann (*op cit.*, pp 209, 212) underlines the facts that in Palestine the title of "Savior" could not easily be applied to Jesus since "Jesus" means "Savior" (see Matt. 1, 21). It would then have been necessary to repeat the name "Jesus" itself; but in the Palestinian Church they already had the conviction that Jesus was not only called Savior (*Ieschoua − Jesus*), but that this is who he was" (p. 212).

4. Note the parallel expression *"Good News of peace"* (Eph. 6, 15) which in turn refers to Is. 52, 7: "Welcome, welcome on the mountain heights the messenger that cries, All is well! Good news brings he, deliverance cries he, telling Sion, Thy God has claimed his throne!"

5. It would be interesting to study here the progression of praise motifs in the various Eucharistic anaphoras: they all culminate in the fact of Salvation. Thus the anaphora attributed to St. Basil: "Thou indeed art Holy and most Holy.... Thou art worshipped in all thy works.... Thou hast fashioned man from the clay of the earth.... Thou hast not rejected thy creature forever.... Thou hast sent prophets.... When the fullness of time had come, thou hast spoken to us through thine own Son... therefore we remember his meritorious sufferings, his lifegiving Cross, his Resurrection after three days, the resurrection of the dead, his Ascension into heaven, his place at thy right hand, God and Father, his glorious and dreadful coming again..."(From the French of E. Mercenier, *La prière des Eglises de rite byzantin,* t. I, Amay-sur-Meuse, 1937, pp. 259-261).

were to be saved" (Acts 2, 47), and Paul can base his magnificent development of the *agape* (love *) of God (Eph. 2, 1-10)
on the affirmative "it is his grace that has saved you." Theodore
of Mopsuestia translates the traditional faith perfectly when,
explaining the second article of the baptismal credo of his
church, he says: "As soon as they were admired for speaking
about the economy, our blessed fathers indicated straightaway
for whom such an economy was effected, by saying: *For us
men.* But they also added: *For our salvation,* in order that the
goal of the economy might be known." [6]

SALVATION IS A PASCH
A PASSAGE

But of what does this Salvation which Jesus brings us consist? Essentially, it consists of a *passage* from a sinful condition
(with all it implies) to a condition of love (with all it implies),
a *passage* from the world of sin into the world of God. We
have mentioned above the parallel with the Jewish Exodus. In
this connection it is even more illuminating and traditional.
Across the waters of the Red Sea, under the leadership of
Moses, the tribes, sadly oppressed in Egypt, *passed* wondrously
from the land of slavery to the Promised Land with the intervention of the power of God "fighting for them" (Ex. 14, 14).
In the same way under the leadership of Christ Jesus, men,
frightfully subdued by sin, *pass* into divine spheres with the
intervention of the power of God, who is "in Christ, recon-
ciling the world to himself" (II Cor. 5, 19). We are aware of
how many Fathers insisted on this relationship of type between
the Exodus event and the Christian Salvation effected in the
Death and Resurrection of Christ, applied to individuals by
the mediation of Baptismal immersion-emersion. A text from
Aphraates explains it excellently: "On the Passover the Jews
escaped from the slavery of Pharaoh; on the day of the

---

6. *Hom. Cat.*, VII, I, ed. Tonneau-Devreesse, Vatican, 1949, p. 161.

Crucifixion we were delivered from the slavery of Satan. They sacrificed a lamb whose blood saved them from the exterminator; we were delivered by the Blood of the well-beloved Son from our works of corruption. They had Moses for a guide; we have Jesus for Head and Savior. For them Moses divided the sea and had them cross; our Savior opened the depths and broke their gates, when, descending into the depths, he opened them and forged the way at the head of all those who were to believe in him" (Dem., 12, 8; Patrol. Syr. 1, 521-523).[7]

We must slow up on this aspect if we want to understand in depth the mystery of the Eucharist, the "Sacrament of Salvation." For our Salvation is a Pasch, a passage, a movement, accomplished in two powerful moments, a moment of destruction, of deliverance from oppression, and of projection into a wondrous universe, surpassing all that our nature ever assumed could be true, the gift of the unique agape * of God. Hence, Salvation is at once the shore of Egypt, the shore of "servitude" (Ex. 2, 23), and the shore of the Promised Land, the shore of hope and of life. The "passage" from the one to the other demands two interventions of God's power, one by which he breaks the bonds of captivity, the other by which he leads man into the free inheritance of the Promise. An exact notion of Salvation must always take into account these two dimensions.

Salvation Is a Redemption

To characterize the first moment, Deuteronomy, speaking of the Exodus, preferred the verb padah, meaning to set aside and break the bonds (Deut. 7, 8; 9, 26; 13, 6; 15, 15; 21, 8; 24, 18); whereas Deutero-Isaias, thinking especially of the awaited intervention, used principally the verb ga'al, affectively richer since it evokes the action of him who redeems, as a relative, a

---

7. P.J. Danielou. in *Bible et Liturgie*, Paris, 1951, pp. 119-135, has grouped together some texts of the Fathers on this point, in relation to Baptism.

sacred property (Is. 41, 14; 43, 1; 43, 14; 44, 6; 44, 22-24; 47, 4: 48, 17: 48, 20: 49, 7; 49, 26; 51, 10; 52, 3; 52, 9; 54, 5; 54, 8). The nuances of these two terms will pass into the *lutroô* of the language of the LXX and of the New Testament which we translate naturally as "redeem," and its derivatives.

The careful study of the sense of sin and of the entirely interior dimension of the awaited "deliverance" brings forth another verb, *kipper*, whose sense is "to atone." * The priority of the divine initiative is maintained (and firmly), but human collaboration is also accented. In slavery to sin, man is not only passive, he is also active since sin is "his sin." God, whose power put to the service of his plan the forces of nature when it was a question of the material deliverance of Israel, can also assume for the work of spiritual deliverance man himself. This is an admirable refinement of the divine *hesed* (mercy,* goodness) which respects the freedom of the one whom it saves, associating him with his own redemption while demanding of him a concrete expiation as inspired by filial sentiment. As man is active in his sin, he will be the same in his deliverance.

Here again—if not by vocabulary, at least by the theological context—there pierces the figure of the Suffering Servant* whose sacrifice clothes these characteristics with an authentic *Kippur* (expiation *). God raised him up for the Salvation "of many" (the *rabbim.* Is. 52, 14; 53, 11; 53, 12), that is, for the universe of men and of nations; [8] and, offering for the sins of all a sacrifice of expiation, he accomplishes this vocation that he "bears" (Is. 53, 3-5), after having interceded for them: "The Just One, my servant; many shall he claim for his own, win their acquittal, on his shoulders bearing their guilt. . . . He gave himself up to death, and would be counted among the wrongdoers; bore those many sins, made intercession for the guilty" (Is. 53, 11-12). This is a completely inner Salvation, as we see it, in which are joined at once the prepossessing love

---

8. See J. Jeremias, *Polloi* in *Theol. Wörth. zum Neuen Test.*, t. VI, pp. 536-545; L. Sabourin, *Rédemption sacrificielle*, Desclée de B., 1961, pp. 242-246.

of God and the filial response of man, since on the one hand
it is God who raises up the Servant ("my servant," "my elect,"
"I have put my spirit on him," "Yahweh was pleased to destroy
him by suffering"), and on the other hand he "does not resist"
(50, 5), "gives himself over to death" (53, 12). In the same
way, this is a salvation whose dimensions exceed the too nar-
row limits of the chosen race: "Use thee I will," he promises,
"nor with thy service be content, when the tribes of Jacob
thou hast summoned, brought back the poor remnant of Israel;
nay, I have appointed thee to be the light of the Gentiles, in
thee I will send out my salvation to the furthest corners of the
earth" (Is. 49, 6).

This deepening and this broadening of the theme of Salvation does not devitalize the Exodus, the passage. The songs
of the Servant are enshrined in a context of a new Exodus,[9] of
an exalting exit under the leadership of Yahweh to a wondrous
world: "No need for confusion at the time of your going; this
shall be no hasty flight, with the Lord himself to march before
you, the God of Israel to rally you" (Is. 52, 12); "Doubt not,
then, yours shall be a happy departure, a peaceful return;
doubt not mountain and hill shall escort you with their praises,
and the woods echo their applause" (55, 12). God redeems,
he pardons sin, he tears man violently out of his misery ("our
griefs," "our sufferings" and also "our crimes"), but this deliverance does not shut itself up, it is not a finality, it is only
the first age of a vitality before an opening into the total gift
of the inheritance of the Promise. For here we are in a context
of Covenant: God is "engaged" in leading his own into a
universe which the first generations represent under the image
of a bountiful land, a glorious Jerusalem, but whose spiritual
and universal dimension we begin to perceive. The redemption
(through the mediation of the sacrifice of the *Ebed* *) of the

---

9. "It is striking to note to what point the theme of the exodus dominates
the thought of 2nd Isaias; it is so central that it forms the introduction and
conclusion of his work" (E. Jacob, *Théologie de l' Ancien Testament*,
Neuchâtel-Paris, 1955, p. 272).

captive People from its sins is only a prelude to his entrance into this universe. This is a starting point which bears within it the means for a leap into the new Jerusalem.

In choosing to situate his Messianic mystery in the line of a suffering Servant,* of the *Ebed Yahweh*,* Jesus accomplished this redemption by the mediation of his atoning sacrifice. In him meet perfectly the basic initiative of the *agape* * of God —since he is the only-begotten * Son of the Father sent for this: "God so loved the world, that he gave up his only-begotten Son ... so that the world might find salvation through him" (John 3, 16-17)—and the perfect response of man. True son of Adam, by Mary his mother, he sheds his blood "for many to the remission of sins" (Matt. 26, 28).[10] As at the time of the exit from Egypt, in the historical event of his death and resurrection, God "breaks the bonds" which kept humanity chained (*padah*), "redeems a holy property, humanity, because of the very special relationship which unites him to it" (*ga'al*); but because it concerns this time of the exit from the world of sin, he does it by means of the sacrifice of love which, in the name of all his brothers, one man offers in expiation for the sins of all (*kipper*). This aspect of our Salvation is too clearly underlined by Scripture and living Tradition for us to dwell too much on it. Jesus is our Redeemer; he whose death was offered with love has washed the world clean from sin forever. It will suffice us to recall, as major affirmations, Paul's words: "All alike have sinned, all alike are unworthy of God's praise. And

---

10. We cannot speak much here about the fact that Jesus accomplishes in himself the figure of the Servant. We refer to O. Cullmann, *Christologie du Nouveau Testament*, Neuchâtel-Paris, 1958, pp. 48-73; L. Cerfaux, *Saint Paul et le Serviteur de Dieu*, Racueil L. Cerfaux, t. II, Gembloux, 1954, pp. 283-298; J. Giblet, *Jésus Serviteur de Dieu*, Lum. et Vie 36, 1958, pp. 5-34; M. D. Hooker, *Jesus and the Servant*, London, 1959; Simmerli-Jeremias, *The Servant of God*, London, 1957, pp. 79-105; J. Palsterman, *Jesus Serviteur de Dieu d'après le Nouveau Testament*, in *Coll. Mechl.*, 1956, pp. 579-596; F. Gils, *Jesus Prophète d'après les évangiles synoptiques*, Louvain, 1957; L. Sabourin, *Rédemption sacrificielle*, Desclée de B., 1961, pp. 223-225; K. Romaniuk, *De themate Ebed Yahve in soteriologia S. Pauli*, in *The Cath. Bibl. Quart.*, 1961, pp. 12-25.

justification comes to us as a free gift from his grace, through our redemption (*apolutrosis*) in Jesus Christ. God has offered him to us as a means of reconciliation (*hilasterion*), in virtue of faith, ransoming us with his blood" (Rom 3, 23-25. John says: "He, in his own person (the Just One, Jesus Christ, is the atonement (*hilasmos*) made for our sins, and not only for ours, but for the sins of whole world" (I John 2, 2), "God . . . (showed) love for us first, when he sent out his Son to be an atonement (*hilasmos*) for our sins" (I John 4, 10). The Epistle to the Hebrews explains: "He must needs become altogether like his brethren; he would be a high priest who could feel for us and be our true representative before God, to make atonement (*hilaskosthai*) for the sins of the people" (Hebrews 2, 17).

But there it is only one moment of the saving forces, setting us in route toward the final entrance into the inheritance of God. The power of God is exhibited here, together with the power of his *agape* *: a "violent" intervention which the Fathers will have a tendency to dramatize in conceiving it as a settling of accounts with Satan, who has "rights" over man whom he conquered in the drama of the terrestrial Paradise. We are familiar with the famous problem of the "rights of the devil," already slightly present in Irenaeus, and which is going to spread rapidly throughout patristic thought.[11] "See," says Origen, "the truth of St. Peter's word: we have not been redeemed at the price of corruptible silver or gold, but by the precious blood of the only Son. If we have been redeemed for a price, as St. Paul expresses likewise, doubtless we have been bought by someone whose slaves we were and who has reclaimed the price he wanted to liberate those whom he was holding. It is the devil who was holding us, he to whom we had sold ourselves by our sins; he has claimed for our ransom the blood of Christ" (*Comment. in Epist. ad Rom.*, lib. 2, 13;

---

11. Read J. Rivière, *Le démon dans la théologie rédemptrice de S. Irénée*, in *Rech. de Sc. Rel.*, 1913, pp. 57-60; *Le dogme de la Rédemption, essai d'étude historique*, Paris, 1905, pp. 373-394.

P.G., 14, 911; trans.).[12] The baptismal catechesis exploited this theme of the battle with the devil, a battle which terminates in the defeat of this devil.[13] But the power of God is not content with setting us free in Jesus the Messias. It wants to have us "enter into the repose of God." The Epistle to the Hebrews, which insists so much on the redemptive value of the blood of Christ—"offered once for all" (9, 26), "to drain the cup of a world's sins" (9, 28) and "annulling our sin by his sacrifice" (9, 26)—also compares Jesus to Moses leading the People in flight toward the Promised Land (3, 1-19) and returns often to this parallel (8, 5 where the author affirms the Tabernacle erected by Moses is only the shadow, the *skia*, of the sanctuary of Christ: 9, 18-28 where he compares the conclusion of the two Covenants). By his atoning sacrifice Jesus, the first, the precursor (*prodromos*), entered heaven. He "passed right up through the heavens," he "has opened up for us a new, a living approach, to the sanctuary" (6, 19-20; 4, 14; 10, 19-20), drawing along with him the true People of God, in the true Exodus of which Israel and her history were only the shadow (*skia*). We find here again the great figure of the suffering Servant whose atoning sacrifice leads multitudes to salvation. Above we recalled that the Songs of the Servant fit together into a context of exodus. But there is more. The character himself carries in him certain traits borrowed from the

---

12. "As the mighty Word, and true man, who, redeeming us by His own blood in a manner consonant to reason (*rationabiliter*), gave Himself as a redemption for those who had been led into captivity. And since the apostasy tyrannized over us unjustly, and, though we were by nature the property of the omnipotent God, alienated us contrary to nature, rendering us its own disciples, the Word of God, powerful in all things, and not defective with regard to his own justice, did righteously turn against that apostasy, and redeem from it His own property, not by violent means, as the apostasy had obtained dominion over us at the beginning, when it insatiably snatched away what was not its own, but by means of persuasion." (Irenaeus, *Adv. Haer.*, V, 1, 1; *AN*, vol. 1, p. 527)

13. See J. Danielou, *op. cit.*, pp. 34-35.

portrait of Moses as tradition imagines him.[14] Jesus, in the act of his redemptive sacrifice, poses the starting point of a set of forces, for he redeems in order to lead man somewhere.

Salvation Leads into the Communion of Life

This "somewhere" implies the other moment of the saving movement also brought about by the power of God. Let us say. that the experience of salvation is situated in a context of covenant. God chose for himself a People with whom he made covenant in view of a plan which is—as the *Heilsgeschichte* reveals to us—a plan of love. The image of the husband and wife which appears in Hosea (2, 1-3, 5), and is carried on throughout the prophetic tradition (Jer. 2, 1-7; 3, 11-20; 31, 21-22; Ez. 16, 1-63; 23, 1-49; Deutero-Is. 50, 1-3; 51, 17-22; 54, 1-14; Is. 60, 1-21; 61, 10-11; 62, 2-12), illustrates perhaps better this mystery of Covenant than the theme of God the Father of the People (also traditional, cf. Ex. 4, 22-23). For, in this "love covenant," which is the *hesed*,* God searches for a communion between him and his People in view of a still wider communion between him and all humanity, since Israel is chosen as the instrument for the salvation of the world. This communion will become apparent on his part as a gift (*pathan*) of which he alone is the giver: he will lead Israel into the share of his divine gifts. Perhaps we have not sufficiently emphasized the fact that the heritage of the promise to Abraham, material gifts of a long posterity and a luxuriant land for a life freely expanded in peace, security, light and joy,[15] is already an "inheritance of communion." God the Creator and Master of the universe desires to crown his own by giving them in abundance (in all its aspects) of that over which he has complete mastery. It is not mere chance that faith in God the Creator is deepened at the very core of

---

14. See E. Jacob, *op. cit.*, p. 272; L. Sabourin, *op. cit.*, *pp.* 207-208; A. Brunot, *op. cit.*, p. 19.

15. See the excellent study by A. Gelin, *Expérience et attente du Salut dans l'Ancien Testament*, Lum. et Vie, 15, 1954, p. 10 (298).

the experience of the Covenant.[16] But Israel had to discover little by little a new and more essential dimension of this communion.

Indeed, if the breath (ruah*) of human life is like a prolongation of the breath of the divine life itself, thus intimately uniting all life to God—to the point that Job can write: "He has but to turn his thought towards men, reclaiming the spirit he once breathed into them, and all life would fail everywhere; mankind would return to its dust" (Job, 34, 14-15)[17]—we catch a glimpse of a connection between the fullness of life expected in the eschatological age and a fuller gift of the divine ruah.* However, it is not only the material life of individuals which so depends on the gift of the breath of life. The life of the people as such, the pace of history, depends completely on mysterious manifestations of the divine ruah,* whether in the great heroes of the past on whom it "settled" (Judges 14, 6, 19; 15, 14; I Sam. 11, 6; etc.), or in the Davidic king whom it "seizes" (I Sam. 16, 13; see Is. 11, 12), or in the prophets who speak and act "under its grasp" (Ez. 2, 2; 3, 12-14, 24; 8, 3; 11, 1-5, 24; 43, 5; Neh. 9, 28-30; etc.). So that little by little one certainty is affirmed: the end toward which Salvation history forges will consist of a generous effusion of the divine breath (Spirit of God*), a free gift of the power of the very life of God, for a wondrous life, lived in total communion between the God of the Covenant * and the new People so constituted.

The Old Testament does not yet dream of the person of the Holy Spirit, but the reality which will find its definitive expression in Jesus begins to appear in the faith of the People. That is the other dimension of Salvation, also rooted in the agape * of the God of the Covenant *. God saves, he redeems,

---

16. Cf. the studied essay of E. Beaucamp, La Bible et le sens religieux de l'univers, Paris, 1959.

17. In the same line, Job 33, 4; Eccl. 12, 7 and especially Gen. 2, 7, but in this last text the term used is not ruah but nesamah which we meet in Job 34, 14 in parallel with ruah (see also Job 32, 8; 33, 4).

he purifies, in order to be able to lead into the intimacy of his life, and the share of his gifts in the "communion of life.*" This is the wondrous Land of Promise, more exaltant than Davidic Jerusalem. Jeremias and Ezechiel are unsurpassed here, always presenting this communion in connection with the aspect of redemption, of pardon from sin, that we have analyzed above.

Jeremias,[18] who lived the adventure of the poverty of heart and of total openness to the Word of God,[19] seizes upon just how far this "communion *" will go: "A time is coming, the Lord says, when I mean to ratify a new convenant with the people of Israel and with the people of Juda. It will not be like the covenant which I made with their fathers, on the day when I took them by the hand, to rescue them from Egypt; that they should break my covenant, and I, all the while, their master, the Lord says. No, this is the covenant I will grant the people of Israel, the Lord says, when that time comes. I will implant my law in their innermost thoughts, engrave it in their hearts; I will be their God, and they shall be my people" (Jer. 31, 31-33; see 32, 38-42; 24, 7). Here, the redemption from sin (and we know the influence of Jeremias on the portrait of the Suffering Servant) exceeds itself in a yet more marvellous gift; a completely loving intimacy between Yahweh and "his faithful."

Ezechiel—in a quite different context, marked profoundly by liturgical themes—introduces the divine *ruah* * (Spirit of God *) into this intimacy. This is going to become, in the re-established People and in each heart, the breath, the motor principle of a new life: "And then I will pour cleansing streams over you, to purge you from every stain you bear, purge you from the

---

18. See A. Gelin, *Jérémie*, Paris, 1952, pp. 149-193; art. *Jérémie*, in *Suppl. Dict. de la Bible*, 1948, col. 883-887; L. Bouyer, *La Bible et l'Évangile*, Paris, 1951, pp. 85-93; for the general theme of the Old Covenant, see P. Van Imschoot, *L'Esprit de Yahvé et l'Alliance nouvelle dans l'Ancien Testament*, in *Ephem. Theol. Lov.*, 1936, pp. 201-220.

19. "He is also the father of the poor (*anawin*) who have implemented and lived the message which he had embodied in his life," A. Gelin, *Jérémie*, Paris, 1952, p. 183.

taint of your idolatry. I will give you a new heart, and breathe a new spirit into you; I will take away from your breasts those hearts that are hard as stone, and give you human hearts instead. I will make my spirit penetrate you, so that you will follow in the path of my law, remember and carry out my decrees. So shall you make your home in the land I promised to your fathers; you shall be my people, and I will be your God. I will set you free from the guilt which stains you; I will send my word to the harvest, and bid it come up abundantly, to spare you from dearth" (Ez. 36, 25-29; see 11, 19; 39, 28-29). We have to read this text in connection with the allegory of the dry bones (37, 1-14), announcing the eschatological re-establishment of Israel, the recently dispersed Israel: the breath of life will enliven the bones, then "shall I breathe my spirit into you, to give you life again, and shall bid you dwell at peace in your own land. What the Lord promises, the Lord performs; you will know that, he tells you, at last." A long time after these words of Ezechiel, the prophet Joel will sing the great day of the universal outpouring of the spirit of God (Joel 3, 1-3).

The great act of God, inaugurated in the redemptive event of the exodus from Egypt, wills to complete itself in this magnanimous liberality of the God of the Covenant. The fleshly Covenant is going to exceed itself in the new Covenant born of it, enlivened in it. God will not be content with giving his created an inheritance. He will give himself in a mysterious communion of Life.* Salvation goes to this fullness.

If the descent of Christ into death effected the first stage of salvific dynamism, his ascension to the Father in his glory as *Kurios* (Lord *) effects the second. But here we must define very carefully the notions involved and be well understood on them. The theologians of our era have strongly reaccented the event of the resurrection and this is perhaps one of the happiest theological developments of the century. But they insisted perhaps not enough on the necessary relationship between this resurrection event and the "communion of Life *"; and certain writings often give the impression of considering the former as an end in itself. Situated at the very heart of the plan of God, the glorification of Christ (in this term we link the resurrection and ascension) is not a terminal point. On the contrary, it leads necessarily up to the Pentecost and the new era in Salvation history which it opens. We are going on to explain.

On Easter morning, Jesus arose glorious. Certainly this exaltation, inseparably bound to his death as the Servant, constitutes its own glorification. Phil. 2, 6-11—this text to which theology returns ceaselessly and which plunges the theologian in wonder—affirms this truth magnificently: "Being of divine nature (of the *morphe* (the form *) of God), he did not cling jealously to the rank which made him equal to God. But he dispossessed himself, taking the nature (*morphe*) of the Slave [20] and becoming like men. Being comported like a man, he humbled himself even more, obeying right up to death, the death on the cross. Therefore (*diô*), God has exalted him and given him the Name which is above every other name, so that, at the name of Jesus, all, in highest heaven, on the earth and beneath the earth, might bend the knee and that every tongue might proclaim Jesus Christ Lord * (*Kurios*) to the glory of God the Father." The most serious exegetes [21] read

20. We follow here the French translation of L. Cerfaux, *Le Christ dans la théologie de saint Paul*, Paris 1954, p. 288. This translation is taken over by O. Cullmann (*op. cit.*, p. 69), who writes: "Mere *Ebed* is translated by *Doulos*," after E. Lohmeyer (*Gottesknecht und Davidsohn*, Heidelberg, 1945, pp. 3-5, who judges this translation possible. V. Taylor (*The Atonement in the New Testament Teaching*, London, 1945, pp. 65-66) thinks that Paul would have avoided making *Doulos* a title of Christ through respect to the title of Kurios, but that the idea of Christ *Doulos* is one of the governing ideas of his Christology.

21. L. Cerfaux *L'hymne au Christ Serviteur de Dieu*, in *Miscell. histor. Alberti de Meyer*, Louvain, 1946, pp. 117-130; S. *Paul et le Serviteur de Dieu*, in *Studia Anselmiana*, 27-28, 1951, pp. 351-365; *Le Christ dans la théologie de S. Paul*, Paris , 1954, pp. 283-298; O. Cullmann, *op. cit.*, pp. 68-69; V. Taylor, *The Person of Christ in New Testament Teaching London*, 1958, pp. 64-69, 260-276; A. Feuillet, *L'hymne christologique de l'Epitre aux Philippiens*, 2, 6-11, in *R. B.*, 1965, pp. 352-380; P. Schoonenberg, *Il s'anéantit lui-même*, in *Concilium*, 11, 1965, pp. 45-60.

through the lines of this hymn Deutero-Isaias' words relative to the suffering Servant, who "for all his heart's anguish will win their acquittal, on his shoulders bearing their guilt" (Is. 53, 11).

But this relationship itself with him whose sufferings "justify the multitudes" (Is. 53, 11) incites us to plunge this text into the whole context of Pauline theology, more particularly into the theology of the New Adam. If the parallel Adam-Christ emerges in several places in the so-called Epistles of the captivity,[22] we can, following certain exegetes,[23] find him one explanation of our hymn. Paul uses here the Greek term *morphe*, often used concurrently with *eikon* to translate the Hebrew terms *selem* and *demut* which we find in the narrative of the creation of the first Adam: "Let us make man, bearing our own image (*selem*) and likeness (*demut*)" (Gen. 1, 26; see 1, 27; 5, 1-3; 9, 6). The first Adam, created in the image of God, arises through his sin and seeks out total equality with God. In wanting to rise up proudly like this, he breaks the bonds of intimacy, of communion,* instituted by God, and hurls all humanity into sin. On the contrary, Christ, the second Adam, is by his very nature in the *morphe* (the form *) of God, perfect and transcendent image of him whose well-beloved Son (Col. 1, 13), whose Firstborn (Col. 1, 15), he is also. But, far from making a pretext of his complete equality with God in order to raise himself, he lowers himself to the point of becoming the Suffering Servant, bearing the sins of men. Therefore, God exalts him, in his being certainly, but also in his function as the New Adam, as the new principle of life for the new humanity. The *kenose* of Jesus (finding its height in the sacrifice of the cross) thus opens up into the salvation of all humanity in the communion of the restored Life between God and man. The glorification of the Lord Jesus exceeds

22. See L. Cerfaux, *Le Christ dans la théologie de S. Paul*, Paris, 1954, pp. 183-188.

23. L. Bouyer, *Arpagmos*, in *Rech. de Sc. Rel.*, 1951 (*Mélanges Lebreton*, 1), pp. 281-288; O. Cullmann, *op. cit.*, pp. 150-156; see names cited by P. Henry, article *Kenose*, in *Suppl. Dict. de la Bible*, 1950, col. 42-45.

the limits of his own physical person in order to attain to full humanity. Personal exaltation and the salvation of men, far from opposing each other, are thus united in the person of Jesus, the New Adam, the starting point of redeemed humanity led into the final share of the "inheritance of the Father."

The first letter to the Corinthians had already explicitly elaborated this theme. Moreover, it bears out a precision of the highest importance. The New Adam is a "spirit which gives life," a "spiritual" Adam in opposition to the first Adam who was only psychical." We must cite I Cor. 15, 20-22: "Christ has risen from the dead, the firstfruits (*aparche*) of all those who have fallen asleep; a man had brought us death, and a man should bring us resurrection from the dead; just as all have died with Adam, so with Christ all will be brought to life," and 15, 44-48: "If there is such a thing as a natural body, there must be a spiritual body too. Mankind begins with the Adam who became, as Scripture tells us, a living soul; it is fulfilled in the Adam who has become a life-giving spirit. It was not the principle of spiritual life that came first; natural life came first, then spiritual life; then man who came first came from earth, fashioned of dust, the man who came afterwards came from heaven, and his form is heavenly. The nature of that earthborn man is shared by his earthly sons, the nature of the heavenborn man, by his heavenly sons; and it remains for us, who once bore the stamp (*eikon*) of earth, to bear the stamp of heaven."

We cannot linger here on the delicate problems which this last text [24] poses, in which, let us note immediately, we meet the theme of the stamp transmitted to the descendants. However, we have to be clear on its essence. Man, in Pauline anthropology, is created a "living soul," animated by the *psuchè*, the principle of his natural life. This *psuchè*, inherited from the first Adam, leads to death the body which it enlivens. To save us, the Son of God took a physical body, inherited from the first Adam, which in fact led him to death. But this death

---

24. See L. Cerfaux, *Le Christ dans la théologie de S. Paul*, Paris, 1954, pp. 222-223.

was a victory, the victory of life. In espousing death, Christ conquered it. He then arises glorious, having conquered sin (the basic obstacle to the outpouring to man of the communion of Life with God), the New Adam, bearer of the breath of the divine, spiritual * life. In his capacity as the New Adam, he has the power of transmitting this spiritual life. From its bestowal will be born the saved humanity, redeemed and bearing, even in its body, the glory of the resurrection. There, and there only, is effected the saving force whose first moment had been the sacrifice of Jesus the Servant of Yahweh. The Communion of Life with which Jesus (in his singular humanity) arises at the morning of his exaltation will then be passed on to all men. The initial promise of salvation, which the author of the Yahwish tradition states immediately after the drama of the sin of the first Adam (Gen. 3, 15), will have been fully realized. It will be the newfound Paradise. Not a Paradise of earthly goods but the Paradise of total intimacy between God and his own, the Paradise of perfect communion.

We have not yet mentioned the Person of the Holy Spirit. In fact, our text, when it affirms that the risen Christ is spiritual, does not seem to mean anything other than this: the life of Christ unfolds henceforth after the very nature and power of divinity; he has passed completely into the world of the divine life, of God the Spirit.[25] Nevertheless this text must also be plunged into the whole of Pauline theology.

Examining the Christian experience lived "in the Christ the Lord," Paul refers explicitly to the Person of the Holy Spirit. The spiritual New Adam, bearing in his humanity all the divine inheritance (name, glory, immortality), transmits to his own the divine Person of the *Pneuma* (Spirit *) that he might enliven them, transform them in turn into what he is. Let us recall the major affirmations of Gal. 4, 4-7: "When the appointed time came, God sent out his Son on a mission to us. He took birth from a woman, took birth as a subject of the

---

25. L. Cerfaux, *op. cit.*, p. 223: "The life of Christ is hereafter spiritual, it unfolds following the nature and power of divinity, which is Spirit."

law, so as to ransom those who were subject to the law, and make us sons by adoption. To prove that you are sons, God has sent out the Spirit of his Son into your hearts, crying out in us, *Abba, Father*. No longer, then, art thou a slave, thou art a son; and because thou art a son, thou hast by Divine appointment, the son's right of inheritance:". We meet in this text all the balance of Salvation, at the same time man's redemption and his introduction into divine intimacy.

Numerous allusions or declarations (Rom. 8, 9-17; I Cor. 2, 10-16; 3, 16; 12, 11-13; II Thess. 4, 8; Titus 3, 4-7; etc.) oblige us to recognize a proper and entirely personal activity of the Person of the Holy Spirit in the heart of each faithful "redeemed" and in the whole Church. Here is a new projection of the communion of Life: by the saving work of the Person of the well-beloved Son, sent by the Father, humanity receives a mysterious presence of the Person of the Holy Spirit who dwells in it not statically but in transforming little by little each of its members into an authentic adopted son of the Father (in Jesus Christ the well-beloved and First-born Son), thus giving him the right to the inheritance of the Son. In the great day of the Parousia of the Lord, when all will arise in the body, then only will the work of Salvation be completed: "Then, when this corruptible nature wears its incorruptible garment, this mortal nature its immortality, the saying of scripture will come true, Death is swallowed up in victory. Where then, death, is thy victory; where, death, is thy sting? It is sin that gives death its sting, just as it is the law that gives sin its power; thanks be to God, then, who gives us victory through our Lord Jesus Christ" (I Cor. 15, 54-57). Let us say immediately that it is precisely in this intermediate state opened by Baptism (in which the faithful passes into the death and resurrection of the *Kurios* *) and closed by the Parousia (in which the baptized faithful arises in his spiritual body), that is situated the role of the Eucharist, the sacrament of Salvation.

What we have just recorded from Paul is met in fact, but in different theological climates, in the whole New Testament.

The narrative of Pentecost in the Acts of the Apostles is its testimony *par excellence*. In the sign of the wind and the tongues of fire, the Holy Spirit descended on the Apostles. Peter explains for the assembled and overwhelmed crowd the theological sense of the event. He begins by attaching it explicitly to the Old Testament hope for the eschatological gift of the *ruah* (Spirit *) of God as expressed in particular by Joel. The days of Salvation were opened. Indeed, the Jews put Jesus to death, but: "God, then has raised up this man Jesus, from the dead; .... And now, exalted at God's right hand, he has claimed from his Father his promise to bestow the Holy Spirit; and he has poured out that Spirit" (Acts 2, 32-33). In order to participate in this outpouring of the Spirit and thus receive Salvation * (2, 40), one must "be baptized, in the name of Jesus Christ, to have his sins forgiven," and then one receives "the gift of the Holy Spirit" (2, 38). We are squarely in the face of the same mystery as the one revealed above by Paul: at once the pardon of sins and the gift of the Spirit are affirmed, and that is dependent on the glorification of Jesus after his death. The Pentecostal gift of the *ruah* * of Life thus appears like the ripened fruit of the Pasch of Jesus, since it is poured out on the world from the glorified Christ.[26]. The continuation of the history of the Church shows that this gift is not only temporary, that, on the contrary, the whole life of the community depends on it.

With Paul it is evidently John who leads this essential truth to its ultimate depth. We know in John the mystery of Jesus the Savior is presented as a step toward his "elevation *" 3, 14; 8, 28; 12, 32), an expression which brings together at once an allusion to the elevation on the cross in his death and an allusion to his glorious elevation above all creatures in his glorification.[27]

---

26. See H. E. Swete, *The Holy Spirit in the New Testament*, London, 1910, pp. 77-78: "The Pentecostal outpouring was direct evidence that Jesus was with the Father; it was the ripe fruit of the Passion and the Ressurection consummated and crowned by his Ascension into heaven. This great gift had come from the hands of the exalted Christ."

27. See A. Vergote, *L'Exaltation du Christ du croix selon le quatrième*

John always sees Jesus glorified in relation to the gift of the spirit of the new Life.

This is clear in the episode of the discussion with Nicodemus (3, 5 and 3, 14-17) and in affirmations such as John 16, 7: "It is better for you I should go away; he who is to befriend you will not come to you unless I do go (by my death and my Paschal exaltation) but if only I make my way there, I will send him to you," and 16, 14-15: "And the Spirit will bring honor to me, because it is from me that he will derive what he makes plain to you, because all that belongs to the Father belongs to me." The Spirit will give men (in close connection with the departure of Jesus) the inheritance that the Father transmits to the glorified Son in the intimacy of their union. That comes out more clearly from the events of the death of Christ if they are read in the light of the declaration of Jesus at the time of the Feast of Tabernacles. We do not have to enter here into the complex problems which these words of the Lord in John 7, 37-39 pose to the exegete.[28] The strictest reading according to the whole of Johannine tradition appears to us to be that of the Fathers of Ephesus, taken over today by Lagrange, Braun, Dodd, Kohler: "On the last and greatest day of the feast Jesus stood there and cried aloud, 'If any man is thirsty, let him come to me and drink; yes, if a man believes in me, as the scripture says, Fountains of living water shall flow from

---

évangile, in *Ephem. Theol. Lov.*, 1952, pp. 5-23; B.F. Westcott, *The Gospel according to St. John*, Cambridge, 1881, p. 53.

28. Principal studies on the problems which the punctuation of this verse poses and the theological interpretation which results: F. M. Braun, *L'eau et l'Esprit*, R.T., 1949, pp. 5-30; C. Lattey, *A note on John 7, 37-38*, Scripture, 1954, pp. 151-153; A. M. Dubarle, *Des fleuves d'eau vive* in *R.B.*, 1943-1944, pp. 238-241; K. Rahner, *Flumina de ventre ejus*, in *Verbum Domini*, 1941, pp. 327-337; *Flumina de ventre Christi: Dei Patristische Auslegung von Joh. 7, 37-38*, in *Biblica*, 1941, pp. 269-302, 367-403; E. Boismard, *De son ventre couleront des fleuves d'eau vive*, in *R.B.*, 1958, pp. 523-546; M. Kohler, *Des fleuves d'eau vive*, in *Rev. de Theol. et de philos.*, 1960, pp. 188-202; P. Grelot, *Jean 7, 38; eau du rocher ou source du Temple?* in *R.B.*, 1963, pp. 43-52; *de son fleuve couleront des fleuves d'eau vive*, in *R.B.*, 1959, pp. 369-373.

his bosom.' He was speaking here of the Spirit, when was to be received by those who learned to believe in him; the Spirit which had not yet been given to men, because Jesus had not yet been raised to glory. . . ." From the bosom of Jesus lifted up in his Pasch (and not, it seems, from the bosom of the believers) the river of living water of the Spirit, announced to the Samaritan woman, for the new Life in this Spirit revealed to Nicodemus, flows upon the world. Then when John states that after Jesus died, "one of the soldiers opened his side with a spear; and immediately blood and water flowed out" (19, 34), several theologians and exegetes [29] see in that sign the realisation of the prophecy of the Feast of Tabernacles. Already several Fathers had recognized there the very birth of the Church.[30] Perhaps it is necessary to keep the interesting suggestion put forth by Dodd and Hoskyns.[31] In order to describe the death of Jesus, John, instead of the cry mentioned by Mark and Matthew or the prayer in Luke, says "He yielded up (transmitted to them) his Spirit (*paredoken to pneuma*)" (19, 30). Plunged into the theological synthesis of John this little sentence can take on a profound meaning: inclining his head toward Mary and John, Jesus, lifted up on the cross, "delivers" to them the eschatological Spirit, this Spirit of the new Life springing out of his death.[32]

---

29. Thus E. C. Hoskyns, *The Fourth Gospel*, London, 1947, pp. 532-536; C.H. Dodd, *The Interpretation of the Fourth Gospel*, Cambridge, 1953, pp. 428-429; O. Cullmann, *Les sacrements dans l'évangile johannique*, Paris, 1951, pp. 81-83 (does not make direct allusion to our passage, and his vision is especially sacramentarian); F.M. Braun, *op. cit.*, pp. 15-20.

30. One will find some testimonies in B. F. Westcott, *op. cit.*, pp. 284-286, and E. C. Hoskyns, *op. cit.*, pp. 534-536.

31. C.H. Dodd, *op. cit.*, p. 428 and 442, note 1; E.C. Hoskyns, *op. cit.*, p. 532; of the same author *Genesis I-III and St. John's Gospel*, in *Journal of Theol. Stud.*, 1920, pp. 210-218.

32. "The outpouring of the Spirit here recorded must be understood in close connection with the outpouring of the water and the blood. The similar association of Spirit and Water and Blood in I John 5, 8, there are three who bear witness, the Spirit and the water and the blood, and the three agree in one, seems to make this interpretation not only possible, but necessary" (E. C. Hoskyns, *op. cit.*, p. 532).

Evident is the importance of the appearance of Easter evening: "He breathed on them, and said to them, Receive the Holy Spirit; when you forgive men's sins, they are forgiven, when you hold them bound, they are held bound" (20, 19-23). The verb used (*emphusan*), which is found only here in the whole New Testament, refers explicitly to the Greek version of Gen. 2, 7 (the narrative of the creation of man) and of Ezechiel 21, 9 (the dry bones regain life). Leaving aside the problem of the relation between this gift of Easter evening and the Pentecostal gift,[33] let us note all the implications of this text. The mention of the pardon of sins refers us to the first moment of the saving forces, the gift of breath (which is the Holy Spirit) to the creation of the new humanity not *ex nihilo* but from sinful humanity. The little group of disciples, assembled behind "locked doors," receives from the Paschal Christ the "inbreathing" which, as the original core of the new humanity, as the "initial cell," it has charge of spreading to the extremities of the earth and of history: "I came upon an errand from my Father, and now I am sending you out in my turn" (20, 21).

Such is the second moment of this salvific Pasch. Of the first moment: of redemption, we said that it was "violent," engaging all the power of God. We can give the same adjective to the second. It is a moment of re-creation, but of a re-creation "in greater wonder and honor [34]" than the first. In fact, it is no longer a question of creating from nothing the great adventure of natural life. It is a question of taking man out of a sin of hostility and of leading him to the very heart of divine intimacy in the communion of Life. Only the infinite power of the agape of God can realize this wonder. That allows us to understand how the mystery of salvation necessarily binds together these two moments, these two powerful interventions of God, being at once redemption (rooting out of sin) and communion. It consists

---

33. One will find an interesting reflection on this problem in M. J. Lagrange, *Évangile selon saint Jean*, Paris, 1947 (8e édit.) pp. 514-516; H. B. Swete, *op. cit.*, pp. 167-168.

34. Offertory prayer in the Roman Rite.

of the passage of man in the state of sin and death into the state
of intimacy with God and eternal life. Medievbal theology will
express this in distinguishing two effects of grace, one of cure
(*gratia sanans*) and another of super-elevation (*gratia elevans*).[35]
We must regret that current theological teaching has lost a bit of
the dynamic connection between these two effects of grace
(so clearly underlined by Saint Thomas in his scheme of the
justificatio impii). Man, if we keep the balance of the mystery,
is not pardoned and sanctified, redeemed and super-elevated.
He is pardoned, redeemed in order to be sanctified, super-
elevated. A genuine theology of Salvation will have to take into
account without loss these two moments: Salvation does not consist only of redemption, nor only of sanctification. It consists
of a redemption opening into the communion of Life, in a
communion of Life rooted in redemption.

THE CHURCH IS THIS COMMUNION OF LIFE

Salvation is accomplished therefore in communion with
God, and the place of this communion is the risen Jesus, Jesus
Kurios (Lord *). No one has expressed this positive dimension
of Salvation without denying the aspect of redemption from
sin better than Irenaeus of Lyon.[36] When he tries to characterize
the precise goal of the mission of the Son, this term "communion" (*koinoia, communio*) flows spontaneously from his

---

35. "*Anima per gratiam conformatur Deo*" (I, 43, 5, ad 2), but also
"*solum per gratiam fit remissio poenae*" (I-II, 87, 5, ad 2); "*gratia
Spiritus Sancti abundanter dari non debuit antequam impedimentum peccati
ab humano genere tolleretur, consummata redemptione per Christum*" (I-II,
106, 3); "*gratia . . . est quaedam similitudo divinitatis participata in homine*"
(III, 2, 10, ad I), etc.

36. We know how G. Aulen (*Christus Victor*, French translation, Paris,
1949), reacted against the explanation of the soteriology of Irenaeus in the
line of the so-called physical redemption. For him, and this aspect is without
any doubt present in Irenaeus, the incarnation as such is not sufficient; victory
over sin is necessary, by the work of Christ, especially his death on the cross.

pen: "For He fought and conquered; for He was man con-
tending for the fathers, and through obedience doing away
with disobedience completely: for He bound the strong man,
and set free the weak, and endowed His own handiwork with
salvation, by destroying sin. For He is a most holy and merciful
Lord, and loves the human race. He caused man (human nature)
to cleave to become one with God (in his incarnation).... For
it was incumbent upon the Mediator between God and man, by
His relationship to both, to bring both to friendship and concord, and present man to God, while He revealed God to man.
For, in what way could we be partakers of the adoption of
sons, unless we had received from Him through the Son that
fellowship which refers to Himself, unless His Word, having
been made flesh, had entered into communion with us? Wherefore also He passed through every stage of life, restoring to all
communion with God" (*Adv. Haer.* III, 18, 7; *AN*, vol. I, pp.
447, 448). To this text, in which is mentioned at the same
time the personal communion that the hypostatic union creates
in Jesus and the communion of all mankind with God, the
ultimate goal of the former,[37] let us add this magnificent passage
relative to the act of Salvation: "Since the Lord thus has redeemed us through His own blood, giving His soul for our
souls, and His flesh for our flesh, and has also poured out the
Spirit of the Father for the union and communion of God and
man (*in adunationem et communionem Dei et hominis*), impart-
ing indeed God to men by means of the Spirit (*ad homines
quidem deponente Deum per Spiritum*), and, on the other
hand, attaching man to God by His own incarnation (*ad Deum
autem rursus imponente per suam incarnationem*), and bestow-
ing upon us at His coming immortality durably and truly, by

Moreover, Aulen is not without hardening his position. See G. Wingren, *Man
and the Incarnation*, Edinburgh-London, 1959, pp. 112-143; H. Wheeler
Robinson, *Redemption and Revelation*, London, 1942, pp. 245-280. For a
balanced study of this problem, see J. I. Hochban, *St. Irenaeus on the
Atonement*, in Theol. *Stud.*, 1946, pp. 525-557.

37. For a synthesis of the diverse "communions" envisaged by Irenaeus,
see A. Houssiau, *La christologie de S. Irénée*, Louvain, 1955, pp. 204-207.

means of communion with God (*per communionem quae est ad Deum*)—all the doctrines of the heretics fall to ruin" (Irenaeus, *Adv. Haer.*, V, 1, 2; *AN*, vol. 1, p. 527).[38] If we want to understand in depth the mystery of the Eucharist, the "sacrament of Salvation," we must pursue our research and ask ourselves of what precisely consists this communion of Life, the positive aspect of Salvation.

The answer is very simple. This communion of life is nothing more than the Church. So that saying "the Eucharist, the sacrament of Salvation" or "the Eucharist, the sacrament of the Church" amounts to saying the same thing. This is true on the condition of a faithful understanding of the theological reality expressed by the term *Ekklesia*. The Church is indeed nothing more, in the very depths of its essence, than the communion of life of men with the Father and between them in

---

38. "For it was for this end that the Word of God was made man, and He who was the Son of God became Son of man, that man, having been taken into the word (*commixtus Verbo Dei*), and receiving adoption, might become the son of God" (*Adv. Haer.*, III, 19, 1; *AN*, vol. I, p. 448); "He 'was made in the likeness of sinful flesh,' (Rom. viii, 3) to condemn sin, and to cast it, as now a condemned thing, away beyond the flesh, but that He might call man forth into His own likeness, assigning him as [His own] imitator to God, and imposing on him His Father's law, in order that he may see God, and granting him power to receive the Father; [being] the Word of God who dwelt in man, and became the Son of man, that He might accustom man to receive God, and God to dwell in man, according to the good pleasure of the Father" (*Adv. Haer.*, III, 20, 2; *AN*, vol. I, p. 450); "We have given nothing to Him previously, nor does he desire anything from us, as if he stood in need of it; but we do stand in need of fellowship with Him (*nos autem indigemus ejus quae est ad eum communionis*). And for this reason it was that He graciously poured Himself out, that He might gather us into the bosom of the Father (*"et propterea benigne effudit semetipsum ut nos colligeret sinum Patris*)" (*Adv, Haer.*, III, 20, 3; *AN*, vol. I, p. 528); "he is made man among men, visible and tangible, in order to destroy death, make life appear, and effect a communion between God and man" (*Dem. Apost.*, 6; trans. from tr. L.M. Froidevaux, *Sources chrèt.*, pp. 39-40; see *ibid.*, 31, p. 80); "he is true man . . . . recalling man to communion with God, in order that, by means of this communion with him, we might receive participation in incorruptibility" (*Dem. Apost.*, 40, pp. trans.)

Christ Jesus, by the Holy Spirit. We do not have to do research here on the origins and the implications of the formula. It will suffice for our task to elicit the great articulations of this traditional doctrine,[39] too much overshadowed since the Bellarminian reaction to the positions of the Reformation.

The Pentecostal gift of the Spirit, poured out by the Lord Jesus, which is surely a gift of new Life, cannot be compared with the natural gift of life coming from the first man. At the natural level, indeed, each gift of life is disjunctive. At the precise moment when the new living being bears in himself the elements necessary to lead to good the adventure of his existence, he detaches himself from his source. It is also additive. The life of the new living being adds itself to that of the living source, and makes two lives which will be led side by side, often independently the one from the other. If the living source should disappear, the life of the being engendered in it is not affected. Whereas the gift of spiritual Life is assimilative and unitive. Christ gives the Spirit, with which he is overflowing, in attracting others to him. The happiest comparison remains that of an initial cell around which is built little by little a whole organism. Paul will speak of the Body of Christ being built up from its Head, Jesus *Kurios*,* up to the day when, in the glory of the Parousia, "he places his kingship in the hands of God, his Father, having first dispossessed every other sort of rule, authority, and power; his reign, as we know, must continue until he has put all his enemies under his feet, and the last of those enemies to be dispossessed is death. God has put all things in

---

39. This is what we meet in the expressions of St. Thomas Aquinas. Thus: "*Ecclesiae unitas in duobus attenditur, scilicet in connexione membrorum Ecclesiae ad invicem, seu communicatione; et iterum in ordine omnium membrorum Ecclesiae ad unum Caput* .... *Hoc autem Caput est ipse Christus*" (II-II 39, 1); such a text permits the explanation of the contents of the equivalence made by St. Thomas: "*Corpus Christi Mysticum, quod est societas Sanctorum*" (III, 80, 4). On the Thomist vision of the Church, see Y. M.-J. Congar, *Esquisses du Mystère de l'Église*, Paris, 1953, pp. 50-91; *Bulletin d'ecclésiologie*, in *R. S. P. T.*, 1950, pp. 391-392; 1951, pp. 633-635. This was written before the Council. The constitution *Lumen Gentium* has brought back into focus this traditional viewpoint of the Church.

subjection under his feet; that is, all things have been made subject to him, except indeed that power which made them his subjects. And when that subjection is complete, then the Son himself will become subject to the power which made all things his subjects, so that God may be all in all" (I Cor. 15, 24-28).

This "God all in all" of Paul will be expressed in the theology of John by the theme of indwelling,* illustrated in the allegory of the vine. These two themes, that of the Body of Christ and that of the Dwelling in Jesus, the one complementing the other, make it necessary for us to say a few words about them. at the risk of appearing illogical we will linger especially on the Johannine view, more immediatley linked to our subject and also, so it seems to us, more expressive of the depth of the communion of Life in its two dimensions: the vertical dimension of communion with the Father in Jesus, and the horizontal dimension of communion with the brethren in Jesus.[40]

Dwelling in God

For the synoptic tradition, eternal Life belongs to the future, like an inheritance expected at the end of time: "Everyone who has forsaken home, or parents, or brethren, or wife, or children for the sake of the kingdom of God, will receive in this present world, many times their worth, and in the world to come, everlasting life" (Luke 18, 29-30; see Matt. 7, 13-14; 18, 8-9; 19, 29; 25, 46; Mark 10, 29-30). Paul himself who, as we shall see, insists on the actual presence of the gift of the Spirit and of Salvation which it bears, conceives, however, the Christian life as a situation of tension: we are saved, we already have Life, but we are still waiting, for the plenary gift

---

40. On this Johannine theology of the communion of life we can consult P. Bonnetain, *Grâce selon la doctrine Johannique*, in *Supp. Dict. de la Bible*, t. III, 1938, col. 1106-1124; J. Dupont, *Essais sur la christologie de saint Jean*, Bruges, 1951, pp. 61-234; L. Bouyer, *La Bible et l'Évangile*, Paris, 1951, pp. 193-208; C.H. Dodd, *The Interpretation of the Fourth Gospel*, Cambridge, 1953, pp. 187-200.

of which we have only the *arrhes* * Rom. 6, 20-23; I Tim.
1, 15-16; 6, 11-12; II Tim. 1, 1; 1, 9-10; Titus 1, 1-2; 3, 7;
etc.). This is a very delicate theology upon which we shall
often have to return. John, and this is his original contribution
to the theology of the Church as communion of Life, sees
eternal Life as a reality not awaited for the future but already
given to those who by faith and the new birth by water and
the Spirit have passed into Jesus: "God has given us eternal
life, and this life is to be found in his Son. To keep hold of
the Son is to have life" (I John 5, 11-12; see John 1, 12; 3, 36;
5, 24, 38, 44, 46, 47; 6, 29, 30, 35, 40, 47, 64, 69, etc.). Even
more, for John, since the faithful already has Life, and Life
eternal, death has lost all importance: "He who believes in me,
though he is dead, will live on, and whoever has life, and has
faith in me, to all eternity cannot die" (11, 25-26; see 6, 50-51;
8, 51). The final resurrection which Jesus promises (6, 40, 54)
will be for the believer what, according to John, it was for
Christ, less a radical novelty than the epiphany, the breaking
out, of the Life already present but yet veiled by the conditions
of the flesh.[41]

From the first instant, in a mysterious but real way, the
fullness of the new Life surges in him who receives Christ and
goes to the source of the new birth. He becomes then a man
"born of the Spirit" (John 3, 6, 8), "born of God" (I John 5,
1; 2, 29; 3, 9; 4, 7), a "child of God" (*teknon theou*) (John
1, 12; I John 2, 10; 3, 1; 5, 2),[42] "the seed of God (*sperma*

---

41. "The evangelist agrees with popular Christianity that the believer will
enter into eternal life at the general resurrection, but for him it is a truth of
less importance than the fact that the believer already enjoys eternal life, and
that the former is a consequence of the latter" (Dodd, *op. cit.*, p. 148, *see*
also the fine analysis on pp. 364-367).

42. We borrow from B.F. Westcott (*The Epistles of St. John*, London
1906, pp. 122-124), the following remarks on the difference between teknon
and uios, child and son. In itself, even in biblical language, the term *teknon*
calls forth a community of nature (II. P. 1, 4) that the term *uios* does not
necessarily imply: *uios* can designate solely the object of a paternity of
affection (of the kind of an adoption, for example), and it is in this sense that
in the Old Testament the People of God are called Sons of God, the messianic

theou) dwells in him" (I John 3, 9). This transformation is in Christ, as in passing to the core of the mystery of Jesus. For this new birth and the new relation to God (relation of *teknon*, of child) which results from it operate surely by the reciprocal dwelling of the faithful in Jesus and of Jesus in the faithful. The faithful communes with the inheritance of the Father (and we shall see that this communion is not only of a static order but is active in the plane of Life) by the mediation of his dwelling in Jesus, himself in living and transcendent communion with him whose Son he is by a very particular title, rendered capable (by his paschal sacrifice) of leading his brothers to a genuine participation in his own fullness.

This theme of indwelling is constant in John,[43] but it attains its full height in the allegory of the vine (John 15, 1-17). Jesus does not say: "I am the trunk and you are the branches," he says: "I am the vine, you are its branches" (15, 5). He does not say of the branch that it is "on him," he says that it is "in him" (15, 4-5). We seize on the nuance and its

---

king Son of God also. The term *uios* often puts the accent on the dignity, the privileged relation to a person of great quality; the term *teknon* insists especially on the derivation of life, implying in the one who is the beneficiary an element of similitude with the one who is the principle. On the problem of the vocabulary of sonship, see E. Huntress, *Son of God in Jewish Writings prior to the Christian Era*, in *The Journ. of Bibl. Lit.*, 1935, pp. 117-123; J. L. McKenzie, *Divine Sonship and Individual Religion*, in *The Cath. Bibl. Quart.*, 1945, pp. 32-37; *The Divine Sonship of Men in the Old Testament*, ibid., 1945 pp. 326-339; *The Divine Sonship and Covenant*, Ibid., 1946, pp. 320-331.

43. "He who eats my flesh, and drinks my blood, lives continually in me, and I in him" (John 6, 56); "one who claims to live in him. . ." (I John 2, 6); "the influence of his annointing lives on in you . . . " follow those lessons and dwell in him; yes . . . dwell in him" (2, 27-28); "a man born of God does not live sinfully because the *sperma tou Theou* dwells in him" (3, 9); "when a man keeps his commandments, it means that he is dwelling in God, and God in him. This is our proof that he is really dwelling in us, through the gift of his Spirit" (3, 24); "if we love one another, then we have God dwelling in us" (4, 12); "where a man acknowledges that Jesus is the Son of God, God dwells in him, and he in God. . . he who dwells in love dwells in God, and God in him", "we are in the True God, in his Son Jesus Christ" (5, 20).

importance: Christ Jesus is the whole vine, the trunk as well as the branches; he is the one into whom the faithful (those who "believe in him" in the strong sense which clothes the term *pistis* in John) have passed (precisely by this *faith* and, we shall come back to it, the vitality which it stirs up leading to Baptism and to the Bread of Life). Between Jesus and the faithful there exists not simply the relation vitally uniting the trunk to the branches but the relation uniting the branches to the vine. The faithful are in Jesus in the way that the branches are in the vine, having only the vine for their *raison d'etre*.

This relation implies several consequences: on the one hand the life which bears in it the branch and the fruit which this life makes it produce have no source but the vine, on the other hand in each branch the vine is present. It is the same for the Christian; his eternal Life (already present in him) and the fruits which it bears already have no other source than Jesus, and on the other hand, in him as in each of his fruits, it is Jesus in the integrity of his mystery, who is present and acting.

Then we must say that between Christ and the faithful there exists a mysterious circumincession, very well expressed by the idea of dwelling: "The branch that yields no fruit in me, my Father cuts it away; the branch that does yield fruit, he trims clean, so that it may yield more fruit ... you have only to live on in me (*meinate en emoi*), and I will live on in you. The branch that does not live on in the vine can yield no fruit of itself; no more can you, if you do not live on in me. I am the vine, you are its branches; if a man lives on in me, and I in him, then he will yield abundant fruit; separated from me, you have no power to do anything. If a man does not live on in me, he can only be like the branch that is cast off and withers away. . . . As long as you live on in me, and my words live on in you, you will be able to make what request you will, and have it granted. . . . You will live on in my love, if you keep my commandments, just as it is by keeping my Father's commandments that I live on in his love." It is noteworthy that in this text, which aspires to express the totality of the saving love of Jesus for his disciples and to enunciate to them the great commandment of fraternal charity, the term indwelling comes back ceaselessly as the most apt translation of the reality of the union of Jesus and his own. And we shall note that it is a question of dwelling (*menein*) not in one place, or statically, but rather in a living person, not temporarily but permanently. In the opening verses of the Gospel according to Saint John, the incarnation was presented in these terms: "The Logos was made flesh (man), and came to dwell *eskenosen*) among us." In the singular humanity of Jesus a mysterious communion was in operation: the Son of God, with his divinity, his glory, his fullness, all the favorable grace and the faithfulness of God,[44] assumed human values in view of Salvation. Since the Pasch this process has been prolonged—in a different way, to be sure, since between the faithful and God, there does not exist the unique bond created by the hypostatic union [45]—no longer simply as the way of Salvation but as the goal of Salvation. Christ (the Son of God and brother of men, in all the complexity of his mystery) dwells in the new humanity which is the Church and the Church dwells in him. This is the make-up of Salvation.

But the reflection of John goes much further. This dwelling in Jesus goes, in fact, beyond itself; it becomes a dwelling in the Father: "Where a man acknowledges that Jesus is the Son of God, God dwells in him, and he in God . . . he who dwells in love dwells in God, and God in him" (I John 4, 15-16);

---

44. The "full of grace (*charis*) and truth (*aletheia*)" of John (1, 14) answers to the Hebrew binomial *hesed we emet*. The association of these two terms characterized the God of the saving Covenant, the God of the design of love; *hesed* calls forth the forever fresh power, never weakened, always compassionate, always inventive of new ways, of the love of Yahweh toward his People; *emet* calls forth the solidarity, the fidelity of this same love. See Ps. 25, 10; 40, 11; 57, 3, 10; 61, 8; 89; 115, 1; 138, 2, etc. In Jesus it is this love of Covenant, therefore of communion, which meets humanity. We see the importance of this remark.

45. This point has been clarified well by Y. M.–J. Congar, *Le Christ, Marie et l'Église*, Desclée de B., 1955, pp. 67-80; and especially *Dogme christologique et Ecclésiologie, vérités et limites d'un parallèle*, in *Chalkedon*, t. III, in collaboration, Wurtzbourg, 1954, pp. 239-268.

"We are in the true God, in his Son Jesus Christ" (5, 20; see 3, 9; 4, 12). We meet here the first (and the most essential) dimension of the mystery of the Church, the communion of life with the Father in Jesus by the mediation of the gift of the Spirit,[46] a dimension which we qualify as vertical.

For this Jesus in whom we live, and who lives in us, belongs at the root to an even more profound universe of dwelling: he lives in the Father and the Father lives in him; and it is this actual dwelling of the Father in the Son, of the Son in the Father, which has, in fact, presided over the whole saving work of Jesus. This inter-Trinitarian dwelling is rooted in the strictest unity: "I am in the Father and the Father is in me" (John 14, 10-11; see 10, 30; 10, 38; 14, 20; 17, 11, 21), and comes to light in a mysterious living dynamism of mutual knowledge and mutual love. Certainly, John is not speaking explicitly of meta-historical Trinitarian relations within the Godhead. He considers the Father-Son relations only in connection with the historical mission of the Son. But his affirmations open perspectives on the intradivine intimacy, and we know how living Tradition will lean on them to deepen its faith in the Trinity of Persons. Moreover, it is of little importance here, since it is in Jesus, Son of God in his incarnate state, that the Christian lives. The Father knows the Son and the Son knows the Father (John 6, 48; 7, 29; 8, 55; 10, 15); the Father loves the Son and the Son loves the Father ("You have loved me before the creation of the world," 17, 23-26; 3, 35; 14, 30; 15, 9); the Father glorifies the Son and the Son glorifies the Father (12, 20-28;

---

46. "He will bring honor to me (the Spirit of truth), because it is from me that he will derive what he makes plain to you. I say that he will derive from me what he makes plain to you, because all that belongs to the Father belongs to me" (John 16, 14-15). But this gift of the Spirit is explicitly linked by John to the glorious exaltation of Jesus: "He was speaking here of the Spirit, which was to be received by those who learned to believe in him; the Spirit which had not yet been given to men, because Jesus had not yet been raised to glory" (John 7, 39). The sense of this last verse is independent of the problem of punctuation posed by the whole passage and of which we have spoken above (note 1, p. 35).

13, 31-32; 17, 1-5). When the faithful passes into the Son to dwell there, he is at the same time introduced into this transcendent dwelling of the Father and the Son with all its network of Life: "On that day you will understand that I am in my Father and you in me and I in you" (John 14, 20); "That they may all be one; that they too may be one in us, as thou, Father, art in me, and I in thee. . . . And I have given them the privilege which thou gavest to me, that they should all be one, as we are one; that while thou art in me, I may be in them, and they may be perfectly made one. So let the world know that it is thou who hast sent me, and that thou hast bestowed thy love upon them, as thou hast bestowed it upon me. This, Father, is my desire, that all those whom thou hast entrusted to me may be with me where I am, so as to see my glory, thy gift made to me, in that love which thou didst bestow upon me before the foundation of the world . . . so that the love thou hast bestowed upon me may dwell in them, and I, too, may dwell in them" (17, 21-26).

We are here perhaps face to face with the most beautiful and most compact text of the whole Bible; and it is to be regretted that the commentaries so often mutilate it, being content with insisting on the aspect of unity without showing forcibly enough how this unity is realized in dwelling in the Father and is expanded in mutual knowledge and love, thus plunging the faithful into the universe of the intradivine intimacy. Here is the ultimate goal of Salvation, of the long economy led by the Word of Yahweh incarnate in Jesus to the end of time: "If anyone loves me he will keep my word and my Father will love him, and we will come to him and we will make in him our dwelling" (14, 23). In Jesus the Christian meets the Father. In the midst of their personal relations a profound communion of Life links Father and Son. Just as a mutual love seals up this communion of Life, so the reciprocal love of the Son and men establishes a bond of communion between him and them, making them meet the Father and Son in the communion of Life. In the Son men know the Father and are known by him (14, 7-8; 17, 1; I John 2, 3; 2, 13-14;

4, 8; 5, 20); in the Son, men love the Father and are loved by him (17, 26; 16, 27; 14, 21; I John 4, 9-10; 4, 19); in the Son, men glorify the Father and are glorified by him (15, 8; 17, 22). Because they are in Jesus, they are also in the Father. This majestic truth finds its strongest expression (which will never be surpassed) in 17, 21: "As thou, Father, art in me, and I in thee, that they "should also be one in us." [47] "One in us" (*autoi en emin*): this is the most intimate communion possible between God and man. Here it is a question of a real communion in Life: divine energy traverses the faithful in order that his works be those of God himself. But that is through a concrete historical person, in whom this communion springs perfectly, Jesus the Christ. One sees into what depth Salvation in Jesus leads us.

We have just spoken of Salvation. Sin did not have the sole effect of separating us from living communion with God. It has also set us one against another: the murder of Abel by Cain his brother after the sin of Adam and Eve is an expression of that drama. The sacrifice of Jesus, in its turn, will not limit its efficacy to this vertical communion which we have just spoken about. It will always resolve "in Jesus," the unity of men, a horizontal communion.

Here again Johannine theology represents a summit. For John, Salvation (in its positive aspect of projection into the world of God) is at the very same time both indissociably the communion

---

47. C. H. Dodd (*op. cit.*, pp. 196-197) writes: "It is clear that for the evangelist, as for Hellenistic writers whom I have cited, the idea, *en Theo*, with its correlative, God in us, stands for the most intimate union conceivable between God and men. But it clearly does not mean for him, as it does for some of them, an impersonal inclusion, or absorption, into the divine, conceived pantheistically; nor does it mean, as for some others, an ecstatic possession by a divine *afflatus*. It is so far like the former that it involves a real community of being, a sharing of life; and it is so far like the latter that it is a dynamic relation and not a static one, producing the effects of an incursion of divine energy through which men may speak the words and do the works of God. But it is unlike both in being a personal relation with a living God, mediated through a concrete, historical personality, in whom that relation is original and perfect.

of Life with the Father in Jesus and the communion of Life with the brethren in Jesus. All this constitutes for him the essential nucleus of the mystery of the Church. Speaking to his faithful, even in his own name, he makes clear to them: "What is it, this fellowship of ours? Fellowship with the Father, and with his Son Jesus Christ . . . if we claim fellowship (*koinonia*) with him, when all the while we live and move in darkness, it is a lie, our whole life is an untruth. God dwells in light; if we too live and move in light, there is fellowship (*koinonia*) between us, and the blood of his Son Jesus Christ washes us clean from all sin" (I John 1, 3-7). Even more, the state of *agape* toward the brethren, the state of fraternal love, is for John the only sign capable of giving to man the certainty of his entrance into the communion of Life with the Father: "Remember that we have changed over from death to life (dynamism of the salutary act), in loving the brethren as we do; whereas, if a man is without love, he holds fast by death. A man cannot hate his brother without being a murderer, and you may be sure that no murderer has eternal life dwelling in him. God has proved his love to us by laying down his life for our sakes; we too must be ready to lay down our lives for the brethren" (I John 3, 14-18).

It is easy to seize on the ultimate reason of this necessary communion of men among themselves—realized by a love which is not only theoretical but active, since John gives the example of him who sees his brother in need and withholds help when he is rich—as a fruit of salvation. We have just seen how, passed into Christ, the faithful was trained, by the very rhythm of the life of Christ, in a genuine communion of Life with the Father.

Communicating with this Life, he is also vitally touched by the current of love, of obedience full of love, of total fidelity to the Father's design which bears the mystery of Jesus; and, fundamentally, he cannot, in his turn (but always in Jesus), fail to espouse this design. This design is essentially a design of *agape*, of love of men. Then, in the very instant that he passes into God, the Christian passes into the love of men, that he finds in the Father. John can then write: "If we love one another, God dwells in us, in us his love is accomplished" (I John 4, 12); "accomplished" in us first but also by us in the world. The Communion of Life with the Father flourishes therefore in Communion of Life with the brethren, the one does not go without the other, and these two dimensions integrate Salvation necessarily and inseparably. We understand now the profound sense of the "commandment of brotherly love" given by Christ in the very context of the allegory of the vine: "If you keep my commandments, you will live in my love, as I have kept the commandments of my Father and I dwell in his love. . . . Here is my commandment: love one another as I have loved you. . . .What I command you is that you love one another" (15, 10-17; see also I John 5, 3; 3, 11-12; 3, 23; 4, 21). It is not a question of an unexpected order to an already established Communion of Life, but of the very law of this Life. In Christ, the faithful meets all his brothers, not in the accidental fashion of the edges of a pyramid meeting only in the fine point uniting the whole, but rather in the fashion of concentric circles whose surfaces cover each other. In each of his brothers who have passed "into Jesus," he meets Jesus and the Father; in Jesus and his Father he meets all his brothers. The paschal gift of the Spirit, aim of the sacrifice of Jesus the Servant of God, has effected this wondrous *koinonia* (communion *). In this encounter in Jesus of the vertical communion with the Father and of the horizontal communion with the brethren, we recognize the Mystery of the Church.[48] For the Christian

---

48. This theology of the Church as Communion of Life dominated the admirable Commentary on the First Epistle of St. John of St. Augustine. Read in the edition of P. Agaësse, *Sources chrétiennes,* 75, 1961, the introduction, pp. 87-102. Let us cite this passage which, concerning the theme of husband and wife, takes up this concept of the Church as communion: "That bridegroom's chamber was the Virgin's womb, because in that virginal womb were joined the two, the Bridegroom and the bride, the Bridegroom the Word, and the bride the flesh; because it is written, 'and they twain shall be one flesh;' and the Lord saith in the Gospel, 'Therefore, they are no more twain but one flesh.' And Isaias remembers right well that they are two: for speaking in the person of Christ he saith, 'He hath set a mitre upon me as upon a bridegroom, and adorned me with an ornament as a bride.' One seems to

Salvation consists then in passing at the same time into the Father and into communion with his brothers. In short, the living forces of Salvation come to a head in the Church.

Incorporation into Christ the Head

Paul expresses the same reality (which is essentially at the base of faith) under another form, by his theology of the Church, the Body of Christ the Head.[49] In his sacrifice Jesus accomplished Salvation: henceforth, men have access to the Father (the vertical dimension of Salvation), and also the barrier of hostility which separated them is reversed (the horizontal dimension). "But now you are in Christ Jesus; now, through the blood of Christ, you have been brought close, you who were once so far away. He is our bond of peace; he has made the two nations one, breaking down the wall that was a barrier between us, the enmity there was between us, in his own mortal nature. He has put an end to the law with its decrees, so as to make peace, remaking the two human creatures as one in himself; both sides, united in a single body, he would

---

speak, yet makes Himself at once Bridegroom and Bride; because 'not two, but one flesh:' because 'the Word was made flesh the Church is joined, and so there is made the whole Christ, Head and Body"' (In *I am Epist. Joan.*, tract. 1, 2; *NP-N* vol. VII, p. 461.) See also in the same sense *In Joan. Evang.*, tract. 9, 10. This has been equally vigorously clarified by H. B. Swete, *The Holy Catholic Church: The Communion of Saints*, London, 1916.

49. The major references here are L. Cerfaux, *La théologie de l'Église suivant S. Paul*, Paris 1948, pp. 201-218, 243-259, 276-280; *Le Christ dans la théologie de S. Paul*, Paris, 1954, pp. 264-266, 320-322; P. Benoit, *Corps, Tête et Plèrome dans les épîtres de la Captivité* in *R.B.*, 1956, pp. 5-44, taken up in *Exégése et Théologie*, t. II, Paris, 1961, pp. 107-153; collation of the book of J.A.T. Robinson, *The Body*, in *R.B.*, 1957, pp. 581-585, taken up in *Exégèse et Théologie*, t. II, Paris, 1961, pp. 165-171; L. Malevez, *L'Église Corpus du Christ, sens et provenance de l'expression chez S. Paul*, in *Sciences Rel.* (ie., *Rech. de Sc. Rel.*), 1944, pp. 27-94; H. Schlier, *Le Temps de l'Église, Tournai*, 1961, pp. 169-193, 291-309 (revival of former articles); B. M. Ahern, *The Christian's Union with the Body of Christ in Cor., Gal. and Rom.*, in *The Cath. Bibl. Quart.*, 1961, pp. 199-209; J. Havet, *La doctrine paulinienne du Corps du Christ*, in *Lit. et théol. pauliniennes*, D. d. B., 1960, pp. 185-216.

reconcile to God through his cross, inflicting death, in his own person, upon the feud. So he came, and his message was of peace for you who were far off, peace for those who were near; far off or near, united in the same Spirit, we have access through him to the Father" (Eph. 2, 13-18).[50] Jesus, the restored new Adam, carries in him the breath of the new Life which is alone capable of enlivening this restored humanity of the brethren. But this new humanity, precisely because of the entirely transcendent quality of the bond uniting it to its source (to its principle, therefore to its Adam) and uniting between them each of its members, cannot conceive itself uniquely in the scheme of a human society, of a group of men united by the pursuit of a single goal, indeed, in the scheme of natural humanity in which all possess the same specific nature from the same common ancestor, but, however, multiplied according to individuals and really existing only in this multiplication, since the species does not exist as such.

The studies of H. Schlier, of Msgr. Cerfaux and of P. Benoit[51] have shown how this concept of the Church as a mere "social body" weakens the great Pauline intuition. The new humanity is constituted in coming to unite itself really and physically, but sacramentally and mysteriously, to the singular humanity of Jesus the Lord. Salvation is effected by the union of the body and soul of the faithful with the personal soul and body of the risen Jesus, so that at the end of the process we find not the life of Jesus and the life of the faithful, but the life of Jesus in the faithful. One breath of life (the *Pneuma* exalting the humanity of Christ) enlivens at the same time Jesus and each of the baptized. There where several living organisms

---

50. One will note that the text opens on the theme of the indwelling: "Thus you are no longer exiles, then, or aliens; the saints are your fellow-citizens, you belong to God's household. Apostles and prophets are the foundation on which you were built and the chief corner-stone of it is Jesus Christ himself. In him the whole fabric is bound together, as it grows into a temple, dedicated to the Lord; in him you too are being built in with the rest, so that God may find in you a dwelling-place for his Spirit" (2, 19-22).

51. References given in note 2, p. 59.

are touched by the one, same breath of life, there is a single body. The same here: the whole of the Baptized forms a single body, the Body of Christ, in and by the Holy Spirit given by Jesus. We cannot linger here on this point but one sees the realism of this doctrine and the light that it projects on the mystery of Salvation. The sacrifice of Jesus is accomplished in a wondrous *koinonia* (Communion *): on the one hand, his personal humanity is itself inundated, transfixed completely by the inheritance of divinity, on the other hand, men, in coming to meet in him as members, receive a participation in this fullness which he bears; he is really "God all in all" (I Cor. 15, 28).[52]

In the Epistles of the captivity, Paul again makes clear this doctrine in emphasizing the role of Christ in this progressive establishment of his Body. He is the Head of the Body, because—we meet here, it seems, the Greek views of medicine at the time of Paul—he is the source of the vital influx:[53] "In Christ the whole plenitude of Deity is embodied, and dwells in him, and it is in him that you find your completion; he is the fountain head from which all dominion and power proceed ... you, by baptism, have been united with his burial, united, too, with his resurrection, through your faith in that exercise of power by which God raised him from the dead.

---

52. "Unity is manifested even better if we look at things on the side of Christ. And besides, in the domain of Christian things, it is a reality: not only are we like a body, but we really belong to Christ, and since his life is ours, we are truly members, and Christ is the principle of unity and life between us as the body of which we are members. Baptism consecrated us to the body of Christ, and the Eucharist identifies us with this body of Christ to which it refers us, in such a way that Christ is really, for all Christians, their body. Christians are a body, not by the simple law of comparison, but in a sacramental and mystical realism" (L. Cerfaux, *Le Christ dans la théologie de S. Paul*, Paris 1954, p. 265).

53. P. Benoit, *Corps, Tête et Plérome dans les épîtres de la captivité*, in R. B., 1956, pp. 25-31, studies the problem of the two senses of the word *kephale* — that of the vital principle and that of the hierarchical principle — in Pauline theology. He chooses a passage (without exclusiveness) from the hierarchical sense to the sense of vital principle.

And in giving life to him, he gave life to you too, when you lay dead in your sins, with nature all uncircumcised in you. He condoned all your sins ... (he who insists on a false humility which addresses its worship to angels) takes his stand upon false visions; his is the ill-founded confidence that comes of human speculation. He is not united to that head of cure, on whom all the body depends, supplied and unified by joint and ligament, and so growing up with a growth which is divine" (Col. 2, 10-19; see 1, 15-20; Eph. 1, 22; 4, 15).

One cannot conceive of a stricter union on the one hand between Jesus and the baptized, on the other hand between each baptized and his brother. Already the Epistle to the Corinthians had strongly emphasized this: "A man's body is all one, though it has a number of different organs; and all this multitude of organs goes to make up one body; so it is with Christ. We too, all of us, have been baptized into a single body by the power of a single Spirit, Jews and Greeks, slaves and free men alike; we have all been given drink at a single source, the one Spirit. The body, after all, consists not of one organ but of many" (I Cor. 12, 12-27; see 6, 12-20; 10, 17; Rom. 12, 3-8). All are brothers because all are enlivened by the same Spirit, sprung from the same source of vital influx; belonging all to the same Body; therefore living of one Life, proportionately the same with all, and in the Head, and working for the fruits fundamentally attributable to all. Salvation ends in the Church.

Adopted Sonship in Jesus the Only-Begotten

Enlivened by the Spirit which he received at Baptism "in the death and resurrection of Christ" and which dwells in him as its temple,[54] changed by this Spirit, in the way by which a

---

54. This theme of Temple has been studied with much detail by Y. M.–J. Congar, *Le Mystère du Temple*, Paris, 1958 (especially, for the immediate point aimed at here, pp. 183-205). A complete enough pneumatology is missing in Catholic theology; for the essence of the problem, refer to the very crowded pages of L. Cerfaux, *La théologie de l'Église suivant S. Paul*,

member is without cease under the immediate influx of the current of life (under pain of being detached from the body and of being corrupted), the faithful becomes "in Jesus" (in the very strong sense that we have just used) the adopted son of the Father, for the inheritance of glory. He is thus engaged in a dynamism of progressive deepening which will find its total bloom only at the moment of the Parousia. This is an important point for our subject and we have to go into depth a little here.

What is understood by this title "adopted son," expressing the very special relation of communion with the Father into which the gift of the Spirit leads us?

"Through faith in Jesus Christ you are all now God's sons (*uioi*). All you who have been baptized in Christ's name have put on the person of Christ; no more Jew or Gentile, no more slave and freeman, no more male and female; you are all one person in Jesus Christ. And if you belong to Christ, then you are indeed Abraham's children; the promised inheritance is yours. Consider this; one who comes into his property while he is still a child has no more liberty than one of the servants, though all the estate is his; he is under the control of guardians and trustees, until he reaches the age prescribed by his father. So it was with us; in those childish days (*nepioi*) of ours we toiled away at the schoolroom tasks which the world gave us, till the appointed time came. Then God sent out his Son (*uios*) on a mission to us. He took birth from a woman, took birth as a subject of the law, and made us sons by adoption (*uiothesia*). To prove that you are sons (*uioi*), God has sent out the Spirit of his Son (*uios*) into your hearts, crying out in us, *Abba, Father*. No longer, then, art thou a slave, thou art a son; and because thou art a son, thou hast, by Divine appoint-

Paris, 1942, pp. 120-131; *Le Christ dans la théologie de S. Paul*, Paris, 1954, pp. 209-236. The most complete synthesis remains that of the Anglican theologian and exegetist H. B. Swete, *The Holy Spirit in the New Testament*, London, 1910 (especially pp. 283-360). One will find interesting notations and numerous references in C. Spicq, *Vie morale et Trinité Sainte selon saint Paul*, 1957, pp. 49-71.

ment, the son's right of inheritance" (Gal. 3, 26; 4, 7). The vocabulary itself, and the use of the word Son (*uios*), obliges us to see in this sonship like a prolongation of the personal relation uniting the Son to his Father; we are adopted as sons in the Son. Elsewhere, the same insistence is met, in connection, this time, especially with the theme of inheritance: "Those who follow the leading of God's Spirit are all God's sons (*uioi*); the spirit you have now received is not, as of old, a spirit of slavery, to govern you by fear; it is the spirit of adoption (*uiothesia*), which makes us cry out, *Abba, Father*. The Spirit himself thus assures our spirit, that we children (*tekna*) of God; and if we are his children, then we are his heirs too; heirs of God, sharing the inheritance of Christ; only we must share his sufferings, if we are to share his glory" (Rom. 8, 14-20). There is no possible doubt, everything here evokes a very great intimacy, which bears all the affection with which Paul generally charges their Father-Son relationship,[55] and which the mention of inheritance again emphasizes.

Nevertheless it is only the question of adopted sonship (Rom. 8, 15, 23; Gal. 4, 5; Eph. 1, 5); this is an important distinction since not only does it avoid any pantheistic tendency but especially accents again the procession of love undergirding the divine initiative of Salvation. Only the sonship of Christ Jesus is unique and natural;[56] to characterize ours Paul christianizes an old Greek juridical term, that of adoption (*uiothesia*):

---

55. Even when it is situated in the simple plane of human paternity, Paul does not see it solely under the angle of the relation of origins (the father is he who gives life.), but he charges it with all the implications of the paternity of affection (educative, provident, moved by love). Thus I Thess. 2, 11; I Cor. 4, 15; Gal. 4, 2. In the same way when he speaks of the Father-Son relations: Col. 1, 13 calls him well-beloved Son (with the pregnant sense of this adjective in Biblical language); see also Eph. 1, 6.

56. This natural sonship is affirmed in texts like Rom. 1, 3, 4, 9, 10; 8, 3, 29; I Cor. 1, 9; II Cor. 1, 19; Gal. 1, 16; 2, 20; 4, 4, 6; Col. 1, 13; I Thess. 1, 10. On the relations between the two sonships, Christ's and our own, see L. Cerfaux, *Le Christ dans la Théologie de S. Paul*, Paris, 1954, pp. 329-341.

God has chosen us, in the only Son, as his sons, when indeed we had no right to it, when nothing in us could postulate this honor and its consequences.

Moreover, the purely juridical contents of the term are passed by here: incorporation into Christ the Head in the title of member, being truly vivified by the same breath of Life as his, causes a new reality, not a simple juridical title, in the Christian. "In Christ" the faithful participates truly, (although mysteriously), in the mystery of God. He becomes a son in the Son, thus a communicant of the divine inheritance. Paul puts that in the picture through several converging traces. Thus: "All those who from the first were known to him, he has destined from the first to be moulded into the image of his Son, who is thus to become the eldest-born among many brethren" (Rom. 8, 29-30; see I Cor. 15, 48-49; II Cor. 4, 4-6; Col. 1, 15); for the Bible image does not only say similitude (two eggs or two twins are not the image one of the other), but also natural derivation.[57] Another indication in the same sense: "My little children, I am in travail over you afresh, until I can see Christ's image formed in you!" (Gal. 4, 19). Moreover, Paul says that the Christian is "regenerate" in the Spirit of Christ (Titus 3, 5-6; I Cor. 4, 15), that he has become a "new creature" (Gal. 6, 15; II Cor. 5, 17; Eph. 2, 10; 4, 24).

All this tends toward the sense of a real bond uniting the Christian to Christ and through him to the Father, a bond that is realized by incorporation into him who, in his resurrection, has become the Head of the new humanity. Medieval theology, especially in its Thomist synthesis, rendered perfect account of this Pauline foundation by the doctrine of capital grace: all grace given to men and integrating them thus in the Church "derives from the plenitude and the eminence of the grace of Christ" (see III, 8, 5), so well that "in the incarnate Son" God

---

57. See J. B. Lightfoot, *The Epistle of St Paul to the Colossians*, London, 1880, pp. 144-146.

accords to the faithful "a certain similitude of the natural eternal sonship of his only-begotten * Son." [58]

The Situation of Tension Proper to Salvation

There is the realistic vision that Paul makes of Salvation to which the death and resurrection of Christ introduce the faithful: in the unique reality of the Body of Christ, and always in vital reference to the person of the glorified Jesus, man enters into a close spiritual Communion of Life with the Father (who adopts him as a son) and with other men (who become his brothers). But at the core of this majestic view Paul is going to assume, more than John does, a historical dimension of progress. We saw above how for John eternal Life was given at once in the reception of Christ by the faithful. Strengthening his idea somewhat, one could characterize thus the progress of the new Life in the Christian: the veil (again "of the world") covering this glory in him will become more and more tenuous and fragile, up to the day when, at the Parousia,* it will be torn away completely. It is less a progress in Life itself than in what presently prevents it from being manifested in all its fullness. Paul, on the contrary, will put progress in this Life

---

58. It would be necessary to cite here St. Thomas of Aquinas, III, 23, on the sonship of Christ. St. Thomas studies there in a very realistic fashion, also very close to the Pauline basis, the problem of the adopted sonship of Christians. It is very much to be regretted that this question is so often hurried over in current teaching, as much in the tracts on Christ as well as in those on divine grace. Let us bring into relief the following affirmations: "*Sicut per actum creationis communicatur bonitas divina omnibus creaturis secundum quandam similitudinem, ita per actum adoptionis communicatur similitudo naturalis filiationis hominibus secundum illud Rom. 8, 29: Quos praescivit conformes fieri imaginis Filii sui*" (III, 23, 1, ad 2); "*adoptari convenit soli creaturae rationali; non tamen omni, sed solum habenti caritatem, quae est diffusa in cordibus nostris per Spiritum Sanctum, ut dicitur Rom. 5, 5. Et ideo Rom. 8, 15 Spiritus Sanctus dicitur Spiritus adoptionis filiorum*" (III, 23, 3,). We are far, in these very strong expressions, from the diluted solution often given in leaning on a badly understood theology of Trinitarian appropriations.

itself, first given in the seed, then gradually developing to its full bloom in the glory of the resurrection of the flesh. This is a passage from the possession of the *"arrhes"* * of glory to the possession of total reality.

For our heritage as "adopted sons in Jesus the well-beloved Son" is nothing more than the sharing of the proper glory of Christ the Lord, itself a participation in the glory of God: "We are children of God; and if we are his children, then we are his heirs too; heirs of God, sharing the inheritance of Christ; only we must share his sufferings, if we are to share his glory. Not that I count these present sufferings as the measure of that glory which is to be revealed in us.... The whole of nature, as we know, groans in a common travail all the while. And not only do we see that, but we ourselves do the same; we ourselves, although we have already begun to reap our spiritual harvest, groan in our hearts, waiting for that adoption which is the ransoming of our bodies from their slavery" (Rom. 8, 17-23.

In the train of the risen Christ, and in him, all our being, body as well as spirit, will, as it were, become radiant with the glory of God. This glory which in Scripture designates the splendor and the radiance of the divine power of Yahweh, even having the characteristics of a divine attribute, is incommunicable of itself. To say that man, when he perceives the totality of the inheritance, will become "a glorious being" (I Cor. 15, 43; II Cor. 3, 18; Phil. 3, 21), is to affirm the intimacy of the communion of Life to which Salvation has introduced him: "It is to heaven that we look expectantly for the coming of our Lord Jesus Christ to save us; he will form this humbled body of ours anew, molding it into the image of his glorified body, so effective is his power to make all things obey him" (Phil. 3, 21). The Father will give us for an inheritance a portion (in a mysterious fashion whose concrete modalities we are not familiar with) of this total communication of his divine goods which at the day of resurrection he gave to the singular humanity of him who was also his own only-begotten * Son. Incorporated into

Jesus we poor redeemed creatures will be transfixed by the glory of God in the privilege of immortality.

This future glory is not however, completely of the future. Indeed, we already possess its *arrhes*.* Here we touch upon one of the most delicate aspects to discern well, Pauline soteriology. In the course of this work, we will often have to return to this to deepen it, for there its source takes on the dimension of tension proper to the Christian experience which characterizes the present state of the Church, the Pilgrim Church on the way to the fulness of the glorious eschatological Church. Everything has already been given at the very instant of incorporation into Christ the Head. However, everything is yet awaited because it has all been given in the germ which—although it already contains all the fruit—has not yet attained its full blossom. It will find it only ecclesially, at the moment when, at the time of the Parousia * of the Lord, the whole Body of Christ, in a single instant, will be resurrected. The ultimate glory of the definitive manifestation of the Head will coincide with the ultimate blossoming of the seed of life which this Head has infused in his members. It will be, in the strictest sense of the term, the Day of the Church.

We wait for that time, not as for a completely unknown future, not blindly, but in the certitude of Christian expectation which knows that that which it awaits is already present for it. Scholastic theology will express this existential situation of the Christian by the thesis—which one would like to see more often explained and analyzed by the manuals—"grace is the beginning of glory in man." [59] Beginning, *inchoatio,* not simply a verbal announcement, a promise of which the realization is sure, but on the contrary a real presence although without the final bloom, the authentic foundation already bearing the ultimate goal although it has not yet emerged from the seed.

This is what the Pauline vocabulary evokes: "We possess

---

59. II-II, 24, 3 ad 2.

the first-fruits (*aparche*) of the Spirit and groan in wait
for the redemption of our body" (Rom. 8, 23); "He has put
in our hearts the *arrhes* * (*arrabon*) of the Spirit" (II Cor.
1, 22; see Eph. 1, 13-14; II Cor. 5, 5). Transposed outside
the juridical domain, in the register of life, the notion in question here calls forth the presence of the oak in the acorn, of
the adult in the child. It is that which permits us to grasp
the whole complexity of the Christian situation, for the Christian is already saved, already belongs to the Kingdom of God:
the pagans are saved (Rom. 11, 11), the "Day of Salvation"
is already here (II Cor. 6, 2), "we have already risen with
Christ" (Col. 2, 12), "seated with Christ in heaven" (Eph.
2, 5), as well as "our life is hidden with Christ in God" (Col.
3, 5). And in spite of everything we "await Salvation" (see
Phil. 3, 20; 2, 12), we "will be saved" (Rom. 5, 10), we
"will be glorified with him" (Rom. 8, 17), we "shall inherit
the Kingdom of God" (I Cor. 6, 9-10; 15, 50; Gal. 5, 21; Eph.
5, 5; Col. 3, 24; Tit. 3, 7), and even more we "await our
Savior, the Lord Jesus Christ who will transfigure our body of
misery in order to conform it to his body of glory" (Phil.
3, 20). Is this a contradiction? No, it is quite simply a description of the state of tension characteristic of the present age
of the Church, an age of faith in which all is present, although
in "mystery," in the certitude which the Word of God establishes and not in the evidence of vision.

The Parousia * will be like the developer revealing in all
its clarity what was, however, impressed in the depths of our
beings but was not released from the natural quality of our life:
"Risen, then, with Christ, you must lift your thoughts above,
where Christ now sits at the right hand of God. You must be
heavenly-minded, not earthly-minded; you have undergone
death, and your life is hidden away now with Christ in God.
Christ is your life, and when he is made manifest, you too will
be made manifest in glory with him" (Col. 3, 1-4). Right up
to the great resurrection, accomplished under the refulgent
light of the glory of Christ the Son of Man, our bodies buried
in death will not yet partake of the communion in the divine

inheritance: glory, immortality, joy and peace, which constitute the divine inheritance, will be given to them only at the precise instant when, according to the plan of the Father, the entire Church will have attained its definitive proportions. The bonds of interdependence and of mutual solidarity of the members of the Body of Christ the Head go that far. By Baptism the faithful is received, for salvation, into a living Body, not into an agglomeration of individuals; he is by that inscribed in the tension of the whole Church toward the ultimate blossoming of the arrhes * of Salvation; and he will penetrate himself in totality into the inheritance of the Promise only in communion * with his brothers, in the glory of the Parousia of the Lord the Head. The mystery of Salvation, begun in the pardon of sins through participation in the redemptive sacrifice of Christ the Servant, is accomplished in a total communion of men with the Father and among themselves in Jesus the Lord, in the gift of the Holy Spirit. In short, it is accomplished in the glorious Church arising from the tombs for eternal Life at the appearance of its Lord. This is the wonderful power of the *agape* * of God, surpassing all that Ezechiel himself, conscious however of the depth of the *hesed we emet* (mercy and fidelity *) of Yahweh, could foresee.

THE SACRAMENTAL ORGANISM,
THE MEANS OF THIS COMMUNION

In the Church "the means of Salvation"—in particular the sacramental organism, intimately joined to the ministry of the Word since it is a question of the "sacraments of the faith"—are situated entirely in the tension opened by the Pasch of Jesus and which will be resolved only at the Parousia.* For it is necessary that the perfection of Christ the Head, his capital grace, concentrating in it the whole inheritance that the Father reserves for men, attain them little by little, be infiltrated little by little in the sons of the first Adam in order to infuse in them the full breath * of the new Life.

Let us not forget—this point also merits more consideration by the theologians—that the new humanity does not render the former useless; the goodness and the beauty and the grandeur of Creation are not all eliminated or scorned or diminished by Salvation. And the new Adam pours out his Life only on those who have already received the great gift of natural life as a descendant of the first Adam. Then, the Body of Christ must be built up in proportion to the growth of this natural humanity and its expansion, as much historical as geographic. But this "extensive" construction does not suffice. God, in his supernatural economy, respects the conditions and the laws of his natural creature. Man penetrates only progressively into the values which make him whole. That takes place on all levels: physical (he arrives only little by little to his adult stature), intellectual (he discovers only little by little the intelligible content of the beings that surround him and the sense of his own mystery), affective (the evolution of the feelings and the will of man is, we know, one of the most complex, and psychology discerns many stages in it), moral (man conquers himself, puts his passions in order, really "takes himself in hand" only slowly, in an effort which indeed lasts all one's life). He progresses in the same way on the Christian level: the seed given in the initial act of the "new birth" will be developed gradually in the faithful by a slow process of deepening; all the more since the faithful lives (in spite of his Salvation) as a sinner before winning in his own life (in communion with all his brothers) the war against evil, the war of which the decisive battle has been won on the cross by Christ but which is not by that completely extinguished.[60] The Christian will pass only slowly into the totality of the communion of Life, and that in the fore, ceaselessly defending himself against the forces of evil in a battle which will be

---

60. We recognize the analogy given by O. Cullmann, *Christ et le temps*, Neuchâtel-Paris, 1957, especially pp. 100-101. We will have to return to this point, which is why we do not dwell upon it at great length here.

terminated only at his death. Extensive growth (geographical and historical) and intensive growth (qualitative), such are the two major pulsations of the Body of Christ * up to the Parousia.*

Christ wanted the Church itself, under its continual influx, to bear the responsibility of this twofold growth and be armed in special ways, homologous to its nature. It is a body being constructed, renewed and "saved" in living connection with the Head and through the power of the Spirit who vivifies it at its core. Here takes place, in necessary connection with the Word and the hierarchical ministry, the sacramental organism dominated by the Eucharist. Our sacraments thus appear to us in all their complexity. On the one hand, they are oriented, as it were, toward their ultimate end, their *raison d'etre*, toward Salvation which, as we have shown above, is identified in fact with the Church as communion of Life; the gift of the initial seed of Salvation, the depth of this initial gift, the constant purification of the faithful. On the other hand, they are of the Church, they find in it at once their source and their power.

This last point must be underlined. Speaking of the gift of baptismal grace, Saint Thomas does not reason in the following fashion: because he was pardoned from his sins and has received the gift of the new Life, the faithful is incorporated into Christ and becomes a member of the Church. He says this, on the contrary: because he is incorporated into Christ the Head and has become a member of the Church, the faithful receives the new Life and, in it, the pardon of his sin.[61] We

---

61. "*Per baptismum aliquis incorporatur Passioni et Morti Christi, secundum illud Rom. 6. 8: "Si mortui sumus cum Christo credimus quia simul etiam vivemus cum Christo." Ex quo patet quod omni baptizato communicatur Passio Christi ad remedium ac si ipse passus et mortuus esset*' (III, 69, 2); "*poena Passionis Christi communicatur baptizato inquantum fit membrum Christi* (note the expression), *ac si ipse poenam illam sustinuisset ideo ejus peccata remanent ordinate per poenam Passionis Christi*" (III, 69, 6, ad 1; see III, 69, 3: "*conveniens est ut id agatur in membro incorporato quod est actum in Capite;*" III, 69, 4: "*a Capite autem Christo in omnia*

see the nuance and its extreme importance. Entrance into the ecclesial Body of Christ is not ontologically posterior to the gift of grace; it constitutes, on the contrary, its immediate cause. And our author explains himself clearly: "Only the members united to their head live and receive from him sense and movement; then it is necessary that by Baptism man be incorporated into Christ as his member" (III, 69, 5). In the gift of Life, the joining to the Head, therefore the incorporation, is fundamental.[62] That brings us back to affirm that the baptismal grace of entrance into the Body of Christ is an ecclesial grace: the new Life blossoms from the Church, the Church acting only in connection with its Head. We meet the great patristic theme of Mother Church bringing forth and nursing her sons, and espoused by Christ. What Saint Thomas says here of baptismal grace is valuable for all sacramental grace: it comes from the Church but is oriented toward the Church. This is the perfect translation, this time in the plan of the means of Salvation, of the tension which we revealed above to be at the very heart of the mystery of the communion of Life in the pilgrim stage of the Church. Under the power of the Spirit of the Lord, the Church (not the Head alone, nor *a fortiori* the members alone, but the Head in living conjunction with the members) develops and purifies itself. It is a transposition to the supernatural level of the analogy of the life of the body: the living being, under the *impulsus* of its immanent principle, gives to himself the growth and the continuance of existence; even more, from the initial cell, the embryo gives to itself its own organs.

---

membra ejus gratiae et viritutis plenitudo derivatur.... Unde manifestum est quod per baptismum aliquis consequitur gratiam et virtutes;" III, 69, 6, etc.).

62. We have there a trace of the interesting research on the very complex theology of character: it is anterior to baptismal grace, and has a real causality in it; structural incorporation into the Church (yet without the gift of grace) is the effect of character. And this incorporation is the cause of the derivation of the grace coming from the plenitude of Christ the Head.

The sacramental organism is situated therefore at the core of the saving Church and sacramental grace appears to us thus quite simply as a diffusion—by the mediation of this sacramental organism—of the ecclesial communion of Life which the Lord Jesus unleashes for his brothers.[63] This is the mystery of ecclesial Salvation, emanating from the Church (present already in all its intensity in the Paschal Jesus) and ending up in the Church (the eschatological Church having actualized in its members the plenitude of the Paschal Jesus).[64]

Therefore, when we speak here of the Eucharist, the Salvation of the Church Pilgrim, will be necessary to replunge ceaselessly our conclusions into the vast context that we have just evoked in this chapter. The sacrament *par excellence* (by *antonomase*, says Saint Thomas),[65] the center of the whole sacramental organism,[66] the end of Christian initiation,[67] the Eucharist is the privileged means in which, by the eating of the body of our Lord Jesus at the end of the reactualization of his sacrifice as the Servant,* the Church on earth penetrates more into the communion of Life, but this on the one hand

---

63. We recognize here a theology of sacramental grace in the line of John, of Saint Thomas, not in that of Cajetan. This theology seems to be realized perfectly at once only in the texts of Saint Thomas (on which it immediately relies) and in the foundation of living Tradition. Its importance is more evident for an ecclesiology centered on the communion of life in Jesus *Kurios*.

64. This aspect has been developed and deepened by P. Congar, *Jalons pour une Théologie du laicat*, Paris 1954, pp. 211-218: "Christ is the Alpha and the Omega of all relationships of men with God, and these must be relationships of communion (to become the "communional" temple of God). But he is the Alpha for all only by all his *acta et passa in carne* (St. Thomas), while he is the Omega with us, not only in his fleshly body born of Mary and crucified, but in his "communional" body which we constitute with him and in him — and he in us" (p. 211).

65. III, 73, 4, ad 2.

66. St. Thomas goes even as far as to write: "*Eucharistia est quasi consummatio spiritualis vitae et omnium sacramentorum finis*" (III, 73, 3); "*nec aliquis habet gratiam ante susceptionem hujus sacramenti vel nisi ex*

serves to withdraw it little by little from the world of sin, and on the other hand serves in intensifying its hope for the definitive Day of the Parousia.

aliquo voto ipsius, vel per seipsum, sicut adulti, vel voto Ecclesiae sicut parvuli" (III,, 79, 1, ad 1).

67. At least in the ancient discipline, and still now in the case of the Baptism of an adult: *"Nisi graves urgentesque causae obsint, adultus baptizatus statim Missae sacrificio assistat et sacram communionem percipiat,"* in C. J. C., 753, 2.

CHAPTER II

THE EUCHARISTIC BODY
OF THE LORD JESUS

Of all the sacraments, the Eucharist has the signal privilege of making present, really although sacramentally, the sacrificial act of Jesus the Servant and, at the end of the ecclesial offering of this sacrifice, of giving us to partake of the true body and blood of Jesus, our Lord. In participating mysteriously in the Pasch of Christ in this way, we are put in possession of the divine inheritance of the communion of Life in the risen Jesus.

By saying in the risen Jesus, we affirm explicitly that, under the signs of bread and wine the body and blood of the risen *Kurios* * are indeed present in the oblation. It is most important to capture the realism of this assertion and to plunge it into the theological climate of the preceding chapter in asking ourselves a question: why must the Eucharistic body of Jesus be his glorious body? Does such a necessity justify itself theologically? It is a delicate problem, on which the specialists are far from being in complete accord [1] and which, in fact, engages a whole Christology.

THE EUCHARISTIC BODY OF JESUS
IN THE LOGOS-FLESH CHRISTOLOGY

Indeed, one can grapple with the mystery of Jesus from two different angles. John, in the opening lines of his Gospel,

---

1. Dom A. Vonier himself refuses to see in the Eucharistic body the risen body of Jesus. Thus he writes: "The Eucharistic body and blood of

opens the way to a contemplation which is especially pivoted on the dynamism of the incarnation (but, we are anxious to emphasize from the start, not exclusively): the Logos-flesh movement. For "the Logos (the Word *) was made flesh and dwelled among us," after having figured preeminently in the Creation ("by him all was made and without him not anything was made, of all being he was the life").[2]

In that presentation of Christ-Mystery, not to grant to the historical events in the life of Jesus, especially to his death and resurrection, an essential echo in his own individual humanity, will be a great temptation, so confounding to our minds is this taking on of our impoverished humanity by the very Person of the divine Logos.* It is therefore a danger not to insist enough on his passage as *pneumatic* (spiritual) and the transformation that this produces in his body and soul. Right from the incarnation, the flesh of Christ, transfixed by the power of the Logos, is lifegiving and divine. His cross, whereon he conquers sin and death, dissolves the sole obstacle which prevents us from receiving in all its intensity the divine inheritance, especially the Spirit of the New Life, which, as Logos, he has the power to give us. In short then, the accent is on the "wondrous blending," the marvelous and total impregnation of the whole humanity of Jesus by his Logos essence. All this is complete from the moment of his incarnation, thus

---

Christ represent fully and with perfect fitness that phase of his existence where he died on the cross; they represent in no way that other phase of his existence where he lives gloriously in heaven." *Key to the Doctrine of the Eucharist*, Newman Press, 1959.

2. On the interpretation, as the history of Salvation, of what we call the Prologue of John, see C. H. Dodd, *The Interpretation of the Fourth Gospel*, Cambridge, 1953, pp. 263-296; *La Bible aujourd'hui*, Tournai-Paris, 1957, pp. 112-113 (we know that the position of Dodd on the origins conceived as myths creates a problem in Catholic exegesis); E. Boismard, *Le prologue de saint Jean*, Paris, 1953, pp. 99-175. On the creative role of the Word, see C. Spicq, *Le Siracide et la structure littéraire du prologue de saint Jean*, in *Memorial Lagrange*, Paris, 1940, pp. 183-195; J. Giblet, *La théologie du Logos selon l'évangile de saint Jean*, *La Parole de Dieu en Jésus-Christ*, in collaboration, Casterman, 1961, pp. 85-120.

sanctifying in him the flesh, realizing in his own Person this communion of Life, the goal of the Economy of Salvation.

His death and resurrection appear then more like conditions required in order that we, in our turn, might enter into a share of this communion. Let us repeat that it is a question of emphasis. The necessity of the redemptive death is never doubted or even lessened (on the contrary, the living consciousness of the state of sin and of the tragic situation which it sweeps away incite us to insist on this necessity). The majesty of the resurrection is never diminished. But on the other hand, the vigorous understanding of the depth and realism of the union of the Logos and the flesh makes the highest truth out of the fact of deification, of elevation, even of transformation which must result in the singular humanity of Jesus, from the instant of the incarnation. One can immediately imagine what a look into the firmly enunciated *kenose* of Paul would bring to such a theology.

This Christological thread runs through the Greek tradition of Alexandrian inspiration, but we meet it already with Irenaeus of Lyon, in whom it is so strongly designed that one could make him the holder of a purely "physical" theory of the redemption.[3] Athanasius of Alexandria seems to be a privileged

3. See A. D'Ales *La doctrine de la récapitulation en saint Irénée,* in *Rech. de Sc. Rel.,* 1916, pp. 185-211, which appears to be a typical example. One knows the reaction of G. Aulen, *Christus Victor,* French trans., Paris, 1949. As major texts of Irenaeus let us cite: "For it was for this end that the Word of God was made man, and He who was the Son of God became the Son of man, that, man, having been taken into the Word, and receiving the adoption, might become the son of God. For by no other means could we have attained to incorruptibility and immortality, unless we had been united to incorruptibility and immortality. But how could we be joined to incorruptibility and immortality, unless, first, incorruptibility and immortality had become that which we also are, so that the corruptible might be swollowed up by incorruptibility, and the mortal by immortality, that we might receive the adoption of sons?" *Adv. Haer.,* III, 19, 1, *AN,* vol. I, p. 449). "Therefore, he united man with God and effected a communion between God and man, for we would not have been able, in any way, to receive a share in incorruptibility if he had not come to us. For, if

witness of this soteriology which, while quite retaining the
soteriological value of Christ's Pasch, is especially attached to
the theme of the image of God restored by the coming of the
Son in the flesh.[4] This is an evident dependence on Irenaeus:[5]
"For the Word, perceiving that no otherwise could the corruption of men be undone save by death as a necessary
condition, while it was impossible for the Word to suffer
death, being immortal, and Son of the Father; to this end
He takes to Himself a body capable of death, that it, by partaking of the Word Who is above all, might be worthy to
die in the stead of all, and might, because of the Word which
was come to dwell in it, remain incorruptible, and that thence-
forth corruption might be stayed from all by the Grace of the

---

incorruptibility had remained invisible and hidden, it would have been of no
use for us; it was made visible, therefore, in order that, in all respects, we
might receive a participation in this incorruptibility. And because in the first
creature, Adam, we had all been chained to death for disobedience, it was
necessary that the chains of death be broken by the obedience of him who
was made for us. Because death had reigned over the flesh, it is necessarily
by the intermediary of the flesh that it be abolished and that man be freed
from its oppression. The Word was therefore made flesh so that, by means
of the flesh — thanks to which he had obtained power, the right of possession
and dominion — sin might be abolished and no longer be found in us.
And this is why our Lord took a body identical with that of the first creature:
to fight for the fathers and conquer in Adam that which in Adam had
struck us" (*Dem Apost.*, 31: L. M. Froidevaux, *Sources chrét.*, pp. 80-82,
trans.) One will note the balance of this last text. We have cited it *in
extenso* because it seems to us typical of the fashion of Irenaeus.

4. See J. N. D. Kelly, *Early Christian Doctrines*, London, 1960, pp. 377-
380: "The dominant strain in Athanasius's soteriology is the physical theory
that Christ, by becoming man, restored the divine image in us; but blended
with this is the conviction that His death was necessary to release us from the
curse of sin, and that He offered Himself in sacrifice for us;" H.E.W. Turner
(*The Patristic Doctrine of Redemption*, London, 1952, pp. 70-95, especially
pp. 87-95), writes on this subject some penetrating phrases which emphasize
the force of the theology of Athanasius.

5. This dependence is underlined in P. Camelot, *Athanase d'Alexandrie,
Contre les païens et sur l'incarnation du Verbe, Sources chrét.*, Paris, 1947,
thus pp. 59-60, 65-73, 231 note 2.

Resurrection. And thus He, the incorruptible Son of God, being conjoined with all by a like nature, naturally clothed all with incorruption, by the promise of the resurrection. For the actual corruption in death has no longer holding-ground against men, by reason of the Word, which by His one body has come to dwell among them" (*De Jncarn.*, 9, 112a-c; *NPN*, 2nd series, vol. IV, pp. 40, 41). "The body, then, as sharing the same nature with all, but by virtue of the union of the Word with it, was no longer subject to corruption according to its own nature, but, by reason of the Word that was come to dwell in it, it was placed out of the reach of corruption" (*De Jncarn.*, 20, 132b, *NPN*, 2nd series, vol. IV, p. 47).[6] Nevertheless, how will other men be able to enter into a share of this deified humanity? Athanasius (like John himself) is clear: by the gift of the Holy Spirit through the resurrection. The Letters to Serapion abound in affirmations of this sort: "It is by the Spirit that we are said to be all partakers of God. . . . Now that we are said to be partakers of Christ and partakers of God, it seems that the unction and the seal which are in us are not of the nature of created things but of that of the Son who, by the

---

6. "It was unfitting that they should perish who had once been partakers of God's image. What then was God to do? or what was to be done save the renewing of that which was in God's image, so that by it men might once more be able to know Him? But how could this have come to pass save by the presence of the very Image of God, our Lord Jesus Christ? For by men's means it was impossible, since they are but made after an image; nor by angels either, for not even they are (God's) images. Whence the Word of God came in His own person, that, as He was in the Image of the Father, He might be able to create afresh the man after the image. But, again, it could not else have taken place had not death and corruption been done away. Whence He took, in natural fitness, a mortal body, that while death might in it be once for all done away, men made after His Image might once more be renewed. None other was sufficient for this need, save the Image of the Father" (*De Incarn.*, 13, 120b; *NPN*, 2nd series, vol. IV, p. 43). "It was made manifest to all (at the resurrection) that it was not from any natural weakness of the Word that dwelt in it that the body had died, but in order that in it death might be done away by the power of the Savior" (*De Incarn.*, 26, 141c; *NPN*, 2nd series, vol. IV, p. 50).

Spirit which is in him, unites us with the Father" (*Ad Serap.,* 1, 24.)[7]

The Divine, Life-giving Body of the Logos

One understands then easily that, in this tradition, which we shall call (a little summarily however, for the line of demarcation is not so clear) "Alexandrian," when they speak of the Eucharistic body of Jesus, they are insisting on the fact that this body is the body of the Logos,* therefore the deified body; and that they are often passing over in silence its pneumatical quality, which results from a transformation by the mysterious action of the Holy Spirit.

Witnesses abound, and we will meet them throughout our study. Let us be content here with a quote from Cyril of Alexandria: "The body of the Lord itself was sanctified by the power of the Logos which was united to it; but it was rendered at this point efficacious that in the Eulogy it can communicate to us its own sanctification" (*In Joan.,* 17, 13, lib. 11, cap. 9; *P.G.,* 74, 528; trans.).[8] Saint Thomas Aquinas, without any possible doubt, follows a middle course in the Latin tradi-

---

7. It is even in relying on this sanctifying action of the Pneuma that Athanasius proposed to show his divinity. H.E.W. Turner (*op. cit.,* p. 89), remarks on this important place accorded to the Spirit in the soteriology of Athanasius. But a text like the *Contra Arian.,* I, 46-52, shows well how, for him, the Spirit invades the humanity of Jesus because of the presence of the Logos, under his initiative: "He is not the sanctified, but the Sanctifier; for He is not sanctified by another, but He Himself sanctifies Himself that we may be sanctified in the Truth. He who sanctifies Himself is Lord of sanctification. How then does this take place? What then does he mean but this? viz., "I, being the Father's Word (*Logos*) I give to Myself, when become man, the Spirit (*Pneuma*); and in the same Spirit do I sanctify Myself when become man, that henceforth in Me, who am truth (for thy Word, Logos, is Truth), all men may be sanctified ... (he) gives and receives as man" (*Contra Arian.,* I, 46-48; J. H. Newman, *Select Treatises of St. Athanasius* vol. I, London, pp. 227-229). In the same sense, see Cyril of Alexandria, in *Joan.,* 17, 18-19; lib. 11, cap. 10; *P.G.,* 74, 547-550.

8. The rest of the text cited is also characteristic of the theology of Cyril.

tion (thus Ambrose, *De Myst.*, 58; *De Sacr.*, VI, 1, 4; Hilary
of Poitiers, *De Trin.*, 10, 18-35), which, in spite of the magnificent balance of the *Tome a Flavien of Leo*, is marked by a
very lively sense of the transcendence of the Word in the
complex of the hypostatic union, in this Alexandrine line.
And it is not chance that, expounding on the nature of
Eucharistic grace in the *Summa Theologica*, he leans explicitly,
from the very first article (III, 79, 1), on a citation from Cyril.
For him, all the virtue of the Eucharist comes *"primo quidem
et principaliter"* from what it contains: the Word-made-flesh.
Then commenting on John 6, 55: "He who eats my flesh and
drinks my blood has eternal life and I will raise him up at the
last day," he writes: "The Word raises souls, but the Word-
made-flesh gives life to bodies, and Augustine says: In this
sacrament there is not only the Word in his divinity, but the
Word-made-flesh; therefore, it is equally the cause of the resurrection of both souls and bodies" (*In Joan.*, cap. 6, lect. 7; ed.
Cai, no. 973; trans.). After having divinized the flesh of
Christ, the divine Logos wishes to divinize that of the Christian who really unites himself to the divine flesh of Christ in
the Eucharist.

The Risen Body of the Lord

But is it therefore necessary to conclude from this that,
in the first line of explanation, one would deny that the
Eucharistic body of Jesus, deified by the power of the
Logos, be the risen body of the Lord? We do not think so.
We have in fact emphasized much now, whether in Irenaeus
or in the great Alexandrians, the accent on the divine nature
bestowed in the incarnation, which is not at all in conflict
with faith in the Redemptive work accomplished by the Paschal
event.[9] All are unanimous in recognizing that the resurrection

---

9. For the case of Irenaeus, see J. N. D. Kelly, *op. cit.*, pp. 173-174;
for Athanasius, see P. Camelot, *op. cit.*, pp. 79-86; H.E. Turner, *op. cit.*,
p. 89.

has, at least on Christ's own flesh, the effect of rendering it henceforth incorruptible and impassive, of radiating from it all the glory of his divinity which up to then had been unleashed only for a moment (at the Transfiguration): "He did not suffer that the temple of His body remain long, but having merely shown it to be dead, by the contact of death with it, He straightway raised it up on the third day, bearing away, as the mark of victory and the triumph over death, the incorruptibility and impassibility which resulted to His body ... the Son of God Himself, after an interval of three days, showed His body, once dead, immortal and incorruptible; and it was made manifest to all that it was not from any natural weakness of the Word that dwelt in it that the body had died, but in order that in it death might be done away by the power of the Savior" (Athanasius, *De Incarn.*, 26, 141a-e; *NPN*, 2nd series).[10]

But, above all, they admit especially a certain real bond between this personal resurrection of Jesus and the restoration of human nature. The participation of all in the divinization accomplished in Jesus at his incarnation can be effected only when sin has been expiated and destroyed in their own flesh. Therefore, his personal passage from death to incorruptibility and impassibility draws up as it were, the first step of our own passage from death of sin to the glorious resurrection: "There remained still to be paid the debt of all, for all ought to die, and this was then the principal cause of his coming among us. It is why, after having shown his divinity by his works, it remained to him to offer the sacrifice for all, delivering to death for all the temple of his body, in order to free them and to deliver them all from the ancient transgression; by that he would show himself stronger than death, showing

---

10. "He is the true Son of God, being from Him, as from His Father, His own Word, and Wisdom, and Power, Who in ages later took a body for the salvation of all, and taught the world concerning the Father, and brought death to nought, and bestowed incorruption upon all by the promise of the Resurrection, having raised His own body as a first-fruits of this, and having displayed it by the sign of the Cross as a monument of victory over death and its corruption" (*De Incarn.*, 32, 152c; *NPN*, 2nd series, vol. 5, p. 53).

in his incorruptible body the first-fruits of the general resurrection" (Athanasius, *De Jncarn.* 20, 132a).

The body of Christ can bestow on other men the full consequences of his total impregnation by the divinity of the Logos, only after he has passed glorious through death and emerged victorious. We certainly do not think that this affirmation exaggerates the numerous indications that we meet in this Alexandrine tradition. On the condition, of course, that we do not press them too much and especially that we do not hunt for a disclosure of the nature of the line of causality, we retain the proper balance. For this precision is found only in Thomistic synthesis. As a witness of importance, let us cite here a text of Gregory of Nyssa. One knows Gregory's insistence on the "physical" concept of the redemption and the fact that no where, it seems, does he formally attach our sanctification (for him the goal of Salvation) to the events of the death and resurrection.[11] However, apparent silence does not at all equal a negation, or indeed, a positive exclusion.

In the celebrated *Catechetical Discourse* we find a revealing arrest on the death and resurrection of God-made-man: "For when our nature, following its own proper course, had even in Him been advanced to the separation of soul and body, He knitted together again the disunited elements, cementing them, as it were, together with the cement of His Divine power, and recombining what has been severed in a union never to be broken. And this is the Resurrection, namely the return, after they have been dissolved, of those elements that had been before linked together, into an indissoluble union through a mutual incorporation; in order that thus the primal grace which invested humanity might be recalled, and we restored to the everlasting life, when the vice that has been mixed up with our kind has evaporated through our dissolution, as

---

11. "Assuredly he is not ignorant of the traditional doctrine of salvation by the death of Christ, since he makes brief allusions to it; but never does he formally attach our sanctification to it" (J. Gross *La divinisation du chrétien d'après les Pères grecs*, Paris, 1938, p. 231, trans.). See H.E.W. Turner, *op. cit.*, pp. 90-94.

happens, to any liquid when the vessel that contained it is broken, and it is spilt and disappears, there being nothing to contain it. For as the principle of death took its rise in one person and passed on in succession through the whole of human kind, in like manner the principle of the Resurrection-life extends from one person to the whole of humanity. For He Who reunited to His own proper body the soul that had been assumed by Himself, by virtue of that power which had mingled with both of these component elements at their first framing, then, upon a more general scale as it were, conjoined the intellectual to the sentient nature, the new principle freely progressing to the extremities by natural consequence. For when, in that concrete humanity which He had taken to Himself, the soul after the dissolution returned to the body, then this uniting of the several portions passes, as by a new principle, in equal force upon the whole human race. This, then, is the mystery of God's plan with regard to His death and His resurrection from the dead; namely, instead of preventing the dissolution of His body by death and the necessary results of nature, to bring both back to each other in the resurrection; so that He might become in Himself the meeting-ground both of life and death, having re-established in Himself that nature which death had divided, and being Himself the originating principle of the uniting of those separated portions" (*Disc. Cat.*, 16, 7-9; *NPN*, 2nd series, vol. V, pp. 89-91).[12]

There is no possible doubt; it is by his death and resurrection—considered as moments of his sacrifice[13]—that the

---

12. For the development on the Cross of Christ, see *Disc. Cat.*, 32, 4-6; for the development on the resurrection let us cite this interesting passage: "At that other time He was transfused throughout our nature, in order that our nature might by this transfusion of the Divine become itself divine, rescued as it was from death, and put beyond the reach of the caprice of the antagonist. For His return from death becomes to our mortal race the commencement of our return to the immortal life" (*Disc. Cat.*, 25, 2; *NPN*, 2nd series, vol. V, p. 495). Such phrases must make us very prudent when we are called upon to bear judgment on the theology of Gregory.

13. See the remark of J. N. D. Kelly, *op. cit.*, p. 384: "Both Athanasius and Gregory of Nyssa, while viewing man's restoration as essentially the

God-made-flesh concretely restores the fallen human nature. And the movement of divinization which must be extended to all the race has its origin in these events. Certainly, for Gregory, their necessity is explained less by their own causality than because "He Who had determined once for all to share the nature of man must pass through all the peculiar conditions of that nature" (32, 2; *NPN*, 2nd series, vol. V, p. 499); and, in his theology, the flesh of Christ possesses the same divine power before and after the resurrection. However, it will no longer die. This is the strength which henceforth it can transmit to men by transforming them in it, in its post-victory power. Concretely, whatever the power of life through the presence and the action in it of the Logos was by the perichoresis of the Logos and of humanity, in the plan of God, it could not procure for men the gift of immortality until it had itself integrally espoused their condition.

It is of little importance here that, for Gregory, Christ's death appears more like a condition of Salvation than like a means of Salvation: [14] it marked the flesh of Christ in order that by it we might all be delivered. And the same remark goes for the resurrection.[15] Since the Eucharistic bread effects precisely the actualization of this deliverance in putting us into the closest contact with this incorruptible and immortal body (*Disc. Cat.*, 37, 1-4), it is necessary that the eucharistic body be marked by the mystery of the paschal sacrifice. This is perhaps what Gregory wants to suggest when, in the middle of the development on the power of the Eucharist, he speaks of the "Body which has been shown to be superior to death, and has been the First-fruits of our life," making precise that as "a little leaven assimilates to itself the whole lump, so in like manner that body to which immortality has been given it by God, when

---

effect of the incarnation, were able to find a logical place for the Lord's death conceived as a sacrifice."

14. J. Gross, *op. cit.*, p. 231, note 3.

15. The resurrection is like the primary instance of the return of the whole human race to immortal life, after Christ's victory over death. See *Disc. Cat.*, 32, 3-4.

it is in ours, translates and transmutes the whole into itself"
(*Disc. Cat.*, 37, 3; *NPN*, 2nd series, vol. V, pp. 504, 505).[16]
The historical dimension marks the Eucharistic body itself,
the body of him who conquered death to permit us to conquer it in our turn.

The Thomist synthesis, strongly squared around the metaphysics of the conjoined instrument, will arrive, in spite of its
strong accent on the initial divinization by the presence of
the Word, at conserving the realism of the *acta et passa*
Christi, of the mysteries accomplished in the flesh of Jesus.
For Saint Thomas, in fact, the actions of Christ especially
those which weave his paschal mystery, constitute the efficient
cause of our own Salvation. They are not only the meritorious
moral cause, the worth of which for us is God's concession of
his inheritance through his infinite love in the offering by
Christ of his sacrifice, but also and especially the assimilative,
efficient cause. This point that contemporary theology has
restored to worth appears unquestionable to those who can read
the Summa while plunging it into its context.[17] The historical
mysteries of Jesus still exercise *hic et nunc* in the Church their

------

16. L. Meridier (French translator of Athanasius) seems to us, however,
to warp the text and he thought of Gregory when he translates: "It is
precisely this glorious body which is shown superior to death" (p. 175),
which many authors repeat; the immediate context does not authorize this
addition to the text.

17. The signal studies on this point are: H.M. Bouesse, *La causalité
efficiente instrumentale de l'humanité du Christ et des sacrements chrétiens,*
in *R.T.,* 1934, pp. 370-393; 1938, pp. 256-298; J. Lecuyer, *La
causalité efficiente des mystères du Christ selon saint Thomas,* in *Doctor
Communis,* 1953, pp. 91-120; F. Holtz, *La valeur sotériologique de la
résurrection du Christ selon saint Thomas,* in *Ephem. Theol. Lov.,* 1953
pp. 609-645; J. Gaillard *Pérennité des mystères du Christ selon saint
Thomas,* in *R.T.,* 1957, pp. 540-542 (extract of a chronicle on the Liturgy);
M. Matthijs, *Mysteriengegenwart secundum S. Thomas,* in *Angel.,* 1957,
pp. 393-399; G. Van Roo, *The Resurrection of Christ Instrument of Grace,*
in *Greg.,* 1958, pp. 271-285; J.H. Nicholas, *Reactualisation des mystères
rédempteurs dans et par les sacrements,* in *R.T.* 1958, pp. 20-54; J. Hamer,
Le Christ est ressuscité, in *L'Église et les églises,* t. II, Chevetogne, 1955,
pp. 438-468 (same ideas taken in *R.S.P.T.,* 1959, pp. 722-723); C.E. O'Neill,

efficient capacity through the mediation of faith and the sacraments of the faith: [18] not solely the humanity (which lives in the risen Jesus), but the historical events accomplished in it and by it. We grasp the nuance and its importance for our subject. Christ reaches men of all times and of all places through

The Mysteries of Christ and the Sacraments, in *The Thomist*, 1962, pp. 1-53. For the more general problems of the *Mysteriengegenwart*, besides the studies of Nicholas, Matthijs, O'Neill noted here, see J. Sohngen, *Le rôle agissant des Mystères du Christ*, in *Q.L.P.*, 1939, pp. 79-107; Th. Filthaut, *La théologie des Mystères*, Paris, 1954 (complete dossier of the controversy); Maison Dieu, no. 14, 1948: Dom Odon Casel, *La doctrine du mystère chrétien* (note the studies of D. Dekkers et P. Ch.-V. Heris); B. Neunheuser, *Mystery Presence*, in *Worship*, 1960, pp. 120-127.

18. The affirmations of Saint Thomas concerning the present efficacy of the *acta et passa* of Jesus are numerous. Let us recall the most important: "*Quasi instrumentaliter ea quae sunt humanitatis ut resurrectio, passio, et alia, ad effectum divinitatis se habent. Sic ergo resurrectio Christi non causat resurrectionem spiritualem in nobis quasi causa principaliter agens, sed sicut causa instrumentalis*" (*De Ver.*, 27, 3, ad 7); "*actiones ipsius ex virtute divinitatis fuerunt nobis salutiferae utpote in nobis gratiam causantes et per meritum et per efficaciam quandam*" (III, 8, 1, ad 1); "*caro ejus et mysteria in ea perpetrata operantur instrumentaliter ad animae vitam*" (III, 62, 5, ad 1); "*omnes actiones et passiones Christi instrumentaliter operantur in virtute divinitatis ad salutem humanam*" (III, 48, 6); "*in facto esse mors consideratur secundum quod jam facta est separatio corporis et animae . . . hoc autem modo mors Christi non potest esse causa nostrae salutis per modum meriti sed solum per modum efficientiae. Inquantum scilicet nec per mortem divinitas separata fuit a Christi carne, et ideo quidquid contingit circa carnem Christi, etiam anima separata, fuit nobis salutiferum virtute divinitatis unitae*" (III, 50, 6); "*Sicut mors Christi efficienter operata est nostram salutem ita etiam et ejus sepulturam*" (III, 51, 1, ad 2); "*resurrectio Christi non est proprie loquendo causa meritoria nostrae resurrectionis, sed est causa efficiens et exemplaris*" (III, 56, I, ad 3); "*ascensio Christi est causa nostrae salutis non per modum meriti sed per modum efficientiae*" (III, 57, 6, ad 1). We would be able to multiply the citations and extend them to the mystery of the birth of Christ (III, 37, 1, ad 1), of circumcision (III, 37, 1, ad 2, ad 3), of the baptism in the Jordon (III, 39, 1), etc. For Saint Thomas the mysteries accomplished in the flesh of Christ are all efficient instrumental causes of our Salvation, and for him the field of efficient instrumental causality outflanks that of meritorious causality which is extinquished with the death of Christ since one can procure merit only when one is *viator*. Our texts

the instrumentality of the acts of his life in their reality as historical events.

How is this possible? In order to be able to act with an instrument, it must be present hic et nunc. The mysteries of the life of Jesus, inasmuch as they are events, did they not unfold in a special place and in a bygone time? The instant of the resurrection will never be able to reappear in its historical reality, and besides, it can no longer last nowadays. . . .

Here there intervenes the genial transposition which Saint Thomas made the metaphysics of instrumentality undergo. Certainly, in their human reality, the acts of Christ were transitory acts, accomplished once for all and fleeing with the instant in which they were realized. However, the human nature which accomplished them was mysteriously united to the very person of the Word of God, assumed by it as a conjoined instrument, for the work of Salvation. Then it operated under the instrumental power infused in it by the divinity.[19] Then, the principal cause, God, raised the proper action of this human instrument to make it produce a relevant definitive effect of divinity, bearing in it, nevertheless, the proper mark of the instrument. In a painting of Van Gogh

---

are equally clear on the fact that it is not solely the humanity of Christ which is assumed as the instrument, but the historical acts accomplished by it and in it.

Now these historical mysteries meet us through the mediation of faith and of the sacraments of the faith: *"passio Christi licet sit corporalis habet tamen spiritualem virtutem ex divinitate unita. Et ideo per spiritualem contactum efficaciam sortitur, scilicet per fidem et fidei sacramenta"* (III, 48, 6, ad 2; see III, 49, 1, ad 4, ad 5; III, 62, 5, ad 2).

19. *"Dare gratiam aut Spiritum Sanctum convenit Christo secundum quod Deus, auctoritative; sed instrumentaliter convenit ei secundum quod homo, inquantum scilicet ejus humanitas instrumentum fuit divinitatis ejus. Et ita actiones ipsius, ex virtute divinitatis fuerunt nobis salutiferae, utpote gratiam in nobis causantes et per meritum et per efficientiam quandam"* (III, 8, 1, ad 1); *"duplex est efficiens, principale et instrumentale. Efficiens quidem principale humanae salutis est Deus. Quia vero humanitas Christi est divinitatis instrumentum, ex consequenti omnes actiones et passiones Christi instrumentaliter operantur in virtute divinitatis ad salutem humanam"* (III, 48, 6).

the final effect attains to the zone of the spiritual and of the genius, making the one who contemplates it participate in a typically human experience, when the brush by itself could only make a spot of color where the hand which guided it printed the mark of man. The same here, the final effect of the work of Christ rules itself according to the conditions of God, assuming the historical act for an effect sprung from Jesus in his God-man complexity. In the service of God, the historical event participates in divine eternity and in divine ubiquity, and by that its effect can join all times and all places.[20] Then, although between the past mystery and the individual who today receives Salvation there is no longer any sensible, corporal, temporal, immediate contact, the salvific power of this mystery will be able to operate nevertheless, the *virtus divina* having made the event participate in its own nonsubmission to time. Saint Thomas himself writes: "Christ's Passion, although corporeal, has yet a spiritual effect from the Godhead united: and therefore it secures its efficacy by spiritual contact—namely, by faith and the sacraments of faith..." (III, 48, 6, ad 2; Fathers of the English Dominican Province, *Summa Theologica*, vol. II, p. 2287).

What will this effect be in the individual? A mysterious assimilation in the event itself, realizing an effective inclusion of the faithful in Christ. If, in its instrumental symbiosis, the principal efficient capacity comes from God, the exemplariness comes precisely from the human action effected by Jesus under this divine influx. In us God is going to stamp, by the mediation of the historical event of which the efficacy

---

20. *"Sicut alia quae Christus in sua humanitate fecit vel passus est, ex virtute divinitatis ejus sunt nobis salutaria, ita et resurrectio Christi est causa efficiens nostrae resurrectionis virtute divina, cujus proprium est mortuos vivificare. Quae quidem virtus praesentialiter attingit omnia loca et tempora. Et talis contactus virtualis sufficit ad rationem hujus efficientiae"* (III, 56, 1, ad 3); *"cum Deus sit causa principalis nostrae resurrectionis, resurrectio vero Christi sit causa instrumentalis, resurrectio nostra sequitur resurrectionem Christi secundum dispositionem divinam quae ordinavit ut tali tempore fieret"* (*In I Cor.*, cap. 15, lect. 2: edit. Cai, no 915).

remains, that which is accomplished in Jesus by this event. The affirmations of Saint Thomas are constant on this point.[21] Under the influx of the events which wove the human salvific mystery of Jesus, we are going to relive his mystery in our personal life, and thus conform ourselves dynamically to him. Here, and we grasp it right away, is manifested the sacramental symbolism of which we shall speak again: the sensible sign (words and gestures) do not tend only to "illustrate" the grace given, but also to recall the efficient cause (the historical event of the life of Jesus) into which the Christian will be assimilated by this grace.[22] Thus the whole Christian life is lived literally in the Mystery of Christ. And if that is true of all events of Jesus's existence, it is moreover imperative to put an order among them and affirm that, *par excellence*, that is realized in the paschal event of the death and resurrection.

By the efficient power (instrumental) of the passion and death of the Savior, our sins are pardoned, our death destroyed;[23] by the efficient (instrumental) power of the resur-

---

21. "*Secundum rationem efficientiae quae dependet ex virtute divina, communiter tam mors Christi quam etiam resurrectio est causa tam destructionis mortis quam reparationis vitae; sed secundum exemplaritatem mors Christi (per quam recessit a vita mortali) est causa destructionis mortis nostrae, resurrectio vero ejus (per quam inchoavit vitam immortalem) est causa reparationis nostrae vitae*" (III, 56, 1, ad 4); "*resurrectio Christi est causa exemplaris nostrae resurrectionis quod quidem necessarium est non ex parte resuscitantis qui non indiget exemplari, sed ex parte resuscitatorum quos oportet illi resurrectioni conformari... licet autem efficientia resurrectionis Christi se extendat ad resurrectionem tam bonorum quam malorum, exemplaritas ejus se extendit proprie solum ad bonos qui sunt facti conformes filiationis ejus*" (III, 56, 1, ad 3).

22. "*Per baptismum autem homines sepeliuntur Christo, id est conformantur sepulturae ejus. Sicut enim ille qui sepelitur ponitur sub terra, ita ille qui baptizatur immergitur sub aqua*" (*In Rom.*, cap. 6, lect. 1: edit. Cai, no 474). We will be permitted to refer to our study *La triple dimension du signe sacramentel*, in *N.R. Théol.*, 1961, pp. 225-254 where we have explained this aspect at length.

23. III, 56, 1, ad 4 (Already cited, See note 21); "*passio ejus habet quandam divinam virtutem dimittendi peccata*" (III, 49, 1, ad 2); "*passio Christi licet sit corporalis sortitur tamen quandam spiritualem virtutem ex*

rection of the Lord, we are restored to the new Life which is the life of grace.[24] But the death of Jesus is at the same time the pattern of our own death to sin and by that to death, and his resurrection the pattern of our entrance into the new Life and of our own bodily resurrection at the day of the Parousia.[25] For we are going to die physically partaking the death of the Lord and rise in his resurrection: "Christ's Resurrection is the cause of ours through the power of the united Word, who operates according to His will. And consequently, it is not necessary for the effect to follow at once, but according as the Word of God disposes, namely, that first of all we be conformed to the suffering and dying Christ in this suffering and mortal life; and afterwards may come to share in the likeness of His Resurrection" (III, 56, 1, ad 1; Dominican Fathers, vol. II, p. 2325). This is realized, being given our nature, at both the corporal level and the spiritual level. Justification, as envisaged by St. Thomas, with its two moments of death to sin and of projection into the world of God, appears to us thus wholly situated in the dynamism of the paschal event, passage from death to resurrection, accomplished under the efficacy of both the death and resurrection. A rather ignored text explains this most fully: "Two things concur in the justification of souls, namely, forgiveness of sin and newness of life through grace. Consequently, as to efficacy, which comes of the Divine power, the Passion as well as the Resurrection of Christ is the cause of justification as to both the above.

---

divinitate cujus caro ei unita est instrumentum; secundum quam virtutem passio Christi est causa remissionis peccatorum" (III, 49, 1, ad 2, *see the body of the argument*).

24. III 56, 1, ad 4 (Already cited; See note 21); *"in justificatione animarum duo concurrunt, scilicet remissio culpae et novitas vitae per gratiam. Quantum ergo ad efficientiam quae est per virtutem divinam tam passio Christi quam resurrectio est causa justificationis quoad utrumque. Sed quantum ad exemplaritatem, proprie passio et mors Christi est causa remissionis culpae per quam morimur peccato; resurrectio autem Christi est causa novitatis vitae quae est per gratiam sive justitiam"* (III, 56, 2, ad 4).

25. St. Thomas examines this problem in a special, article, III, 56, 1.

But as to exemplarity, properly speaking (*proprie*) Christ's
Passion and death are the cause of the forgiveness of guilt, by
which forgiveness we die unto sin: whereas Christ's Resurrection is the cause of newness of life, which comes through
grace or justice" (III, 56, 2, ad 4; Dominican Fathers, vol.
II, p. 2327). For Saint Thomas, then, the historical mystery of
the resurrection intervenes in the act of justification.

The sacraments, and very particularly the Eucharist, which
dominates them as their living center, have for their end
precisely the realization or the deepening of this justification,
the entrance of man into the divine heritage in Jesus. Which
obliges us to conclude (without, it seems to us, warping the
fundamental intention of our author) that in them the efficacy
of the historical resurrection of the Lord is at work. Moreover,
in a capital article which aims at establishing the necessary
and close connection between the sacramental institution and
the passion of Christ, Saint Thomas takes good care to recall:
"Justification is ascribed to the Resurrection by reason of the
term to which (*ad quem*) which is newness of life through
grace. But it is ascribed to the Passion by reason of the term
from whence (*a quo*), i.e. in regard to the forgiveness of sin"
(III, 62, 5, ad 3; Dominican Fathers, vol. II, p. 2359). This
is a precious indication. The Thomist (and medieval) treatment of the passion and death signifies no positive exclusion
or even dimming of the salvific value of the resurrection event
(see III, 66, 10, ad 3). It is content with grasping the redemptive dynamism at its point of origin, where there springs
forth the great soaring which will lead him to the end. That is
to say that in the sacramental effect of the Eucharistic Bread,
the efficacy of the resurrection will enter into play. The
Christian will pass positively into the world of the divine inheritance by the action in him (by means of this Eucharistic
Bread) of the historical act of Jesus passing into the world of
glory, after being buried in the death of the Servant.

We have established then, too quickly I fear, an important
point: even the explanation of the more "physical" type of the
mystery of Salvation accords a choice place to the paschal

event in its two key stages of death and resurrection. By return a mysterious action of this event is recognized in the Eucharist. But it is necessary to pursue our investigation a little further. For the realism of the Gospel texts obliges us, in spite of its perpetual recourse to the divine Person of the Logos, to affirm a necessary role of the person of the Holy Spirit in the sanctification of the faithful and, more precisely, in his sanctification by contact with the Eucharistic Body of the Lord.

The Mysterious Action of the Holy Spirit

That, even and perhaps especially, for tradition that we call Alexandrian here, the Person of the Holy Spirit plays an essential role in the process of the sanctification of the faithful, we do not have to show, it is so evident.[26] The admirable *Letters to Serapion* of Athanasius, in order to establish the divinity of the Spirit, rely on the fact of his sanctifying work. Certainly, in the total divine work, be it the question of Creation or of divinization, the three Persons act in common: "In fact, the Father does all things by the Word in the Spirit, and it is thus that the unity of the Holy Trinity is safeguarded" (*Ad Serep.*, 1, 28). But in this community of action, Athanasius does well to preserve the dynamic order and the personality of each of the Three.

It is not a question of (as a whole theological current, making ill use of Saint Thomas, has understood it in barricading itself behind the term "appropriation") a disappearance of the personalities to the point that only the divine essence dwelled in the cause. In the common work, each Person guards his own characteristics: the operation comes from the Father, by the Son, is accomplished in the Spirit. We have to lend a great deal of attention to this formula, constant in all of Tradition,

---

26. See J. Galtier, *Le Saint Esprit en nous d'après les Pères Grecs*, Rome, 1946; J. Gross, *La divinisation du Chrétien d'après les Pères Grecs*, Paris, 1938; H.B. Swete, *The Holy Spirit in the Ancient Church*, London, 1912.

ek, dia, en [27]: three actors but in a unity of order.[28] Our entrance into the divine inheritance, explains Athanasius, can be accomplished only in the Person of the Holy Spirit: "The grace and gift accorded in the Trinity are given on the part of the Father, by the Son, in the Spirit. In fact, the same as the grace accorded comes from the Father by the Son, thus there can be no communication of the gift in us if it is not in the Holy Spirit, for it is in participating in him that we have the love of the Father and the grace of the Son and the communication of the Spirit itself" (*Ad Serap.*, 1, 30).

We meet such a view in this whole tradition. The sanctification of man by the perception of the mysterious activity of the Logos can only be done in the Holy Spirit delivered to the world in connection with the event of the resurrection of the Lord. Let us be permitted some characteristic affirmations, taken again from Athanasius: "It is also by the Spirit that we are all said to be partakers of God . . . now that we are said to be partakers of Christ and partakers of God, it appears that the unction and the seal which are in us are not of the nature of created things but of that of the Son who, by the Spirit who is in him, unites us to the Father" (*Ad Serap.*,

---

27. We have made on this point a rather close investigation into the Tradition of the Church. We met the formula in the major documents of this Tradition, under the pen of the most important Fathers. We will be permitted to refer to our *Leçons sur le Mystère de la Trinité des Personnes divines, pro manuscripto*, Livre second, Ottawa, 1961, pp. 122-127, where we have reported the most characteristic witnesses.

28. This point will be taken up again by Saint Thomas and it seems to us that we have there the principle permitting us to seize upon the connection between the mystery of the Trinity of Persons and that of action *ad extra*. We have tried to show it in a typed thesis, *L'Ordre de Dieu, source et exemplaire de l'ordre du monde*, Le Saulchoir, 1957. E. Bailleux (*La Création, oeuvre de la Trinité selon Saint Thomas*, in *R.T.*, 1962, pp. 27-50) has just treated it in a way that appears very correct to us, for him who is concerned with the mystery of Creation. One will still see C. Strater, *Het begrip "appropriatie" bij S. Thomas*, in *Bijdragen*, 1948, pp. 1-41, 144-186.

1, 24); "in him (the Spirit) the Word glorifies creation, and in conferring sanctification and sonship by adoption, leads men to the Father . . . in him the Word sanctifies created things; he in whom creation is sanctified can not himself be outside the divinity of the Father" (1, 25). Sanctification is, one will note, always attributed to the Logos, but we would make it precise that the Logos sanctifies "in the Holy Spirit present in him." Present, certainly, in Christ from the instant of the incarnation (for he is inseparable from the Logos), nevertheless not always exercising his activity on men but only after the event of the Pasch.

From there to affirm that, if the Eucharistic bread sanctifies the faithful who eats it, it does not hold this power uniquely from the presence in it of the divine Logos, but—in indissoluble union with the Logos and in radical dependence on him—of the mysterious action of the Holy Spirit, the step is easy. Did the Fathers of this tradition do it? To answer is extremely delicate. We have to mistrust premature conclusions. Thus, Athanasius himself, in the fourth letter to Serapion, writes: "To the feeding of how many men would his body suffice yet in order that it become also the nourishment of the whole world? But here is why he makes mention of the ascension of the Son of man into heaven: it was to root them up from the thought of the body and make them understand henceforth that the flesh of which he spoke is a heavenly food come from on high and a spiritual nourishment (*pneumatiken trophen*) given by him. He says in fact: "The words that I have spoken to you are spirit and life," which is the same as saying: What is shown and given for the salvation of the world is the flesh that I bear; but this very flesh, with its blood, I will give to you spiritually as nourishment, so that it may be distributed spiritually (*pneumatikos*) to each of you and become for all a safeguard in view of the resurrection and eternal life" (*Ad Serap.*, 4, 19).

At first sight, one could see there an affirmation of the presence of the Holy Spirit in the Eucharistic bread. But the immediate context informs us about the sense that we must give to

"spiritual": "it is of himself that he said: The Son of man;
and: The Spirit; to indicate by the first his corporal being
and, by the name Spirit, to manifest his spiritual, immaterial
and very visible divinity" (4, 19). Spiritual food means
then food bearing the divinity which is Spirit, this divinity
which Jesus as Logos has in him. Spiritual body is the same
then as "body of him who is equally God." Moreover, in this
section of the epistle, it is a question of blasphemy against the
Spirit which is not pardoned when blasphemy against the Son
of man is remitted. Athanasius seeks to show that "it is in so
designating himself that the Savior said the whole word"
(4, 18: beginning), that "it is he whom the two blasphemies
attain" (4, 19), that "naming the Spirit in opposition to his
corporal being he indicated his own divinity" (4, 19). The text
of John (which is worth for us this reflection on the Eucharist)
is invoked in order to support this exegesis.[29] Nevertheless the
mention of the ascension of Christ forbids us a too 'physical'
interpretation: perhaps one must see there an index of importance accorded to the historical dimension. The Eucharistic
body would then be the bread of immortality, because it is the
body of the glorified Lord, made forever possessor of incorrupti-

---

29. Here, moreover, is how this text is introduced: "This particularity
of terminology I have noted also in the Gospel according to John, when the
Lord, discoursing on the eating of his body and seeing that many were
scandalized by it, says: "This scandalizes you? And when will you see the
Son of man going up there where he was before? It is the Spirit who gives
life, the flesh is worth nothing. The words which I have said to you are
spirit and life." Here also, in fact, he said the two: flesh and Spirit, about
himself, and he distinguished the Spirit (of his being) according to the flesh
in order that (his auditors), believing not only in him who appeared in him
but also in him who was invisible, might learn that the things of which he
speaks are not body but spirit." And the text which we comment on is
followed by the lines: "Thus again the prophet, contemplating the Word-
made-flesh, says: 'The Spirit of our face, Christ the Lord,' for fear that
deluded by the exterior appearance one thinks that the Lord is pure man,
but that in hearing also (the word) Spirit one might recognize that he who
is in the body is God."

bility,[30] "trophy of its victory over death" (*De Incarn.*, 26).[31]

With Gregory of Nyssa, the author of the second *Homily of Pseudo-Chrysostom on the Pasch*, and Cyril of Alexandria, we meet an attempt at synthesis permitting the reconciliation of this simultaneity of the action of the Logos and of the action of the Person of the Holy Spirit. There is in the sacramental regime an adaptation to human nature composed of body and spirit. The Logos-made-flesh sanctifies the human body, the Holy Spirit sanctifies the human soul: "Since man is compound and not simple by nature, being composed of two elements, a sensible body and a spiritual soul, he warrants equally a twofold treatment, homogeneous with each of the two parts: by the Spirit (in the case of baptism) the spirit of man is sanctified, by water—itself sanctified—the body is sanctified" explains Cyril (*In Joan.*, 3, 5; lib. 2, cap. 1; *P.G.*, 73, 244; and "Purification in the Spirit finds its perfection in the sanctification which the body of the Savior, bearer of the power of the Logos who inhabits it causes in us (*In Matt.*, 8, 15; *P.G.*, 72, 389). Nevertheless (we shall come back here) Cyril slows up especially on the action of the Eucharist on the body of man, by contact with the flesh of Christ given life by the Logos.[32] It is not necessary then to press these formulas.

---

30. P. Batiffol (*Études d'Histoire et de Théologie positive, L'Eucharistie, la Présence réelle et la Transsubstantiation,* 10e edit., Paris, 1930, p. 324) thinks so.

31. In a long section of the treatise *De Incarnatione Verbi,* that cannot be reproduced here, Athanasius slows up on the effects operated in the world by the resurrection of Christ (27-32).

32. On the theology of sanctification according to Cyril see J. Bahe, *La sanctification d'après saint Cyrille d'Alexandrie,* in *Rev. d'Hist. Eccles.,* 1909, pp. 30-40, 469-492; B. Fraigneau Julien, *L'inhabitation de la sainte Trinité dans l'âme selon Cyrille d'Alexandrie,* in *Rech. de Sc. Rel.,* 1956, pp. 135-156; G. Giudici, *La dottrina della grazia nel Commento ai Romani di S. Cirillo d'Alessandria,* Rome, 1951; J. Gross *op. cit.,* pp. 285-297. In relation with the Eucharist see J. Mahe, *L'Eucharistie d'après saint Cyrille d'Alexandrie,* in *Rev. d'Hist. Ecclés.,* 1907, pp. 677-696; A. Struckmann, *Die*

If now we pass on to Saint Thomas Aquinas, we are struck by certain affirmations, treating strongly of the role of the Person of the Holy Spirit in the sacramental efficacy. Thus, in the *Summa Theologica*, in the treatise on baptism, at the precise moment where he compares the baptism of water, the baptism of desire and the baptism of blood, a phrase comes back several times: "The Baptism of Water (sacramental)... derives its efficacy, both from Christ's Passion and from the Holy Spirit" (III, 66, 11, ad 1; Dominican Fathers, vol. II, p. 2391). He goes even as far as making precise: "Baptism of Water has its efficacy from Christ's Passion, to which a man is conformed by Baptism, and also from the Holy Spirit, as first cause" (III, 66, 11; p. 2391), "The power of the Holy Spirit operates in baptism through a certain hidden virtue" (III, 66, 12; trans.).

Seen in the whole Thomist context of the capital grace of Christ, these remarks appear very illuminating to us. In fact, on the one hand, for Saint Thomas, Christian grace given to the members of the Church derives from the plenitude of the capital grace of Jesus (III, 8, 5); on the other hand, this capital grace of Jesus (as moreover all grace) is for him properly (in

---

Eucharistielehre des hl. Cyrill von Alexandrien, Paderborn, 1910. For Gregory of Nyssa, see the remarks of H.E.W. Turner, *op. cit.*, pp. 93-95. Let us cite, as characteristic, the following text: "But since the human being is a twofold creature, compounded of soul and body, it is necessary that the saved should lay hold of the Author of the new life through both their component parts. Accordingly, the soul being fused into Him through faith derives from that the means and occasion of salvation; for the act of union with the life implies a fellowship with the life. But the body comes into fellowship and blending with the Author of our salvation in another way .... What, then, is this remedy to be? Nothing else than that very Body which has been shown to be superior to death, and has been the First-Fruits of our life" (*Disc. Cat.*, 37, 1-3; *NPN*, 2nd series, vol. V, p. 504). Replunge this affirmation into the context of the theory of Gregory on the knowledge of God and union with God, and also of his anthropology. See A.A. Weiswurm, *The Nature of Knowledge according to St. Gregory of Nyssa*, Washington, 1952; J.P. Cavarnos, *Gregory of Nyssa on the Nature of the Soul*, in *Greek Orth. Theol. Rev.*, 1955 pp. 135-151. On the Pseudo-Chrysostom see P. Nautin, *Homélies pascales*, II, París, 1953, pp. 42-49.

the strong sense which he gives to the reality of appropriation)[33] the work of the Holy Spirit. This last assertion is the consequence not only of the fact that he generally denominates grace by the expression "grace of the Holy Spirit" (thus I-II, 106, 1, corpus, ad 1, ad 3; I-II, 106, 2; I-II, 106, 3; III, 72, 2, etc.), but especially of his explicit analysis of the relation between the hypostatic union and this plenitude of grace, with which the humanity of Jesus superabounds, what he furthermore designates under the name of capital grace (III, 7, 13).

One knows how much in his treatise on divine Missions (I, 43, 1-8), in profound harmony with all living Tradition, he has shown magnificently that the order of activity of the divine Persons *"ad extra,"* in the history of Salvation and the Christian vocation of each baptized, was conformed to their intimate and eternal order of origin. Because the Spirit proceeds from the Son, his work presupposes that of the Son. And that is true at the very interior of Jesus's own personal humanity: the plenitude of grace, caused in him by the Holy Spirit as by his immediate principle, presupposes *"ordine naturae"* the assumption of the flesh and the soul of this son of man by the divine Person of the Son.[34] Therefore, since the incarnation, in radical dependence on the presence of the Logos in the singular humanity of Christ, the person of the Holy Spirit causes in

33. On the Thomist sense of appropriation, the finest pages remain those of P. H. Dondaine, *La Trinité,* t. 2, Paris, 1950, pp. 409-423. See also C. Strater, *op. cit.,* and the reaction (in our opinion acceptable only with difficulties without certain nuances, in spite of what it brings to the problem) of A. Patfoort, in *R.T.,* VIII, 1947-1953, pp. 864-877.

34. *"Unio humanae naturae ad divinam Personam quam supra diximus esse ipsam gratiam unionis, praecedit gratiam habitualem in Christo, non ordine temporis sed naturae et intellectus. Et hoc triplici ratione. Primo quidem secundum ordinem principiorum utriusque. Principium enim unionis est Persona Filii assumens humanam naturam, quae secundum hoc dicitur missa esse in mundum quod humanam naturam assumpsit. Principium autem gratiae habitualis, quae cum caritate datur, est Spiritus Sanctus, qui secundum hoc dicitur mitti quod per caritatem mentem inhabitat. Missio autem Filii, secundum ordinem naturae, prior est missione Spiritus Sancti, sicut ordine naturae Spiritus Sanctus procedit a Filio, et a sapientia dilectio. Unde et unio*

him the plenitude of capital grace (III, 7, 9). Veiled in him up to the resurrection, this grace radiates from his glorious being ever since Easter morning,[35] and can then (without cease, since it must last, under the efficacious action of the Holy Spirit, not only as the original cause but also as the preservative cause of the created reality that it is)[36] "derive" in men (*in 2 ad Cor.,*

---

personalis, secundum quam intelligitur missio Filii, est prior, ordine naturae, habituali gratia, secundum quam intelligitur missio Spiritus Sancti" (III, 7, 13). It is necessary to remark how close this argument is (essential for the Thomist treatise on the capital grace of Christ) to the Biblical foundation.

35. *"Ipsa glorificatio qua Deus glorificatus est in Christo, est meritum quo Christus secundum quod homo glorificatus est in semetipso, id est in gloria Dei. Et hoc fuit quando humana natura, deposita infirmitate per mortem crucis, accepit gloriam immortalitatis in resurrectione. Unde ipsa resurrectio fuit principium quo inchoata est ista gloria . . . humanitas Christi in resurrectione glorificata est ex conjunctione divinae naturae eam assumentis in Persona Verbi, quia hoc dicitur in Ps. 15, 10: Non derelinques animam in inferno, nec dabis Sanctum tuum (qui est Sanctus sanctorum) videre corruptionem. Debetur etiam Christo homini talis gloria inquantum est Deus. Nos etiam intantum gloriam resurrectionis habebimus, inquantum participes sumus divinitatis, Rom. 8, 11: Qui suscitavit Jesum Christum a mortuis resuscitabit et mortalia corpora vestra propter inhabitantem Spiritum ejus in vobis . . . . Illud ergo quod emittit radios claritatis ad humanitatem Christi est Deus, et sic humanitas Christi clarificatur a gloria divinitatis ejus, et humanitas Christi inducitur in gloriam divinitatis non per transmutationem naturae sed per participationem gloriae, inquantum ipse Christus homo adoratur tamquam Deus . . . . Dicit "Et Deus clarificatus est in eo": idest si ita est quod gloria divinitatis ad gloriam humanitatis redundet, Deus clarificavit eum, idest fecit participem suae gloriae, eum ad suam gloriam assumendo . . . Et sic duplex est gloria Christi. Una quae est in humanitate ejus a divinitate derivata; alia est divinitatis ad quam quodammodo assumitur humanitas; sed aliter et aliter. Nam prima habuit principium temporis, et ideo de ipsa loquitur in praeterito dicens: Et Deus clarificavit eum in semetipso, quod fuit in die resurrectionis. Secunda gloria est perpetua quia ab aeterno Verbum Dei est Deus, ad quam humanitas Christi assumpta in perpetuum glorificatur . . . "* (In Joan., cap. 13, lect. 6; ed. Cai, 1828-1829). See in the same sense *In Heb.,* cap. 5, lect. 2; ed. Cai, 260; III, 54, 3, third reason): *"Est dispensative factum ut ab anima gloria non redundaret in corpus ad hoc quod mysterium nostrae redemptionis sua passione impleret. Et ideo peracto hoc mysterio passionis et mortis Christi, statim anima in corpus, in resurrectione resumptum, suam gloriam derivavit.*

cap. 1, lect. 5, nº 44). This will be done by contact with the paschal event which "faith and the sacraments of faith" (III, 48, 6, ad 2) will render possible. Such is, it seems to us, the authentic Thomist thought on the connection between Logos and Holy Spirit in the work of the Gift of New Life in Jesus. It is a position, one sees, profoundly rooted in the Alexandrian line, but arriving at respecting, with at once much realism and flexibility, the affirmations of the revealed truth. For Saint Thomas, Christian grace wears well its proper name *"gratia Sancti Spiritus."* But it blossoms both in Christ and (by him) in the Church, in dependence on the presence of the Logos. This dependence is not only accidental, not only belonging to the economy. It comes from the eternal order of origin by which the Spirit proceeds from the Son in the mystery of the Trinity of Persons.

All that Saint Thomas will say in the Commentary on the Gospel according to Saint John, a very important theological document in our opinion, of the mission of the Holy Spirit goes in this sense. Thus, commenting on John 16, 7: "If I do not depart, the Paraclete will not come to you, but if I depart I will send him to you," and 7, 39: "The Spirit had not yet come because Jesus had not yet been glorified," he has recourse to a reason of fitness. From the instant of his conception Jesus possessed the Spirit and *"non ad mensuram,"* but in plenitude. However, certain motives prevented him from giving the Spirit immediately to his disciples: their lack of disposition, his own presence rendering useless the sending of another divine Person, the danger that one should think *"quod homo esset qui*

Et ita factum est corpus illud gloriosum." One will remark that in the text of the Summa, Saint Thomas leans on the fact that, since the incarnation, at least the human soul of Jesus is glorified (see III, 14, 1, ad 2): at the resurrection the glory of this soul shines through the body; there is then a partial glorification of humanity in the hypostatic union; this glorification becomes integral only in the Paschal mystery.

36. All created reality dwells without cease under the influx of the first cause which is God not only in the mystery of the unity of essence, but also in that of the Trinity of Persons.

daret Spiritum Sanctum," the necessity of safeguarding the unity of the Church and of avoiding popular enthusiasms around certain Apostles to the detriment of the attachment to his unique Person (*In Joan.*, cap. 16, lect. 2; edit., Cai, 2088-2090; cap. 7, lect. 5, 1091-1096). To which is added a more profound reason of fitness, that Saint Thomas takes up here in relying on John Chrysostom: the Spirit, being a gift of God, could be delivered only to friends. Therefore, it was necessary that the reconciliation by the sacrifice of the cross reconcile us with God and make us his friends before we could enjoy the Person of the Gift of God (cap. 7, lect. 5, 1096).[37] He maintains firmly with Scripture therefore that Christian vivification comes from

---

37. The commentary on I Cor. 15 is to be noted. Saint Thomas comments thus on the verse, "the first man is terrestrial, come from the soil, the second man comes from heaven:" *"Vere primus homo factus in animam viventem quia de terra, Gen. 2,7: 'Formavit Dominus hominem de limo terrae,' et ideo dicitur esse terrenus id est animalis; secundus homo, scilicet Christus, factus est in spiritum vivificantem quia de caelo, quia divina natura quae fuit huic naturae unita de caelo est. Et ideo debet esse caelestis, id est talem perfectionem debet habere qualem decet de caelo venire, scilicet perfectionem spiritualem, Joan. 3, 31: 'Qui de caelo venit super omnes est ....' Secundus homo dicitur de caelo non quod attulerit corpus de caelo, cum de terra assumpserit, scilicet de corpore Beatae Virginis, sed quia divinitas quae naturae humanae unita est, de caelo venit, quae fuit prior quam corpus Christi"* (In I ad Cor., cap. 15, lect. 7; ed., Cai, 995). The accent is clearly put on the hypostatic union, which does not prevent Saint Thomas from affirming some lines before (we do know why now): *"Primus homo factus est in animam, novissimus in spiritum. Ille autem in animam viventem solum, iste vero in spiritum viventem et vivificantem. Cujus ratio est: quia sicut Adam consecutus est perfectionem sui esse per animam, ita et Christus perfectionem sui esse inquantum homo per Spiritum Sanctum. Et ideo cum anima non possit nisi proprium corpus vivificare, ideo Adam factus est in animam non vivificantem sed viventem tantum; sed Christus factus est in spiritum viventem et vivificantem, et ideo Christus habuit potestatem vivificandi. Joan., 1, 16 et Joan., 10, 10. Et in symbolo: Et in Spiritum Sanctum vivificantem"* (*ibid.*, 993). Christ gives life by the Holy Spirit, but in the whole context this relation to the Holy Spirit is put in immediate dependence on the hypostatic union. This is a perspective which is perhaps not a warping of the text; compare it with L. Cerfaux, *Le Christ dans la théologie de saint Paul*, Paris, 1954, pp. 222-223.

the Spirit; but instead of insisting on the fact that at the moment of his glorification, Jesus—according to the expression of the Acts of the Apostles—"is put in possession of the Holy Spirit" (Acts 2, 33), that he becomes then a "spiritual body" (I Cor. 15, 45-49); he upholds that from the moment of the incarnation of the Logos this plenitude of Spirit was in Jesus but that it finds its integral radiation at once in his own humanity and in other men, only from the paschal event. We grasp the nuance of all this.

That permits us to understand well, in giving it all its force, this text taken from the treatise on grace: "As in the person of Christ the humanity causes our salvation by grace, the Divine power being the principal agent, so likewise in the sacraments of the New Law, which are derived from Christ, grace is instrumentally caused by the sacraments, and principally by the power of the Holy Spirit working in the sacraments" (I-II, 112, 1, ad 2; Dominican Fathers, vol. 1, p. 1141).

We are able to interpret better certain affirmations of the Commentary on Saint John, relative to the role which the Holy Spirit plays in the Eucharistic eating. We are thus led back into the very heart of our subject. It is a question of the commentary on John 6, at the verse, "He who eats my flesh and drinks my blood has eternal life, and I will raise him up at the last day." After having shown that by the Eucharistic bread the faithful deepened his union both with the person of Christ and with the assembly of the Church, he adds: "He who thus partakes has eternal Life and I will raise him up . . . at the last day. In fact, he who eats and drinks *spiritualiter* becomes a partaker of the Holy Spirit (*fit particeps Spiritus Sancti*) by which we are united to Christ in the union of faith and love, and by which we become members of the Church; the Holy Spirit is for us a resurrection" (cap. 6, lect. 7, 973). The same idea reappears further on in the commentary: "He eats *spiritualiter*,[38] by comparison simply with the *res* signified, who, by

---

38. Some precisions are necessary. First on the position of Saint Thomas concerning the "spiritual and sacramental" eating. In the line of Augustine

the union of faith and love, is incorporated into the mystical Body; for love makes God dwell in man and man in God . . . this is what the Holy Spirit does, according to I John 4, 13: by that we know that we live in God and God in us, for he has given us his Spirit" (cap. 6, lect. 7, 976).

Can one be any more precise on this relation between the Eucharistic body and the Holy Spirit? Saint Thomas hardly stops there, but reveals to us besides, in the commentary on the same chapter, certain interesting indices. "The flesh is nought, it is the Spirit who gives life," affirms Christ; his commentator explains: "It is manifest that the flesh of Christ, inasmuch as united to the Word and to the Spirit, is worth much and in many ways. . . . Then it is necessary to say that the flesh of Christ, considered in itself, is worth no more and profits no more than any other flesh. For if, by intelligence, one separates it from the divinity and from the Holy Spirit, it has no greater power than any other flesh. But let the Spirit and divinity come in, then it serves several ends, since it makes those who receive it dwell in Christ: it is in fact the Spirit of love by which man dwells in God, according to I John 4, 13. . . . Also the Lord says: this effect (eternal life which I promise you), you must not attribute to the flesh considered

---

he distinguished between the simple material reception of the sacrament and the reception made with faith and love only this latter gives to the faithful the "*res tantum,*" that is to say, the typically Eucharistic grace, and the first leads only to nothing. See III, 80, 1. It can even happen that, by a "*votum*" animated by love, one may perceive the "*res tantum*" without receiving sacramentally (sensibly) the body of Christ (always however a reference to the Sacrament). Each time "*nec frustra tamen adhibetur sacramentalis manducatio, quia plenius inducit sacramenti effectum ipsa sacramenti susceptio quam solum desiderium*" (III, 8, 1, ad 3).

Let us again make precise the nature of the twofold Eucharistic "*res.*" There is a "*res contenta et significata,*" that is Christ really present under the species of consecrated bread and wine, and a "*res signata sed non contenta,*" that is the Church, the body of Christ, that the sacramental signs represent because they make the faithful "pass into" it, but which they do not really contain.

in itself for thus the flesh is worth nothing; but if you attribute it to the Spirit and to the divinity joined to the flesh, thus it procures eternal life, according to Gal. 5, 25: If we live by the Spirit we progress also by the Spirit." Then he adds: "The words which I have spoken to you are spirit and they are life," which signifies that they must be referred to the Spirit united to the flesh, and, thus comprised, they are life, the life of the soul. For just as the body lives its corporal life by the corporal spirit, thus the soul lives its spiritual life by the Holy Spirit, according to Ps. 103, 3: "Send thy Spirit and all will be created" (Cap. 6, lect. 8, 993). It is not easy always to grasp whether it is a question of the Holy Spirit or simply of the Spirit as identified with divinity,[39] and the various editions render us hardly any service. However, is seems clear to us, both from the entirety of the text, and from explicit allusions, that Saint Thomas truly intends to speak here of the third divine Person. In the Eucharist the faithful receives at once the real flesh of Christ, both the Word and the Holy Spirit, but in their relations of Salvation: the radical union remains that of the Logos and the flesh, bearing fruit however in the active presence of the Spirit. And if the Eucharist is (we will return to this) the sacrament of the unity of the Church, that depends on this mysterious action in it of the Spirit of love; if it is equally the sacrament of the resurrection, that depends again on this presence of the Spirit; we have heard Saint Thomas himself say it (cap. 6, lect. 7, 973).

After this long investigation, without which the remainder of our research would have lacked seriousness, we can now advance a conclusion. Even the Christological tradition that we have called Alexandrian, the most marked by the perspective of a "physical" redemption, recognized in the Eucharistic bread a mysterious but real efficacy of the paschal event. This nourish-

---

39. In the Latin tradition, the Spirit often designates divinity *ut sic*. Thus this text of St. Ambrose, *De Myst.*, 58: "The body of God is a spiritual body; the body of Christ is the body of the Divine Spirit, for the Spirit of Christ, as we read: "The Spirit before our face is Christ the Lord" ' (ed., Roy Joseph Deferrari, *The Fathers of the Church*, Washington, 1963, vol. 44, p. 27).

ment, in fact produces its effect of grace only in connection with the work of the Holy Spirit. We have seen Saint Thomas define that if this Spirit, from the instant of the incarnation, in dependence on the presence of the Logos in the flesh, caused in Jesus the plenitude of habitual grace called *capital*, it could cause in men a participation in this plenitude (by derivation) only in relation with the death and resurrection. The Eucharistic body then is the body of the risen Lord Jesus. Otherwise it would not be able to radiate into others its own divinization by the Spirit.

THE EUCHARISTIC BODY OF JESUS
IN THE MAN-GOD CHRISTOLOGY

Up to here, we have spoken only of the first traditional way of approaching the mystery of Jesus, in the radiation of the Johannine theology and of the descendant Logos-flesh movement. But if Pauline theology, often, as in Gal. 4, 4-5, makes its own this "descendant" vision, it ordinarily prefers the ascendant Man-God scheme instead. Not that it pretends that Jesus, an ordinary man, would have been made God only at the moment of his resurrection; but, very attentive to the diverse "moments" of the unfolding of his earthly mystery, it stops on the fact that the Son of God, become the Servant,* receives his glorious state of *Kurios* * only at the moment of his resurrection.[40] Then only his humanity plunges totally into the world of the Spirit, and he is made the new Adam capable of propagating this new Life, of which he becomes (at this instant of his exaltation) in his pneumatic body the principle, the starting point. We recognize, threaded among these words, texts like Rom. 1, 3-4: "His Son, descended, in respect to his human birth, from the line of David, but, in respect to the

---

40. See L. Cerfaux, *Le Christ dans la théologie de S. Paul*, Paris, 1954, pp. 57-71 (especially 65-71), 85-93, 127-248.

sanctified spirit that was his, marked out miraculously as the Son of God by his resurrection from the dead: our Lord Jesus Christ;" Phil. 2, 6-11: "His nature is, from the first, divine, and yet he did not see, in the rank of Godhead, a prize to be coveted; he dispossessed himself, and took the nature of a slave, fashioned in the likeness of men, and presenting himself to us in human form; and then he lowered his own dignity, accepted an obedience which brought him to death, death on a cross. That is why God has raised him to such a height, given him that name which is greater than any other name; so that everything in heaven and on earth and under the earth must bend its knee before the name of Jesus, and every tongue must confess Jesus Christ as the Lord, dwelling in the glory of God the Father;" Acts 2, 33: "Exalted at God's right hand, he has claimed from his Father his promise to bestow the Holy Spirit; and he has poured out that Spirit." Here, the insistance is less on the divine assumption of the humanity of Jesus, from the incarnation, than on the marvelous transformation operated in it at the moment of the glorification, at the end of the sacrifice of the cross. Therefore, the emphasis is less on the ontological constitution of Christ than on his historical work. The state of *kenose* retains the attention more than in the other perspective; as well as up to the resurrection event, we are considering Jesus (indeed the Son of God) solely in his behavior as son of man called by God on a saving mission in the messianic line. The paschal exaltation, in inundating this singular humanity with the plenitude of the divine inheritance, proclaims that this Messiah was not an ordinary man but the First-Born Son of the Father (Col. 1, 13-20).

Then there is treated the "newness of life," the "transformation of sinful men," the "new humanity," indeed the "new Adam," only in relation with the risen Jesus. He has, in his state of *kenose*, espoused at this point the human condition that, up to the redemption from sin by his own sacrifice as the Servant, he is considered as belonging to the psychic world, to the world of the first Adam: "God sent his own Son with a flesh like

unto that of sin, and in view of sin" (Rom. 8, 3).[41] Whence
the radical importance, both for the personal humanity of
Jesus and for our own, of the resurrection: it is this which
accomplishes the entrance of humanity into the inheritance
and the communion of Life with God.

This perspective is prominent we know, in the School of
Antioch, and will sometimes provoke excesses, sources of
grave crises for the Church.[42] This school will insist so much
on the human dimension of the mystery of Christ that it will
have the tendency to attribute to him the autonomy of a human
person; we take care to say tendency, for it would be a very
unjust judgment to make heresiarchs of all the Fathers of this
great School, to which exegesis and theology owe so much.
Moreover, the affirmations of these Fathers are infinitely more
nuanced than what, in underlining with a dark trace the
fringe positions, we present here under the name of the Antiochan
tradition.[43] In short, we are in a new theological context, not
contradictory to the first, but bearing a new look on the same
mystery. Athanasius, Cyril of Alexandria, Gregory of Nyssa
attributed to the union of the flesh of Christ with the Logos,

41. See J. A. T. Robinson, The Body, A *Study in Pauline Theology,*
London, 1955, pp. 37-38.

42. The best synthetic study of the theology of the School of Antioch
remains: R.V. Sellers, *Two Ancient Christologies,* London, 1954, pp. 107-201.
Here, as in the case of the Alexandrian tradition, we use the expression
"Antiochan line " to designate the whole Christology giving to the humanity
of Christ and to his acts their full value, sometimes at the risk of putting in
the shadow the presence in this humanity of the divine Person of the Logos.

43. The history of doctrine has shown how, under expressions which are
often equivocal in certain false, lapidarian affirmations, the most incriminated
Fathers of Antioch were often, in fact, attached to the traditional faith and
respected it. On Paul de Samosate see R.V. Sellers, *op. cit.,* pp. 118-122, 130-
132; H. de Riedmatten, *Les Actes du procès de Paul de Samosate,* Fribourg,
1952. For the Post-Nicene Fathers see R. Devreesse, *Essai sur Theodore de
Mopsueste,* Cite du Vatican, 1948; J. L. McKensie, *Annotations on the
Christology of Theodore of Mopsuestia,* in *Theol. Stud.,* 1958, pp. 345-373;
F. A. Sullivan, *Further Notes on Theodore of Mopsuestia,* in *Theol. Stud.,*
1959, pp. 264-279.

from the first moment of his conception, his lifegiving power, to the point that one could wonder what value they attached to the events of the Pasch in this process of Salvation. Theodore of Mopsuestia, and with him the Fathers of Antioch, reserve this power to the risen spiritual humanity of the Lord: at the end of his history, in the act of the resurrection, Christ receives with the plenitude of the Spirit the power of radiating onto his human brothers this immortality and this glory which he possesses and which transforms his own humanity. The question that this new accent will pose to Tradition is the following: does not one thus put too much in the dark the essential fact that the person of Jesus is the unique Person of the Logos, capable then of acting divinely from his incarnation?

The Eucharistic Body of the Lord,
a Spiritualized (Pneumatical) Body

We guess immediately the rebound of this theology of the Antiochan type (here again we are in the face of this elementary but useful designation) on the problem which preoccupies us, that of the nature of the Eucharistic body of Jesus. This body can be only that of the risen Jesus, the pneumatic body mysteriously transformed by the effusion in it of the Spirit of the New Life at the moment of his resurrection. The witnesses are too limpid to make it necessary to analyze them in detail. It will suffice to recall some major affirmations of him who appears to us the greatest witness of this School on this point—Theodore of Mopsuestia. We take them from the *Catechetical Homily on the Mass*: "Truly, in giving the bread, he did not say: This is the figure of my body, but: This is my body; and in the same manner for the cup, not: This is the figure of my blood, but: This is my blood; because he wanted us to look no longer to the nature of the bread and the cup, once they had received grace and the coming of the Holy Spirit, but rather that we take them for the body and blood of our Lord. For it was not even of its own nature that the body of our Lord possessed immortality and the power of giving immortality, but it is the Holy Spirit that bestows these characteristics. And it is by the resurrection from the dead that it received union with divine nature and became immortal and the cause of immortality for others. Consequently, our Lord, after he had said: Whoever eats my body and drinks my blood will live forever, as he saw the Jews murmur and doubt these words—thinking that by means of a mortal flesh it is not possible to assume immortality—added, in order to resolve this doubt promptly: If you see the Son of man ascend to where he was before, as one would say: Now this does not seem assured to you, because it is of my body that that is said, but when you see me risen from the dead and ascending into heaven, it is certain that these words will no longer be hard and choking, because, by the facts themselves, you will be convinced that I have passed into an immortal nature; if I were not so, I would not ascend into heaven either. And to explain from where that will come to him, he promptly added: It is the Spirit which gives life but the body serves for nothing. That, he says, will come to him by the nature of the lifegiving Spirit, by which he will be transferred to this state, will become immortal, that he might bestow immortality on others also; which he himself did not have, and which to others he could not give as coming from his nature, because the nature of the flesh is powerless for a gift and an aid in that. But, if the nature of the lifegiving Spirit made the body of our Lord of this nature of which formerly it was not . . ." (*Hom. Cat., XV*, 1st on the *Mass*, 10-11).

Theodore, in the following homily, comes back on the same theme: "The body of our Lord Christ, who is of our nature, was first mortal by nature, but by means of the resurrection it passed into an immortal and unchangeable nature. When, therefore, the bishop says that this bread and this wine are the body and blood of Christ, he reveals clearly that they have become so by the coming of the Holy Spirit and that by him they have become immortal; because the body of our Lord also, when it was anointed and it received the Spirit, is thus clearly shown. In the same manner now again, when the Holy Spirit comes, it is we believe as a kind of unction by unexpectedly coming grace that, the presented bread and wine received. And from that time we believe them to be the body and blood of Christ, immortal, incorruptible, impassive, unchangeable by nature, as it came upon the body of our Lord by means of the resurrection" (*Hom. Cat., 2nd on the Mass,* 12). We understand that, in a context of impassioned polemic, stiffening and falsifying gravely the very nuanced thought of Theodore,[44] his opponents were able to make of him the holder of the theory according to which Jesus could not have been God from the moment of his conception. But, for us in holding to the Eucharistic problem, there is no doubt: for him the Eucharistic body, a body which sanctifies and immortalizes him who eats it, can be no other than the pneumatical body as it had become at the resurrection. The Eulogy presents to us the *risen* Lord.[45]

It is a pneumatical body, therefore a body transfixed and transformed by the Holy Spirit. Theodore recognizes the role of the Holy Spirit, not only in the accomplishment of the Eucharistic body of the Lord (on this point he has affirmations which are precious for the problem of the epiclesis but which we cannot consider here), but also and especially in the divinizing effect of this body. And here he meets the major conclusions of the Alexandrian tradition. In fact, on the

---

44. See R. Devreesse, *Essai sur Théodore de Mopsueste,* Cite du Vatican, 1948, pp. 243-258; J.N.D. Kelly, *Early Christian Doctrines,* London, 1960, pp. 307-309 (very nuanced).

45. "Certainly, if it is capable according to a divine decree of maintaining us in this life, not possessing it itself in its nature, even more when it receives the coming of the Holy Spirit, will it be capable (the bread) of leading us to receive immortality. And it is not on account of its nature that it so operates, but it is because of the Spirit who dwells in it, just as also the body of our Lord, of which this is the figure, received immortality by virtue of the Spirit and gave it to others, although itself of its own nature did not possess it absolutely." (*Hom. Cat., XV, 1st on the Mass,* 12).

one hand: "By the coming of the Holy Spirit, that which is presented becomes the body and blood of Christ" (*Hom. Cat., XVJ, 2nd on the Mass,* 25; p. 573; trans.); on the other hand: "By his body and his blood we partake of the nourishment of immortality, and through them the grace of the Holy Spirit flows toward us and nourishes us in view of making us immortal and incorruptible in hope; by them (the bread and the cup), in an unspeakable manner, he leads us to partake of the gifts to come; then in the purest sense by the grace of the Holy Spirit, without sacraments or signs, we will be nourished and will become perfectly immortal, incorruptible and steadfast by nature" (*ibid.*).

The allusions of Theodore to this action of the Holy Spirit rendered possible by the eating of the pneumatical body of the Lord are numerous, and certain passages of his second homily on the Mass count, without doubt, among the most beautiful witnesses of Tradition on this point. Thus: "The bishop asks that on all those who are assembled come the grace of the Holy Spirit, in order that, as by the new birth (baptism) they were perfect in a single body, they be now strengthened also as in a single body by communion with the body of our Lord, and that in concord, peace, application to good, they emerge as only one; in order that all of us, looking thus toward God with a pure heart, receive not thereby our chastisement but our participation in the Holy Spirit, being divided in our manners of seeing and inclined to discussions, to disputes, to envy, to jealousy, scorning good manners; but that we show ourselves worthy of receiving it, because it is in concord, peace, application to good, and in a pure heart that the eye of our soul looks toward God. And thus we shall be united in the communion of the holy mysteries, and by this we will be joined to our Head, Christ our Lord, of whom we believe we are the body and by whom we obtain communion with divine nature" (*ibid.,* 13; p. 555; trans.); "He will show this love toward us because of which the only Son of God, God the Word, truly willed, only for all our salvation, to assume

one of us [46] in order to raise him from the dead; he had him
ascend into heaven, he joined him to himself and established
him at the right hand of God; he granted also to us a participation in that, and he gave us yet the Holy Spirit of whom
we now receive the first-fruits in the guise of *arrhes*; but then
we will receive him entirely, when we have effectively received
communion with him, the body of our humility having become like to his body of glory" (*ibid.*, 2); a text that we must
read in connection with the following: "Holy and immortal
is this food which is the body and blood of our Lord, and
full of holiness, since the Holy Spirit has descended on it. It is
not all who take this food, but those who have already been
sanctified: this is why it is only the baptized who take it, those
who, by a new birth received in Baptism, have the first-fruits
of the Holy Spirit, and by that have obtained the favor of
receiving sanctification" (*ibid.*, 22).

It is useless to make the list any longer. In the Eucharistic
body, and by it, the Holy Spirit, whose first-fruits were
given at baptism, deepens little by little his work in the Christian right up to the day of the Parousia. This is an interesting perspective on the connection between Baptism and the
Eucharist, as on the fundamental unity of the whole process
of sanctification. We will be permitted to note immediately
how close, in spite of the radical diversity of the starting points
and the very different Christological options, these views are
to those that we have encountered above with Saint Thomas
Aquinas: the diverse traditions meet here in the living Tradition.

Up to here we have mentioned only Theodore of Mopsuestia
as a witness of the Antiochan School. But we find the same
views with John Chrysostom who, addressing himself to his
catechumens and explaining to them the actions accomplished
in Christian initiation, says: "As soon as they have come out
of the pools, they are led to the dreadful table, the source of

---

46. We have here an example of the often dangerous expressions of
Theodore, tending to see in Jesus an integral "human personality."

a thousand favors, where they taste the body and the blood of the Lord and become the dwelling-place of the Spirit" (*Cat. Bapt.*, II, 27; edit. A. Wenger, *Sources chrét.*, p. 149; trans.). Why? John Chrysostom has clearly indicated why: "Our discourse is concerning this Body, and as many of us as partake of that Body and taste of that Blood, are partaking of that which is in no wise different from that Body, nor separate. Consider that we taste of that Body that sitteth above, that is adored by Angels, that is next to the Power that is incorruptible" (*In Ephes.*, hom. *P.G.*, 62, 27-28; *NPN*, 1st series, vol. XIII, p. 63); the whole context of this homily gives to this capital text, very typical of the Antiochan theology, a very great resonance: we receive the glorious body of the *Kurios*.* Also, "That which when angels behold, they tremble, and dare not so much as look up at it without awe on account of the brightness that cometh thence, with this we are fed with this we are commingled, and we are made one body and one flesh with Christ" (*In Mat.*, 82; *NPN*, 1st series, vol. X, p. 495).

The Eucharistic Anaphoras * of the Syrian type bear the imprint of this Antiochan fashion of envisaging the mystery. The Greek *Anaphora* * of Saint James is known to us only in a late text. However, certain of his expressions are to be noted: "Let us pray that the Lord our God, having graciously received them to His altar that is holy and above the heavens, rational and spiritual, for the odor of a sweet spiritual savor, may send down in answer upon us the divine grace and the gift of the all-holy Spirit; having prayed for the unity of the faith, and the communion (*koinonia*) of His all-holy and adorable Spirit, let us commend ourselves and one another, and our whole life, to Christ our God" (communion prayer, *AN*, vol. VII, pp. 546-7). *The Apostolic Constitutions*, in the *Clementine Liturgy of Book VIII*, have the following *epiclesis* * formula: "We beseech Thee . . . (to) send down upon this sacrifice Thine Holy Spirit, the Witness of the Lord Jesus' sufferings, that He may show this bread to be the body of Thy Christ, and the cup to be the blood of Thy Christ, that those who are partakers thereof may be strengthened for piety, may obtain the remission of their sins, may be delivered from the devil and his deceit, may be filled with the Holy Spirit, may be made worthy of Thy Christ, and may obtain eternal life upon Thy reconciliation to them, O Lord (*despota*) Almighty" (*ibid.*, p. 489). We are near the *epiclesis* * of the Byzantine Liturgy of John Chrysostom in the more ancient text: "Make of this bread the precious body of thy Christ in changing it by thy Holy Spirit, Amen; and make of this cup the precious (*timion*) blood of thy Christ in changing it by thy Holy Spirit, Amen. So that they may become for those who partake thereof the purification of the soul, remission of sin, communion (*koinonia* *) of thy Holy Spirit, fullness of the Kingdom, confidence (*parresia*) in thy face, and not judgment and condemnation" (Brightman, *Liturgies Eastern and Western*, vol. I, Oxford, 1896, p. 330; translated from the French of Tillard).[47]

The witness of the Nestorian liturgies in their rite of communion is very interesting for us: "May the grace of the Holy Spirit be with thee (deacon) and with us and with all the partakers of this cup, for ever in the Kingdom of Heaven" says the celebrant in placing the hands of the deacon on the consecrated cup. The deacon introduces the prayer of thanksgiving: "Let us all then who by the gift of the grace of the Holy Spirit have drawn nigh and been accounted worthy and have partaken in the reception of these glorious and holy and lifegiving and divine mysteries give thanks all with one accord and glorify God who gave them. (And they answer:) Glory be to him for his unspeakable Gift" (*ibid.*, pp. 297, 301; translated as above).

Here then is what for the living Tradition of the Church, examined in its two most divergent options, is the nature of the Eucharistic body of Jesus. It is truly a question of the body of the risen Jesus, of the body of the Lord with his mysterious power to deliver to his human brothers the gift of the Holy Spirit, the Spirit of the new Life. Certainly, in the line that we

---

47. This text is very close to the text presently in use (*ibid., p.* 387) and to the text of the Liturgy of Saint Basil cited in parallel in Brightman.

have called Alexandrian (but which is neither solely Greek nor solely attested to at Alexandria), the insistance bears especially on the fact that it is a question of the body of the Logos, whereas in the Antiochan line it bears especially on the fact that it is a question of the spiritualized (*pneumatical*) body of the triumphant Lord; but at their fine point, the two views meet in that both recognize that this body is the body marked by the resurrection event which, at the end of his sacrifice as the Servant, permits Christ to diffuse to others his fullness as the Savior.

THE EUCHARISTIC BODY OF JESUS
IS HIS GLORIFIED BODY

Moreover, the major principles guiding the theological reflection on the Eucharist lead us to affirm the necessity of this glorious presence. It is a delicate problem, we know, one on which the theologians are not in agreement,[48] and which we must examine in turn.

We will do so in relying on two great principles of Eucharistic theology, that of the mode of the presence, that of the nature of the sacrifice. We will thus be able to reflect on the static plan and the dynamic plan of the mystery.

The presence of the body of Christ at the end of his Pasch

One of the key theses of the treatise on the Eucharist is that, *ex vi sacramenti*, therefore in a direct fashion, we possess, by the efficacy of the *"verba sacramentalia,"* by the one the body of Christ and by the other his blood (III, 76, 1; III, 81, 4, ad 2, ad 3; etc.). The Eucharist, in fact, although situated at the summit of the sacramental organism, does not escape its laws. Each sacrament effects what it signifies, gives to the Church what at once its sensible material and its verbal form symbolize and announce. For in the sacramental sign God at once reveals his precise design and realizes it. The words,

---

48. Let us recall the position of Dom A. Vonier, *Key to the doctrine of the Eucharist*, Newman Press, 1959.

"This is my body," "This is my blood, and blood of the New
Covenant poured out for you and for many to the remission
of sins," the words of Christ in his Church, replunged into the
historical context of the celebration of the Last Supper by the
Lord himself, were comprised by the living Tradition of the
Church, in the sense of a real presence of the body under the
sign of bread and of the blood under the sign of wine.

We shall not discuss here the grave problem of the precise
sense of *estin* in the Greek transcription of the words of Jesus,
who spoke Aramaic, a language in which the verb "to be" is
not expressed.[49] We take the Eucharistic formula, as living
Tradition, guided by the Holy Spirit, understands it.[50] It is not
that a new body of Christ and a new blood are created. Quite
simply, without any real change in Jesus himself, the bread and
the wine are converted by divine power into the now existing
body and blood of Christ. By what we call transubstantiation the body that Christ now possesses in *"esse naturale"*
becomes—under a mysterious mode that Thomist theology
translates by the expression *"per modum substantiae"*[51]—present there where the bread was. The bread has lost its profound
being of bread, but for finding the profound being of an already

49. See P. Benoit, *Les récits de l'institution et leur portée*, in *Lum. et Vie*,
31, 1957, pp. 65-69; F.J. Leenhardt, *Le sacrement de la Sainte Cène*,
Neuchâtel-Paris, 1948, pp. 23-38; *Ceci est mon corps*, Neuchâtel-Paris, 1955,
pp. 22-40 (see the C.R. of P. Benoit, in R.B., 1949, pp. 155-158; 1956, pp.
578-583; reproduced in *Exégèse et Théologie*, t. I, Paris, 1961, pp. 244-254);
J. Jeremias, *The Eucharistic Words of Jesus*, Oxford, 1955, pp. 139-165.
It is possible that the disciples had not grasped immediately the whole
bearing of the words of the Lord. Cajetan, in *IIIam*, 75, art. 1, no. 2, upholds
this position. For him the literal interpretation of the words of Christ relies on
the authority of the Church, not solely on an exegetical analysis of the text
which could lead only to a metaphorical sense. The passage was lifted from
the Roman edition of the works of Cajetan by order of Pius V.
50. The fundamental work on this point remains: P. Batiffol, *Études
d'Histoire et de Théologie positive. L'Eucharistie, la Présence réelle et la
transsubstantiation*, lme édit., Paris, 1930.
51. On the sense of this expression, see the fine analysis of M. J. Nicolas,
L'Eucharistie (Je sais, Je crois), Paris 1959, pp. 45-54.

existing reality, the profound being of the body of Christ. We
see the essential differences with the other substantial transformations that we know.[52] And that teaches us how scrupulously
we must preserve our theological explanations of the Eucharist
from theories about other substantial transformations. Here we
plunge into a mystery.

Cajetan (In III, 75, 4) proposes on this point an explanation
which is at once discreet and appeasing. The body of Christ
is not displaced to "descend beneath the bread." It is, on the
contrary, the bread which is rendered present to the being of
the body of Christ as it now exists. Is it necessary to recall
that the presence can be effected in two ways—by a change
effected in reality which becomes present (I was in Paris, I
am now in Rome; I have changed), by a change effected in
another reality which becomes present to me (Peter is coming
to visit me in my cell, here I am present to Peter without
having budged). Here we are in the second case. The profound
being of the bread changes, becomes the actual body of Christ.
Its accidents (once transubstantiation is effected) have henceforth, with this body of Christ, a relation of presence.

Theologians search for examples illustrating this mysterious
reality: the example of the mirror which, in being oriented
toward an object (which remains immobile and unchanged),
reproduces it in itself; the example of the radio, placed in the
way of the waves emitted by a transmittor, which captures
music, but which leaves it intact and capable of being captured
by thousands of other sets. These are defective examples,
which permit us to grasp however somewhat of the presence
"per modum substantiae" indeed of the sole and unchangeable
body of Christ in thousands of consecrated breads. The whole
change takes place in the bread, placed in the zone of efficient
capacity of the body of Jesus. God attracts to the actual im-
movable body of Christ the profound being of the bread, and it is

52. J. de Bacciochi (*Présence eucharistique et transsubstantiation*, in
Irenikon, 1959, pp. 139-160) clarifies the problem. See also Ch. V. Heris, *Le
mystère de l'Eucharistie*, Paris, 1943, pp. 39-82 (which remains in our

changed, whereas the body of Christ remains unchanged. And—
a remark whose importance we shall see in an instant—the body,
thus become present *"per modum substantiae,"* is the body
which Christ possesses now. This principle guides the reflection
of Saint Thomas and permits him to answer questions which
were posed in the Middle Ages: what would have happened if
the Eucharist had been celebrated at the very moment of the
death of Jesus (III, 81, 4), or between this death and the
resurrection (III, 76, 1, ad 1; III, 81, 4)? Questions which
seem to us very trifling but which permit us to grasp the whole
implication of the enunciated principle: the Eucharist gives us
sacramentally the body and blood of Christ in the state where
they are naturally at the precise moment of the celebration; and
if, during this celebration or as long as the real Eucharistic
presence lasts, this body and this blood are modified in themselves,[53] this modification affects the Eucharistic body and blood.

This body which Christ possesses now is his pneumatical
body. And we have already guessed the stake of a reflection on
the nature of this pneumatical body. Of what consists precisely
this state of "glorious body," of "body marked by the resurrection event," of "body transfixed by the inheritance of the
Father," of "body inundated by the Holy Spirit" of which we
spoke above in listening to living Tradition? Tradition does
not give the answer. It is the proper task of theology to
search for it. We must avow that theologians hardly seem to be
worried about this question, however important it may be and
however susceptible to throwing new light on many treatises.

Saint Thomas slowed down on it, in four long articles of
the *Summa* (III, 54, 1-4, *De Qualitate Christi resurgentis*).

---

opinion the most correct and balanced explanation); A.M. Roguet,
L'Eucharistie, Paris, 1960, pp. 368-380.

53. St. Thomas distinguishes (III, 81, 4) between what belongs to the
body of Christ *"secundum quod in se est"* and can be as well attributed to
him *"in propria specie"* only in his sacramental existence (to live, to die, to
suffer, to be informed by the soul, to be inanimated, etc.), and what is
fitting to it only by relation to the exterior bodies and therefore can be
attributed to him *"in propria specie"* but not in his sacramental existence
(to be ridiculed, scourged, crucified, etc.).

Marked by the Alexandrian line and by Latin realism, he insists especially on the identity of this paschal body with the
earthly body, on its integrity, on the fact that henceforth all
the "fruitio divina" which up to then beatified only the fine
point of his soul now invades his flesh. The Gospel verse according to which the risen Jesus enters into the house "through
closed doors" obliges him to a rather surprising assertion. That
the body of Christ can thus traverse walls comes not so much
from the quality of his glorious body as from the power of
the divinity of the Word which is united to it.[54] The same
remark occurs in the Commentary on Saint John: "Christ
accomplishes this action, miraculously, by virtue of his divinity,
and each time that that is produced in the life of the saints, we
must see there a new miracle"; [55] further on he will liken this
case (with Augustine) to the miracle of the walking on the
waters (In Joan., cap. 20, lect. 6; ed. Cai, 2554). The narrative of the appearance to the disciples of Emmaus with his
"and he disappeared before their eyes" also demands explanation. Saint Thomas begins by giving his own concept of the
glorious body: a body under submission to the will of the
human spirit, so completely submitted to it, that it can be
seen when that will so decrees and disappear when it wants
to (for him the act of vision has its source in an action of the
object on the sight organ). But he hastens to add that in the
case of Christ we must also ascribe it to divine virtue, capable
even of making bodies which are not glorious to be seen
(III, 54, 1, ad 2). The state of glory does not seem then for
him to modify intrinsically the humanity of the risen Jesus.

    We understand then that, when it is a question of the
Eucharistic body, the mention of glory appears to him as really
rather accidental although in fact he ranges it among the

---

54. "Dicendum est quod non ex natura corporis, sed potius ex virtute
divinitatis unitae, illud corpus ad discipulos, licet verum esset, januis clausis
interivit" III, 54, 1, ad 1).

55. In Joan., cap. 20, lect. 4; ed Cai, 2527 trans. This text is typical of
the philosophical context into which Saint Thomas fades in order to answer
the question of the nature of the glorious body.

realities belonging to Christ *"secundum quod in se est."* For him the great novelty which the resurrection brings to the body of Jesus is, without doubt, its reunion with the soul after the separation of death. The state of glory affects the Eucharistic body only *"ex reali concomitantia,"* at the same time that it is under the dependence of the soul of Christ—itself present solely in this fashion, because now *"non est sine corpore"* (III, 81, 4, ad 3)—and especially in dependence on the presence (equally *"ex reali concomitantia"*) of the divinity of the Word, inseparable from his humanity (III, 76, 1, ad 1).

However, Scripture incites us to consider with more attention this status of the glorious body of the *Kurios* (Lord *) and to accord to it more importance. In a remarkable study on the Ascension, Father P. Benoit has assembled and analyzed the many elements of the scriptural foundation on this point,[56] and this study seems a determinant one. For Paul, in fact, the glorious Christ lives now in heaven in his own body, and this is a certain affirmation of faith. The Father has raised him (I Thess. 1, 10; I Cor. 6, 14; 15, 15; II Cor. 4, 14; Gal. 1, 1; Rom. 4, 24; 10, 9), the first-fruits "of them that slept" (I Cor. 15, 20). In raising him at the end of his sacrifice, he gave him a pneumatical body, which we understand as spiritualized, reborn in a new life, henceforth incorruptible. Certainly, it is still a question of his real body, "born of a woman" (Gal. 4, 4), of the body with which he lived his earthly life as the Servant and which he delivered from death (Phil. 2, 7-8), but transformed, from "psychic" to "pneumatic" (I Cor. 15, 44-49). To take up the expressions of Benoit, through this is effected in the person of Christ, Head of the Church, Principle of the new Life, "the cosmic renewal which must characterize the eschatological era. The risen body of Jesus is the first cell of the new Cosmos. In it the Spirit has already taken possession of matter, as he must do of all Creation after the Parousia when

---

56. P. Benoit, *L'Ascension*, in *R.B.*, 1949, pp. 161-203, taken up in *Exégèse et Théologie*, t. I, Paris, 1961, pp. 363-411. We cite according to this latter reference.

Christ will sum up definitively all things" (op. cit., p. 386).

It is not simply then a question of a new element, purely accidental, added to the historical body of Jesus, of a simple luminous radiation of divinity, of a pure transparency leaving the "carnal" body intact, like a ray of sun making a crystal iridescent. It is a question of a new physical state. The body of Christ the *Kurios* (Lord *) is no longer corruptible "flesh," bearer of all the weakness inherent in the fallen human condition inherited from the first Adam (Rom. 7, 5). While remaining his real body, born of Mary, it has become under the power of God the spiritual body of the new humanity, the body of the new Adam whence will blossom the life of a restored universe. In fact let us distrust a concept of human Salvation which reserved this to the soul alone, it alone being profoundly transformed and raised by grace. Each man, body and soul, must, for the Bible, benefit from the inheritance of the *Agape* * of the Father; and then new Life, inherited from the new Adam, must consist in a radical renewal as well of the body as of the soul. The Greek dichotomy, especially Platonic, between body and soul, is we know foreign to Biblical anthropology. Then, Jesus the Lord, principle of the new humanity, was in his resurrection transformed body and soul. And, a truth which it is important to underline, what is thus played in this mysterious transformation of the body of Christ corresponds in fact to the very drama which dominates the whole *Heilsgeschichte* *: passages from the world of the flesh to the world of God, from the old world marked by the law of sin and death (Rom. 8, 6-7) to the new world dominated by the Spirit of sanctification and of Life, from the world of disobedience to the world of total communion * with the designs of God, from the world of breaking off with God to the world of partaking of the divine inheritance in the possession of the heritage of adopted sons. It would be necessary to comment here on the whole eighth chapter of the Epistle to the Romans.

The psychic body of Christ and his pneumatical body represent then the two states of the mystery of sinful man, saved by the *Agape* * of God, the end *a quo* and the end *ad quem* of the salvific dynamism. They are two states, then, which—although states of a same and identical body—cannot coexist simultaneously. Moreover, the realism of the Pauline texts incites us to affirm that this penetration by the Holy Spirit of transformed [57] matter is at this point bound to the actual mystery of the *Kurios* * that it gives to his body a new substantial mode, radically inseparable from it. This mode, certainly, philosophical reason does not arrive at discerning. It transcends the backgrounds of his experience, and the gropings of medieval theology make it faith.[58] Nevertheless, it seems necessary to affirm it in a theology careful of respecting the accents of the revealed basis. The glory of the risen Lord, considered in the climate that we have just evoked, cannot consist of a simple accidental modification (in the Aristotelian sense of the term) of itself; it plunges more profoundly into its whole ontology. It transforms his flesh into that of the new Man, while leaving it essentially identical to that which he took from Mary his mother. This is a connection, we see, which is much closer than that affirmed by theology under the title of *lex concomitantiae realis*: of itself the body of Jesus remains separable from his blood and from his divinity (although in fact it is not), of itself the risen body of the Lord Jesus no longer separable from its state of glory, from its pneumatical mode of existence. The realism of the historical events goes as far as the profound permanence of their effect. Today the body of Christ could no longer be his "psychic" body, if the history of Salvation has sense and reality, if his "times and moments" follow the law of all history: it never turns back, and metaphysically it cannot. Henceforth, then,

---

57. P. Beniot, *op. cit.*, p. 410, uses this expression.

58. To realize the hesitations of the great scholastics, it will suffice to refer to Guillaume d'Auxèrre, *Summa Aurea*, Paris IV, *De resurrectione Christi*, cap. *De dotibus resurgentium, quaest.* 2, *De dotibus corporum glorificatorum;* to Alexander of Hales, *Summa Theol.*, Pars IV, quaest 22, art. 1; to Albertus Magnus, *De Resurrectione*, Tract. 2, quaest. 8, art. 2-5; to Thomas Aquinas, IV Sent., dist. 43-49.

there, where the body of Christ will appear, it will appear necessarily spiritualized and glorious, antecedent to all law of concomitance.

This conclusion, which seems to us imposed by an attentive study of the texts of Saint Paul, is confirmed by the Johannine tradition. Here again, the risen body of Jesus, while remaining a human body and a body having lived an earthly existence, bears in it the values of the pneumatical body.[59] If John insists on the proofs that Jesus gives of the reality of his body, he underlines equally the suddenness of the appearances and especially their abnormal mode (John 20, 19, 26). Comparing John 20, 22 ("He breathed on them and said to them: Receive the Holy Spirit") and 6, 62-63 ("And when you see the Son of man go up there where he was before, know that it is the Spirit who gives life and that the flesh will not be able to help you"), Father Benoit (*op. cit.*, pp. 388-389) shows how, for John as for Paul, at the moment of his glorification, Christ takes full possession of the pneumatical state in which, penetrated by the Holy Spirit and transformed by it, he can henceforth dispense (in particular by means of the sacraments) this Spirit himself, the Breath of the new Life.

In short, Gospel tradition sees in the transformation by the spirit of the real body of Jesus, born of Mary and therefore exactly like our own, the triumph of Christ over death, the very place where the mystery of our Salvation is accomplished. This transformation so marks at this point the being of Christ that it is necessary, in order to preserve all the realism of revealed truth, to affirm that it is a question here of an intrinsic modification, of a new substantial mode affecting the body and blood of Christ in their existence as body and blood.

This is why, when—with the theology of Saint Thomas— it is affirmed that *ex vi sacramenti*, under the species of Eucharistic bread is found solely the body of Christ, separated from his blood, under the species of Eucharistic wine the blood of

59. See P. Benoit, *op. cit.*, p. 390.

Christ, separated from his body, it is necessary for us to conclude from this that this body and this blood thus separated sacramentally, being the actual body and blood of Jesus, are the glorious body and blood of the *Kurios* (Lord *). There is no need to return to the *vis concomitantiae* in order to reveal there the value of the resurrection. In the simple plan of the *vis sacramentalis*, which is here the essential plan from which it is necessary to depart and in which it is necessary without cease to be situated in order to arrive at a coherent explanation of the mystery, that is accomplished fully and cannot fail to be realized. Moreover, a last remark seems convincing to us. If the two states of the body of Christ have between them the relation that we have just evoked, would it not be incoherent, indeed contradictory, that simultaneously the sacramental words give us *ex vi sacramenti* the psychic body of Christ, *ex vi concomitantiae* his pneumatical body?[60] This telescoping of the end *a quo* and of the end *ad quem* of the *transitus Christi ex hoc mundo ad Patrem* seems to us admissible only with difficulty if the very heart of the mystery of Salvation consists precisely of the abandonment of the first state for the possession of the second and of all that it implies.

The Sacrificial Body of Jesus Christ

A correct concept of the relations between sacrifice and communion confirms this conclusion and answers the possible objections. A whole theology and a certain spirituality have for a long time separated Eucharistic sacrifice and Eucharistic communion, and we know the difficulties that the liturgical renewal has encountered and still encounters in certain regions on this point. The custom of distributing the communion after or before the Mass, or even entirely outside it, an almost generalized custom toward the beginning of the nineteenth

---

60. This point has already been underlined by Ch. Journet, *La Messe, présence du sacrifice de la Croix*, Desclée de Brouwer, 1957, p. 348.

century,[61] is not the least sign of the poverty of Eucharistic theology. But the movement raised by liturgical studies and the ideas put forward especially by Dom Vonier have made their way: there exist today few theologians who do not admit the essential connection between Eucharistic sacrifice and Eucharistic communion.

Moreover, that concords fully with the evidence of the history of religions. In all the natural religions which possessed sacrifices, the sacrifice is traversed by a communional dynamism.[62] On the one hand, man offers something to the god, puts himself into relation with it by means of an object which belongs to him and which he gives, charging it to signify and to effect after a certain fashion the gift which he makes of all of himself. On the other hand, in return, there is the gift on the part of the god, a gift more difficult to perceive but of which one is quite sure. Thus is established between the faithful and his god, as a current of giving, the encounter of two generosities, the ascendant generosity of the faithful and the descendant one of the god: in short, a communion. We meet these values in the religion of the people of God, of Israel.[63] The religion of Israel, of which the most perfect actualization is sacrifice, does not consist simply of the expression of radically dependent feeling toward Yahweh, the Father of the people who is also Creator of the whole universe. It is no longer simply admiration in face of the marvels of the *hesed we emet* (mercy and faithfulness *) or of Creation. It is also, and intensely, a search for communion with Yahweh, which is inscribed quite normally in the very movement of the Covenant. In the sacrifice, the victim is offered to Yahweh; on the altar he is given his

---

61. See A. Lemonnyer, *Communions à la Messe*, in *Semaines Liturgiques. Cours et Conférences*, VII, Louvain, 1929, pp. 287-294; J. Browe, *Wann fing man an, die kommunion ausserhalb der Messe auszuteilen*, in *Theologie und Glaube*, 1931, pp. 755-762.

62. That has been put to light especially by G. Van der Leeuw, *La religion dans son essence et ses manifestations*, Paris, 1948, pp. 332-352.

63. See R. de Vaux, *Les Institutions de l'Ancien Testament*, t. II, Paris, 1960, p. 343.

part (the choice parts), the sacrifice is accepted; then very often the faithful, in a sacred meal, eat the pieces which remain and thus participate vitally in the sacrifice: this partaking of the same reality reinforces the communion between Yahweh and his own, makes them pass into a state of more actual and more living Covenant. And Biblical tradition sees in this sacrifice of communion the most complete and most perfect sacrifice. The Jewish Passover meal, in the reality of which Christ institutes the sacrament of his own sacrifice,[64] has in contemporary Judaism precisely the value of a "communion": [65] a value which Christ assumes (in leading it to surpass itself) for the memorial (*zikkaron*) of his Pasch. It is to say that, far from being a simple appendix to his sacrifice, communion represents its very finality. This has been felt strongly by Augustine in his celebrated definition whose influence on the Latin tradition has been so powerful. Each sacrificial act aims at the *"societas,"* wants to "make communion." It can be perfect and authentic only when accepted by God: from this acquired acceptance, communion is inaugurated, and, in the

---

64. We do not want to discuss here the problem debated among exegetes: was the Lord's Supper really a Passover meal? Let it suffice us to indicate that we rally around the position of Père Benoit and of Jeremias (*op. cit.*) showing that Christ indeed instituted his Eucharist when he was celebrating the traditional Passover meal. To grasp well how the problem is posed, one will read J. Delorme, *La Cène et la Paque*, in *Lum. et Vie*, 31, 1957, pp. 9-48; as a type of argumentation doubting that the Lord's Supper was a Passover meal, see L. Bouyer, *La première Eucharistie dans la dernière Cène*, in *M.D.*, 18, 1949, pp. 37-47 (especially 43-45). In any case, according to the just remark of M. Thurian, *L' Eucharistie, Memorial du Seigneur*, Neuchatel-Paris, 1959, p. 22, nothing, not even the chronological difficulties, is opposed "to the idea that one considers Jesus as celebrant of the Holy Supper in the course of the Passover meal, and it is certain that it is in a Passover background that the Eucharist was instituted, the elements of the traditional ritual furnishing to Jesus the liturgical symbols of the Holy Supper."

65. See H. Haag (*Pâque*, in *Dict. de la Bible, Suppl.*, t. VI, Paris, 1960, col. 1126-1130), who shows the sacrificial dimension with which this rite was charged from its origins; col. 1138-1141 for its rites in Judaism.

most effected cases, the fact that the victim returns to man charged with divine favor expresses it sacramentally at the same time that it is realized.

Let us apply that to the sacrifice of Christ the Servant. The sorrowful passion must be achieved in the acceptance by the Father of this host which is Jesus immolated, for without this acceptance there is no perfect sacrifice, and the gesture of man is then in vain. The resurrection and ascension of the Lord is the manifest expression of this acceptance by the Father, in which is effected the sacrifice of the incarnate Son by the inauguration of the New Covenant, of the definitive communion of Life between the Father and men. Let us recall Phil. 2, 5-11: "Presenting himself to us in human form, he lowered his own dignity, accepted an obedience which brought him to death, death on a cross: THAT IS WHY (dio) God has raised him to such a height." The risen body of the Kurios * thus becomes the point of the definitive communion between God and men: filled up with the goods of the Promise and, in particular, with the Spirit of the eschatological era, it is physically a reconciliation between the Father and humanity, not a purely juridical reconciliation but a reconciliation of Life, of communion.* In Jesus man made a gift of his whole self to God in an intense movement of love (and not by a simple desire to be pardoned) which ended up in the offering of the fundamental good which is natural life. In raising Jesus, God gives himself totally to his creature in the supreme act of his Agape,* culminating in the gift of the Spirit, the Breath of divine Life. An ascendant movement and a descendant movement thus meet in the glorified humanity of the Lord. This is the "sancta societas," perfect and definitive.

In the Eucharistic celebration the assembled Church, in its structure as the People of God organically bonded to Christ the Head, offers to the Father by the ministry of the priest under the species of bread and wine separated, changed into the body and blood of Christ the ascendant movement of the oblation of the cross. We cannot insist here on this aspect which would lead us too far.[66] Let us underline nevertheless the fact of the connection, by the bias of the intention of the minister (who must, that the sacrament be valid, want to do what the Church wants), between the profound motive animating the Eucharistic assembly and the sentiments of the heart of Christ in the very act of his oblation. The Church is not content with mechanically "redoing" the gestures of Christ, sure of possessing thereby his body and his blood. Rather she enters mysteriously but really by the intention of her minister—in which all the faithful present must participate if their participation is to be integrally true—into the intention of Christ offering himself to the Father. But because his sacrifice (in fact, the historical sacrifice of the death and resurrection event mysteriously represented) is already accepted, she receives in return, in the eating of the victim, communion with the divine inheritance which the Father has given for her. If sacrifice and communion are at this point bound into the very dynamism of the Eucharist, the Eucharistic body of Jesus can be no other than his spiritualized body, the body of the *Kurios*; otherwise, we would not be partaking of the sacrifice accepted by the Father, of the sacrifice whose finality has already been realized. And the Eucharist would lose its most realistic sense. The communional gifts which the Person of the Lord Jesus has been enjoying since his paschal exaltation are thus communicated to us—in a still mysterious fashion, as *arrhes* *—in the very act where, passing into the dynamism of his own sacrifice, we make in him the unique oblation of his death offered in love to the Father. This is effected, we must repeat, sacramentally.

This permits us to answer an inevitable question: are not the separated bread and wine, according to the obvious sense

---

66. The position of Ch. Journet, *La Messe, présence du sacrifice de la Croix*, Desclée de Brouwer, 1957, seems to us the most nearly correct position, the best in accord with the Biblical foundation and with Tradition. Wide perspectives are thus opened to theological reflection on the mystery of the sacramental sacrifice of the Lord Jesus.

of the words of Christ, transformed into the given body and the shed blood, therefore into the Christ in his death state? Is it not then a contradiction to uphold that this separated body and blood, in the sign of the sacrificial death, are the glorious body and blood? Would it be the *epiclesis* (post-consecrational) which would transform them into the spiritualized body and blood, or yet the commixture which would reunite them the one to the other? The answer seems simple to us. We are in a sacramental universe. At the very moment when we offer it, when we present to the Father the human act of Christ, our sacrifice is accepted; it is in fact at this perfect point that there can exist no lapse of time whatever between its offering and its acceptance by the Father. The two plans—the human plan, by which in time we reactualize the human, fraternal gesture of Christ giving to his Father our humanity, in trying to pass personally into this gesture to make it our own *hic et nunc* (since, when he accomplished it historically, he included us all in him, and since it is necessary for us, in our place in time, to enter personally and freely by the mediation of the sacrament into this historical act); and the divine plan, outside of time—coexist. God accepts our sacramental sacrifice at the precise moment when we present it to him as he accepted the historical sacrifice of Christ at the precise moment when he lived it, even if historically a rather long interval of time has separated this acceptance and the gift of glory. We make him a gift of the "given" body and blood, but when he receives this gift (and he receives it at the very moment that it is done) in this sacramental act, he pours out his gifts of friendship. Our offering, thus joined by the benevolence of the Father, is a communial offering, the glorified body and blood of the Lord.

Do we not meet here the Johannine view, not separating death and exaltation, seeing the water of the new Life and the blood of Salvation flow from the transfixed side of Jesus on the Cross? Even seeing (if we must believe certain of his exegetes) in the last earthly breath of Christ the first gift of divine Breath,* of *Pneuma?* In the same act, the two dimensions of the paschal mystery, situated in two different planes since the one is totally human, the other totally divine, meet, without the law of the irreversibility of history being in the least compromised. And the point of this conjunction can be none other than the risen body of the *Kurios,* passed forever into glory. We cut our first argument here.

At the end of this chapter, on which is going to be founded the continuation of our theological reflection, it seems necessary for us to affirm the presence in the Eucharistic bread of the risen body of Jesus, of the body which has become, in the resurrection event, but in radically inseparable connection with the death event, the point of the definitive communion of Life between the Father and men. By the eating of this body, the faithful will be allowed by degrees to resemble him, thus to pass a little more into this new Humanity which is the Church, the Body of the risen Lord, in which is strengthened his communion with the Father and his communion with his brothers. As a ferment, this glorious body is going to transform the Church on earth, rendering it from day to day ever nearer to that heavenly Jerusalem of which the Apocalypse sings: "And I saw in my vision that holy city which is the new Jerusalem, being sent down by God from heaven, all clothed in readiness, like a bride who has adorned herself to meet her husband. I heard, too, a voice which cried aloud from the throne, Here is God's tabernacle pitched among men; he will dwell with them, and they will be his own people, and he will be among them, their own God. He will wipe away every tear from their eyes, and there will be no more death, or mourning, or cries of distress, no more sorrow; those old things have passed away. And he who sat on the throne said, Behold, I make all things new. (These words I was bidden write down, words most sure and true.) And he said to me, It is over. I am Alpha, I am Omega, the beginning of all things and their end; those who are thirsty shall drink—it is my free gift—out of the spring whose water is life" (Apoc. 21, 2-6).

CHAPTER III

THE EUCHARIST AND THE FIRST MOMENT
OF THE SALVATION OF THE CHURCH

The risen body of the Lord, become Eucharistic bread, bread of Salvation, the bearer of the sanctifying dynamism of the Holy Spirit, mysteriously transforms the faithful who eats it. It is a salvific transformation, entirely paschal, by which slowly, but really and surely, the son of Adam, born a poor sinner, passes more and more each day into the Kingdom of God in the risen Jesus. He does this not all alone, however, like an isolated pilgrim; quite on the contrary, in communion with all his baptized brothers, of all times and places, he is admitted to the same table by the invitation of the same Father in heaven. Thus, the whole Church Pilgrim, still of this world and exposed to the assaults of temptation and sin, gains another step in its march toward the Parousia. This is true chronologically of course (since all of human history goes toward the advent of the Son of man), but especially qualitatively. After each Eucharist lived in truth, the assembly of the faithful finds itself nearer this plenitude which will bring it into the glory of its resurrection when Jesus judges the world. It is released a bit more from sin, and is at the same time more rooted in the love of God. The Lord's meal snatches it a little more away from death, transforms it a little more into the society of Life. We recognize in these expressions that which above we called the first step of the Salvation of the Church Pilgrim, its purification. The Eucharist purifies and redeems the Church, not simply in the ecclesial offering of the sacrifice

of Jesus the Suffering Servant, but—in indissociable connection
with this offering—in the eating of the risen body of the Lord.

THE AFFIRMATIONS OF SCRIPTURE

Two scriptural texts especially, both belonging to the narratives of the institution, will impose themselves at this point
on the living Tradition of the Church and provoke in it a
regard for this redemptive value of the Eucharist, Matt. 26, 28
and I Cor. 11, 27-29. The first will lead it to affirm, in an often
very energetic fashion, the role of the Eucharist in the remission
of sins; the second, on the contrary, will lead it to question
itself, sometimes anxiously, on the conditions of purification
prerequisite to the true celebration of the Lord's meal. But both
situate this Eucharist-sin relation in a clearly ecclesial perspective. We must slow up somewhat on these two revealed texts,
whose ecclesiological resonances, as we shall see, we cannot
minimize.

The Blood Shed for the Remission of Sins

First Matt. 26, 28: "Drink, all of you, of this; for this is
my blood, of the new testament, shed for many, to the remission of sins." We know the profound agreement of the four
narratives, witnesses of the two liturgical traditions,[1] on the

---

1. See. J. Jeremias, *The Eucharistic Words of Jesus*, Oxford, 1955, pp.
72-135; P. Benoit, *Le récit de la Cène dans Luc 22, 15-20*, in *R.B.*, 1939, pp.
357-393; *Les récits de l'institution et leur portée* in *Lum. et Vie*, 31, 1957, pp.
49-76; Da Cruz Fernandes, *Calicis eucharistici formula paulina*, in *Verbum
Domini*, 1959, pp. 232-236; B. Cooke, *Synoptic Presentation of the Eucharist
as Covenant Sacrifice*, in *Theol. Stud.*, 1960, pp. 1-44; G.S. Sloyan, *Primitive
and Pauline Concepts of Eucharist*, in *The Cath. Bibl. Quart.*, 1961, pp. 1-13.
We would like to refer again here, subject to modifications on several
points, an article which appeared in *N.R. Theol.*, 1962, pp. 449-474. We can
still consult on the same subject, but in another perspective, D.A. Tanghe,
L'Eucharistie pour la remission des peches, in *Irenikon*, 1961, pp. 165-181.

words of the institution. We know also how the proper explanations of each formula bring us valuable clarifications for the theology of the whole. To the text of Mark—doubtless the most ancient, and which reports these words of Jesus over the cup: "This is my blood of the new testament, shed for many" (14, 24)—Paul (I Cor. 11, 25) and Luke (12, 20) add that it is a question of the blood of the New Covenant, Matthew (26, 28) that this blood will be shed for many to the remission of sins. We have here two notations which are important for our task.

The implications of the word of Christ designating the cup as the blood of the New Covenant can evidently be cleared only by reference to the Old Covenant, that of Sinai. Moreover, the New Testament texts themselves invite us to this by the parallelism of their formulas with those of the narrative of the Sinai Covenant in Ex. 24, 1-11.[2] The Old Covenant, concluded by the mediation of Moses in the blood of the sacrificed bulls sacramentally shed on the altar (the sign of Yahweh) then on the assembled People, had founded the *Qahal*,* the People convoked and assembled by God, in its very entity as the People of God.* The Pasch of Exodus, of which the annual passover meal was to represent the *Zikkaron* (memorial *), was accomplished in this mysterious covenant* concluded with all Israel, and which inaugurated between Yahweh and his People a bond of communion, a bond which the prophets (to underline its solidity and its depth) will often express by the imagery of espousals.[3] It was not, then, an in-

See equally J. Browne, *Die Kommunionvorbereitung in Mittelalter*, in *Zeitschr. für kathol. Theol.*, 1932, pp. 375-415; J. Ryelandt, *L'effet purificateur de l' Eucharistie*, in *Rev. Lit. et monast.*, 1920-1921, pp. 96-127.

2. This has been drawn out very clearly by Benoit, *Les récits de l'institution et leur portée*, pp. 55-57; see B. Cooke, *op. cit.;* V. Taylor, *Jesus and His Sacrifice*, London, 1943, pp. 136-139; H.B. Swete, *The Gospel according to St. Mark*, London, 1927, pp. 335-336.

3. On the value of communion present in the Old Covenant, see E. Jacob, *Théologie de l'Ancien Testament*, Neuchâtel-Paris, 1955, pp. 170-176; P. Van Imschoot, *L'Alliance dans l'Ancien Testament*, in *N.R. Theol.*, 1952, pp. 785-805; C. Spicq, *L'Épître aux Hébreux*, t. II, Paris, 1953, pp. 285-299.

dividual covenant, or the sum of individual covenants, but one Covenant with the *Qahal* (People *) as such, and only in this way with the individual. In the mystery of his own Pasch and by the blood of his own sacrifice (Heb. 9, 12; 12, 24), Jesus is going to conclude the New Covenant (Heb. 8, 6, 13; 9, 15; 12, 24) which was already announced by Jeremias (31, 31-34) and for which the Old was only a preparation. From this *Kaine Diatheke* (New Covenant) will be born the Church, the eschatological People of God that the *Qahal* announced and for whose appearance it was by degrees preparing. Therefore, Jesus prolongs the sense of the ritual paschal meal in changing its contents from a memorial of the Old Covenant (celebrating at the same time the deliverance from Egypt and the act of Sinai) to the memorial of the New Covenant which completes the Old. The cup which he offers to his own bears truly, although mysteriously, the sacrificial blood in which is sealed the mystery of the Church, the definitive communion of Life between God and men, in him and by him: "This cup is the New Testament in my blood' (I Cor. 11, 25). In sharing and drinking this cup they will participate in the reality of the New Covenant and of the Church which it founds. This again is like the Hebrews, for the food of the passover meal deepened and reactualized their belonging to the *Qahal.**

But, according to the word of Jeremias, which the whole Gospel echoes, this New Covenant ought to be concluded in a pardon of sins: "I shall pardon their sin and no longer remember their crimes" (31, 34; see 36, 25, 29). Just as the first Covenant was concluded in an atmosphere of redemption and deliverance, the New would be completed in a still more radical deliverance, as the first could only prefigure. It is the deliverance from sin, the passage from a world of hostility, of breaking with God, to the world of the perfect communion of Life. The Covenant would be situated then at the end of a destruction of sin, and the sacrificial blood in which it would be sealed would bear in it equally a value of pardon. Even more, being given the connection made by Israel between the sacrificial blood and expiation (finding its height in the *Yom*

Kippur which remits the sins of all the People in the "state of covenant") and the fact that Jesus is presented himself as the Servant of Yahweh,[4] why would not this blood of the Covenant be equally the instrument of this destruction of sin, the blood of expiation? The cup would then contain the perfect sign and the perfect cause of the New Covenant, the blood of the communion of Life and of pardon come from God (for Israel blood is a divine element present in creatures, and to give it is to give life), and the blood of expiation come from men into a movement of love. The engaging love of God and the perfect response of man thus meet in Jesus the Son of God and son of man. That comes through especially in the precise formula of Matthew: "This is my blood, the blood of the Covenant, which shall be shed for many to the remission of sin;" and this assertion only makes the affirmations of Mark, Paul and Luke more explicit.[5]

For in the words of Christ reported by the four narratives there pierce here and there the affirmations of Deutero-Isaias concerning the expiatory sacrifice of the *Ebed Yahweh* (Servant of God *).[6] Because he "completes" them, it is he, the innocent, expiating in his own flesh the sins and the crimes of men (Is. 53, 3-5) in order to give back to his brothers peace and friendship with God (Is. 53, 3, 11) while offering his life in expiation (Is. 53, 10). He atones not for some privileged

---

4. Luke 4, 17-21; Matt. 8, 17; 11, 4-6; 12, 18-21; 20, 28. On this problem see O. Cullmann, *Christologie du Nouveau Testament*, Neuchâtel-Paris, 1958, pp. 48-73; M.D. Hooker, *Jesus and the Servant*, London, 1959; J. Gilbert, *Jésus, Serviteur de Dieu*, in *Lum. et Vie*, 36, 1958, pp. 5-34; L. Cerfaux, *Saint Paul et le Serviteur de Dieu*, in *Recueil L. Cerfaux*, t. II, Gembloux, 1954, pp. 439-454; *L'hymne au Christ Serviteur*, in *Miscel. Hist. A. de Meyer*, t. I, Louvain, 1946, pp. 117-130; *Le Christ dans la théologie de saint Paul*, Paris, 1954, pp. 283-298; C.H. Dodd, *According to the Scriptures*, Cambridge, 1953, pp. 92-96; F. Gils, *Jésus Prophète d'après les évangiles synoptiques*, Louvain, 1957, pp. 49-88, 135-137.

5. J. Jeremias, *op. cit.*, p. 114; V. Taylor, *The Gospel according to St. Mark*, London, 1955, p. 546.

6. P. Benoit, *Les récits de l'institution et leur portée*, pp. 57-58; O. Cullmann, *op. cit.*, pp. 59-60.

group but for many (Is. 52, 14; 53, 11-12), that is to say
for all men and all peoples.[7] He becomes thereby "the covenant
of the people and the light of nations" (Is. 42, 6). Then, when
Matthew mentions explicitly "the remission of sin for many"
(*peri pollon*) he only accents the traces of the Ebed * which
we read between the lines of the other revealed narratives:
the poor suffering Servant, delivering his life for the benefit
of the *rabbim*, in order to "justify them while burdening himself
with their sins." There is no possible doubt that the cup of the
New Covenant contains a blood of communion which expiates
sin, the fundamental obstacle to the perfect communion of
Life which this Covenant was instituted to establish.

Paul does not mention here the expiatory role of the blood
although certain manuscripts underline in the words spoken
over the bread the sacrificial dimension of the "crushed body."
But his whole concept of redemption goes in this sense. Let
it suffice us to recall Eph. 1, 7; "In him we find redemption by
blood, the remission of sins," and Rom. 3, 25: "They are
justified by the favor of his grace in virtue of the redemption
accomplished in Christ Jesus: God has exposed him, instrument
of propitiation by his own blood, through faith." [8] Then we

---

7. On the sense of *rabbim* and its equivalent *polloi,* see J. Jeremias, *op.
cit.,* pp. 123-125, 246-252; art. *Polloi,* in *T.W.N.T.,* t. VI, 1959, pp. 536-545;
L. Sabourin, *Rédemption sacrificielle,* Desclée de B., 1961, pp. 252-259.

8. It ought to be translated: "God has exposed him propitiatory by his
own blood." On this important text, see S. Lyonnet, *Conception paulinienne
de la Rédemption* in *Lum. et Vie,* 36, 1958, pp. 47-52; D.E.H. Whiteley,
St. Paul's Thought on the Atonement, in *Journ. of Theol. Stud.,* 1957, pp.
253-255; L. Moraldi, *Sensus vocis hilasterion in Rom. 3, 25,* in *Verb. Domini,*
1948, pp. 257-276; L. Cerfaux, *Le Christ dans la théologie de S. Paul,* Paris,
1954, pp. 113-116. It seems that we see here a direct connection made by Paul
with the *Kapporet,* propitiatory, of the Ark of the Covenant. The pardon from
sins was bound on the day of *kippur* to the aspersion of this plaque of gold,
which was considered the place of the presence of Yahweh, with the blood of
the victims. This expiation was that of the sins of all the *Qahal* (People*).
Christ, by his own blood, erases the sins of all the new People who are called
to become a completed humanity: "All have sinned and are deprived of the
glory of God, and they are justified by the favor of his grace in virtue of the
redemption accomplished in Christ Jesus" (Rom. 3, 24).

do not warp his thought in affirming that for him also the cup of the Covenant "in the blood of Christ" (the partaking of which, together with the eating of the bread, "announces the death of the Lord") sweeps the faithful away from the vice of sin and at the same time effects their communion with Christ and among themselves: "The cup of blessing that we bless is it not the communion of the blood of Christ? The bread which we break is it not the communion of the body of Christ? The one bread makes us one body, though we are many in number; the same bread is shared by all" (I Cor. 10, 16-17).

We can now affirm that the blood of the New Covenant realizes simultaneously two effects, a positive effect of the edification of the Church in its deepest mystery of communion of Life between God and men (in Jesus), the source of the communion of Life of men among themselves (in Jesus), and a negative effect of expiation from sin, of pardon. These are not two attached or successive effects, but rather two faces of a single reality. The second effect is, for the first, demanded by the concrete situation of the beneficiary of this positive gift. For it is necessary to lead man, bound in his sin, to the partaking of the communional gifts, which requires that *ipso facto* this sin be wiped away. In a word, it is a question of a completely paschal Covenant, like the Old. First, the paschal Covenant of Christ: he passes from this world to the glorious world of his resurrection, from the world of sin and death to the world of God and Life. But also in this Pasch of Christ there is the paschal Covenant of the Church: it is "snatched away from the empire of darkness and transferred into the Kingdom of the well-beloved Son in whom is found redemption, remission of sin" (Col. 1, 13-14).

In the Last Supper Christ gives this blood of the New Covenant for his Apostles to drink. In the ritual background of the Zikkaron (*memorial* *) of the old Pasch, which aimed at establishing the faithful, by means of the sacramentality of the foods of the meal, in the situation of collective liberation created by the salvific event of Exodus, he offers them his body and blood under the signs of bread and wine. He does not give these as mere symbols, but rather that in each of his own they realize in the rhythm of human history the effect accomplished once for all in the events of the death and resurrection: the definitive Salvation. The Lord's Meal, renewed right up to the Day of the Son of Man, procures then to each of Christ's brothers a marvelous nourishment which roots him further into the New Covenant, integrates him further into the People of God which is the Church, at the very moment when it uproots him somewhat from the world of sin.

Not Eating and Drinking to One's Condemnation

Nevertheless, if the words of institution affirm even in the Pauline tradition this efficacy of the Eucharist with regard to sin, Paul, at the very end of the exposition in the course of which he reported these words of the Lord, with all the optimism of which they are full, recalls that, however, some conditions are prerequisite in the faithful for the efficacious perception of this salvific fruit. For in virtue of what has been proclaimed in the recollection of the Last Supper of Jesus (*oste*): "if anyone eats this bread or drinks this cup of the Lord *unworthily*, he will be held to account for the Lord's body and blood. A man must examine himself first, and then eat of that bread and drink of that cup; *he is eating and drinking damnation to himself* if he eats and drinks unworthily, not recognizing the Lord's body for what it is. That is why many of your number want strength and health, and now a few have died. If we recognized our own fault, we should not incur these judgments; *as it is, the Lord judges us* and chastises us, so that we may now incur, as this world incurs, damnation. So, brethren, when you assemble to eat together, wait for one another; those who are hungry had best eat at home, *for fear that your meeting should bring you condemnation*" (I Cor. 11, 27-34).[9]

---

9. For the exegesis of this text see E.B. Allo, *La synthèse du dogme*

The primary truth we must derive from this text is that there is a sin, a very grievous sin, in approaching unworthily (*anaxios*) the table where the Lord gives as our food the bread of pardon. We render ourselves guilty then with regard to the body and the blood themselves (11, 27), responsible for the death of Jesus: "To eat the bread to drink the cup after a manner which is not appropriate, which does not respect the deep signification, is to participate in the death of Christ as if one were at the side of those who put him to death, and is to vow oneself to spiritual death, to the condemnation which reaches the world." [10] This is a realistic affirmation, analogous to that of the Epistle to the Hebrews which decrees, but in quite another context, that the unworthy faithful "crucify on their count the Son of God and make a public game of him" (Heb. 6, 6).[11] For in the celebration of the Eucharist, in a mysterious but real way, the drama of the death of the Lord, announced until he comes again, becomes contemporaneous with the faithful so that the attitudes of scorn or refusal or lightness or untruth with regard to the bread and the cup meet beyond the signs the historical reality itself. Then, far from being purified of his sin by the blood of the Covenant, the guilty Christian eats and drinks his own condemnation; the judgment is already exercised on him. And Paul, reckoning on the old

---

eucharistique chez S. Paul, in *R.B.,* 1921, pp. 321-343 (especially 326-330); J. Hering, *La première épître de saint Paul aux Corinthiens,* Neuchâtel-Paris, 1949, pp. 97-105; F.J. Lenhardt, *Le sacrement de la sainte Cène,* Neuchâtel-Paris, 1949, pp. 85-90; A. Grail, *Eucharistie, sacrement de la charité dans le Nouveau Testament,* in *Vie Spir.,* 85, 1951, pp. 369-387.

10. L. Cerfaux, *Le Christ dans la théologie de S. Paul,* p. 104; see in the same sense J. Leenhardt, *op. cit.,* p. 87: "Can one express more strongly and more nearly correctly also the malice of this opposition than in associating him who is rendered guilty with those who have pushed their opposition to the will of Jesus to the point of making him die? This is what the Apostle does in saying that he who participates unworthily in the meal renders himself guilty with regard to the body and blood of the Lord. He participates in the crime of his death."

11. See *Heb.* 10, 19 where it is a question of the "blood of the Covenant."

Jewish belief that sees in sickness and in temporal evils the sign of and the punishment for sin,[12] makes immediate application of it to the case of his readers: because they celebrate the Eucharist unworthily, their own community is struck with certain corporal proofs.

We must then prove ourselves, judge ourselves with truth, realizing lucidly our state before God,[13] in order to reveal if we are worthy of participating in the meal of the Lord. And this judgment each of us can bear by the presence in him of the Holy Spirit.[14]

But what will be the material of this examination of conscience? The immediate context is going to reveal it to us: "He who eats and drinks eats and drinks his own condemnation if he recognize not the body," then if he approaches these foods as ordinary foods or as mere "ritual supplement to a joyous meal," [15] while this bread and wine are become the bearers of the sacrifice of the New Covenant offered to sinners, the true body and true blood of the Lord, uniting definitively to the Father and among themselves men whom sin had ranged against each other after having opposed them to God. Not to recognize the body is on the one hand not to discern in faith that this bread is no longer an ordinary loaf but the body of Christ, on the other hand that this body given by the Lord Jesus the night he was betrayed is the bread of love, the food of the Covenant welding all men together in the mystery of the one Church: "The cup of blessing which we bless is it not the communion with the blood of Christ? The bread which we break is it not the communion with the body of Christ? The one bread makes us one body, though we are

---

12. See Si, 18, 20-21; John 9, 2-3; etc. A. Gelin, *Les pauvres de Yahvé*, Paris, 1956, pp. 24-27; *Le péché dans l'Ancien Testament*, in *Theologie du péché*, Desclêe de B., 1960, pp. 36-37.

13. See W. Grundmann, article *dokimos*, T.W.N.T., t. 2, pp. 258-264.

14 Compare with the other texts where Paul speaks of this self-judgment (*Gal.* 6, 4; *II Cor.* 13, 5).

15. E.B. Allo, *op. cit.*, p. 328; F.J. Leenhardt, *op. cit.*, p. 87.

many in number; the same bread is shared by all" (I Cor. 10, 16-17). The precise case of the liturgical assembly of the Corinthians [16] permits us to make these two lacks of discernment explicit. First as a grave irreverence, because they attach no importance to the meal of the Lord, "each one rushes to take his own meal" (11, 20-21). The Eucharist becomes thus a simple "religious formality after a good dinner," [17] a secondary food quite inferior to the good flesh and to the good wines that each has taken care to bring and with which he is stuffed. Such a reversal of the hierarchy of values betrays a grave indifference.

There is more. In this lukewarmness is manifested another "grave sin" of the ecclesial community of Corinth, precisely its lack of ecclesial sense. It celebrates in a climate which is not that of fraternal love the meal in which the Lord offers to it the blood of the New Covenant, the blood of the love of men for one another and for the Father. It creates thus the atmosphere of a lie, of a violent contradiction between the attitude of Christ and its own "sacrilegious" attitude. In fact, at the very moment when it assembles, there exist schisms, divisions,[18] indeed—which is even more reprehensible—sects, heresies (perhaps those mentioned in the first chapter of the letter) so that the unity of the local Church is torn apart in the celebration of the memorial of the Lord ... death in order "in his person to kill the feud" (Eph. 2, 16). Another expression of ecclesial spirit is equally lacking when in Christ there is neither rich nor poor, neither slave nor free man (I Cor. 12, 13; Col. 3, 11; Gal. 3, 28; Rom. 10, 12), social inequality finds in the Eucharistic synaxis (where fraternal unity ought to be strengthened by the common partaking of the body of Christ) the occasion for his manifestation on the great day: "The one is hungry whereas

---

16. It is a question here for Paul of the liturgical assembly, see Hering *op. cit.,* p. 98.

17. E.B. Allo, *op. cit.,* p. 328.

18. See J. Hering, *op. cit.,* p. 98

the other is drunk ... do you then want to make affront to those who have nothing?" (I Cor. 11, 21-22). In short, everything seems to indicate that the Corinthians' sin, which leads to their condemnation and prevents them from perceiving the redemptive effect of the blood of the Covenant, consists in a lack of discernment of the authentic nature of the Eucharistic bread, being translated concretely by an anti-ecclesial attitude. The mystery of the Eucharist is at this point bound to the mystery of the Church so that in scorning the one, little esteem is shown for the other, so that in sinning with regard to the one, sin is shown with regard to the other.

Scripture thus puts us face to face with two affirmations each of which underlines energetically one of the aspects of the sin-Eucharist relation, but always in close connection with the mystery of the Church. The formula of the institution, especially in Matthew, revealed to us that the Eucharistic cup contained the blood of the paschal Christ realizing in the faithful who drinks it an uprooting from the world of sin to the profit of a more intense inrooting into the Church of God, the People of the New Covenant. The Eucharist snatches the faithful out of sin at the same moment that it inroots him a little more into the Church. The warning of Paul to the brethren of Corinth recalled to us that nevertheless it is not sufficient to receive materially the Eucharistic bread and wine in order that this marvelous efficacy be exercized. We are not in the realm of magic here. It is necessary to discern the body and adopt a practical attitude conformed to this discernment. There exists then a certain climate of sin which puts an obstacle in the way of the salvific action of the Lord's Meal, a climate betraying itself most often in a lack of fraternal love, therefore in a lack of the spirit of Church. The Eucharist, the sacrament of ecclesial communion, produces its effect only in a heart which is *truly* open to the mystery of the Church. For far from violating man, the New Covenant demands his *true* engagement.

These two great scriptural affirmations are going to traverse all of living Tradition, and their balance (often difficult to maintain) is going to lead the Fathers little by little to deepen the close connection existing between the redemptive activity, going on now without ceasing, of Jesus in his Church and in the Eucharistic celebration. Certainly here again the diverse theological temperaments, the Christological options, the pastoral contexts are often going to provoke a more intense concentration on one of the affirmations, apparently to the detriment of the other. But from an attentive investigation into the major documents of Tradition, we derive very clearly the following conclusion: the Eucharist purifies the Church Pilgrim, delivers it from sin, not automatically but by means of the presence in the heart of the faithful of an attitude typically of the Church. It therefore all takes place, we are going to try to show, here in the Church.

That is already clear for Ignatius of Antioch who lets us understand it in texts of capital importance at once for the theology of the Church and for the theology of the Christian Eucharist. Speaking of Docetes, he explains: "They have no regard for charity, none for the widow, the orphan, the oppressed, none for the man in prison, the hungry or the thirsty. They abstain from the Eucharist and from prayer because they do not admit that the Eucharist is the flesh of our Savior Jesus Christ, the flesh which suffered for our sins and which the Father, in His graciousness, raised from the dead. And so denying the gift of God, these men perish in their disputatiousness. It were better for them to love (*agapan*)[19] and so to

---

19. With J.B. Lightfoot and P. Camelot we translate *agapan* by "to love." We do this because of the distant context (6, 2) and especially for reasons of primitive Christian vocabulary. But several interpreters (of which Sahn, Funk, Hefele) prefer to translate it by "celebrate the *agape*" which moreover accords fully with the immediate context. Perhaps in the thought of Ignatius the two senses are in a certain fashion connected ("the word might possibly

rise again. It is well for you to keep away from such persons.
... Shun schisms as the source of troubles.... Apart from
the Bishop, let no one perform any of the functions that pertain
to the Church. Let that Eucharist be held valid which is offered
by the bishop or by one to whom the bishop has committed
this charge. Wherever the bishop appears, there let the people
be; as wherever Jesus Christ is, there is the Catholic Church"
(*Smyrn.* 7, 18, 2; *The Fathers of the Church*, vol. 1, pp.
120-121).

Evidently we must avoid stiffening this text or interpreting
it in the function of a posterior systematization. However,
all the essential elements of the Christian theology of the
Eucharist are present. Let us take first the explicit affirmation
of the fact that the Eucharist really gives us the flesh and
blood of Jesus. Ignatius repeats elsewhere: "take care to participate in only one Eucharist for there is only one flesh of our
Lord Jesus Christ, and one cup to unite us to his blood, one
altar, as one bishop with the priests and deacons" (*Phil.* 4,
1). And this flesh thus given [20] is that "which suffered
for our sins and which in goodness the Father raised," then
the flesh as the instrument of the victory over sin and by
that of our own resurrection (*Tral.* 9, 2). Therefore, the Eucharistic bread is "a remedy of immortality (*pharmakon
athanasias*), an antidote in order not to die but to live in Jesus
Christ forever" (*Ephes.* 20, 2). We will have to come back to
the dimension of hope with which this little phrase is pregnant;
but we have to put into relief here the aspect of "remedy." The
term *pharmakon* normally designates a medicine, a drug destined
to cure a sickness. And if used in the genitive case, it can often
signify the means of obtaining something, however the expres-

---

contain an indirect allusion to the *agape*," J. B. Lightfoot, p. 307); see in the
same letter 8, 2. It is clear that the translation "celebrate the *agape*" would
give a greater bearing to this text.

20. *Te dôrea tou Theou* in our text does not seem to designate in a direct
way the Eucharist, but the redemption of man by the incarnation and the
death and resurrection. Compare with II Cor. 9, 15; Rom. 5, 15-17. See J.B.
Lightfoot, *Apostolic Fathers*, Part 2, vol. 2, London, 1889, p. 307.

sion *pharmakon athanasias* seems to be, in the medical language of the time, a rather lavish technical formula to designate a certain unguent of marvelous curing powers.[21] *Antidotes* used substantively must be translated by counterpoison, a remedy destined to chase out a mortal infection. The little phrase of Ignatius appears to us then theologically very compact. Certainly, the accent is put on immortality, on the "life forever in Jesus Christ," but at the same time one affirms that the Eucharist realizes this effect only by means of a medicinal action on sin, man's poison. Moreover, this letter to the Ephesians puts forward explicitly the idea of Christ the doctor which was frequently found in the first Christian literature: [22] "Heretics are enraged dogs who chew cunningly. You must be guarded from them, for their wounds are difficult to cure. There is only one doctor of the body and the spirit, engendered and unengendered, come in flesh, God, in death true life, born of Mary and born of God, at first passible and now impassible, Jesus Christ our Lord" (*Ephes, 7, 2*). When he speaks of sin—which seems to find for him its most hideous form in heresy and schism—Ignatius describes it spontaneously as a "mortal poison" (*Tral. 6, 2, thanasimon pharmakon*). And that joins his fundamental vision in which death and resurrection, therefore the negative dimension and positive dimension of Salvation, are rarely separated (thus *Tral. 9, 1-2; 11, 2; Rom. 6, 1; Phil. prol.; 8, 2; Smyrn., 2, 1; 5, 3; 12, 2*).

But the thought of Ignatius plunges still deeper into the mystery. For he seizes on the fact that this cure for sin and this gift of incorruptibility by the flesh and blood of the Lord exceed the strictly individual plan and join the Church: "In His body He was truly nailed to the Cross for our sake under

---

21, P. Camelot, *Ignace d'Antioche, Lettres*, Paris, 1951, pp. 90-91, note 2. Père Camelot takes up the conclusion to the investigation of Th. Scherman, *Zur Erklärung der Stelle Epist. ad. Eph. 20, 2 des Ignatius von Antiocheia*, in *Theol. Quartalschrift*, 1910, pp. 6-19.

22. See the texts cited by J.B. Lightfoot, *op. cit.*, p. 47, note 13; A. von Harnack, *Medizinisches aus des altesten Kirche*, in *Texte und Untersuch.*, 8, 1892.

Pontius Pilate and Herod, the tetrarch—of His most blessed passion we are the fruit—so that, through His resurrection, He might raise, for all ages, in the one body of His Church, a standard for the saints and the faithful, whether among Jews or Gentiles. For He suffered all these things for us, that we might be saved" (*Smyrn.* 1, 2; *Fathers*, vol. 1, pp. 118-119). The Eucharistic synaxis welds, around the bishop in the common partaking of the bread of immortality, all the members, called too to communicate in the fate of Christ since "the Head cannot be born without the members" (*Tral.* 11, 2; *Fathers*, vol. 1, p. 105). That is why they must flock together "as to one temple of God, to one altar, to Jesus Christ alone" (*Magn.* 7, 2; *Fathers*, vol. 1, p. 98). "Be zealous, then, in the observance of the one Eucharist. For there is one flesh of our Lord, Jesus Christ, and one chalice that brings union in his blood, there is one altar, as there is one bishop with the priests and deacons" (*Phil.* 4, 1; p. 114). Uniting each of the faithful to the flesh and blood of Christ in a common celebration under the presidency of the bishop, the Eucharist builds up the Church, purifies it from sin and death in order to render it a complete participant in the glory of him who is its Head.

However, it can do that only if it is celebrated in a context of ecclesial love, the sins of schism and heresy, of dispute among brothers having been banished, "filtered" (*Phil.* 3, 2). Ignatius often condemns this sin of division and chicanery. He seems even to lead all sins back there: "And so denying the gift of God, these men perish in their disputatiousness. It were better for them to love and so to rise again.... Shun schisms, as the source of troubles" (*Smyrn.* 7, 1-2; p. 121). A very realistic expression translates his reasoning very well: "Make no mistake, brethren. No one who follows another into schism inherits the Kingdom of God. No one who follows heretical doctrine is on the side of the passion. Be zealous, then, in the observance of the one Eucharist" (*Phil.* 3, 2-3, 1, p. 114). Divisions in the faith, leading to divergencies in the concrete fashion of living the Christian mystery, tear open the Church. Then, "apart from the bishop, let no one perform any of the functions that pertain to the Church. Let that Eucharist be held valid which is offered by the bishop or by one to whom the bishop has committed this charge. Wherever the bishop appears, there let the people be; as wherever Jesus Christ is, there is the Catholic Church. It is not lawful to baptize or give communion without the consent of the bishop. On the other hand, whatever has his approval is pleasing to God. . . . A man who acts without the knowledge of the bishop is serving the devil" (*Smyrn.* 8, 1-9, 1; pp. 121-122). Plunging this realistic affirmation into the whole context that we have just recalled, it is legal to transcribe: the flesh and blood of the Lord produce their effect in the faithful and in the community only if they are received in love, this love being extended to the very rich sense that Ignatius gives it where the ecclesial dimension occupies a choice place. Sin against unity (and by that against ecclesial love) not only makes a screen to their action, but even transforms into an imp of the devil him who ought to be a beneficiary thereby of the blessed passion in which Jesus conquered the demon forever.

This balanced theology, at the border of Patristics, we could find also in Justin and Irenaeus of Lyon [23], so much is it bound to the essential of the doctrine of faith on the Lord's Meal. The Eucharist strengthens the Church in the first moment of of the mystery of Salvation. It delivers the Church from sin little by little by the mysterious power of the body and blood of Jesus the Servant of Yahweh, the risen Lord of Easter

---

23. We have studied the thought of these two Fathers in the article cited, pp. 460-463. Let us cite this text of Justin: "We call this food the Eucharist, of which only he can partake who has acknowledged the truth of our teachings, who has been cleansed by baptism for the remission of his sins and for his regeneration, and who regulates his life upon the principles laid down by Christ. Not as ordinary bread or as ordinary drink do we partake of them" (*Apol.* 1, 66, 1; *Fathers*, vol. 6, p. 105). And this other: "The offering of flour . . . which was ordered to be presented for those cleansed from leprosy, was a prototype of the Eucharistic Bread, which our Lord Jesus Christ commanded us to offer" (*Dial.* 41, 1; *Fathers*, vol. 6, p. 209).

morning. All theological traditions are in accord on this point.
And some soundings into each of them will suffice to show it.

The Alexandrian School is strongly marked at its beginnings
by the thought of Origen. With him, although he believes in
the expiatory character of the Eucharistic blood—which he
compares to the sacrificial blood of the Old Covenant (*In Jesu
Nave*, 1, 1)—the insistence bears principally on the conditions
of purity and holiness prerequisite for whoever should approach
the Lord's table. The texts abound. Let us be content here
with a more typical passage on the redemptive power of the
Eucharistic blood and with another on the necessary dispositions. Commenting on the words of institution as they are
reported by Matthew, he writes: "Receiving the chalice from
his Father and giving thanks, he gives it to those who have
gone up with him (into the upper room) saying: 'Drink,
for this is my blood, the blood of the New Covenant,' blood
which is drunk and shed at the same time. It is drunk by the
disciples and shed for the remission of sins committed by
those who drink it and who shed it. If you wonder how it is
shed, simply think about these other words of Scripture: 'The
love of God has been shed in our hearts.' If, therefore, the
blood of the Covenant has been poured into our hearts for the
remission of our sins, once this drinkable blood is shed in our
hearts, all we have done before in our sins is remitted and
erased" (*In Mat. comment., ser.* 86; *P.G.*, 13, 1735).

In this passage allegory (which in the whole context plays
an important part) seems to us to have only a minimal role,
and we are not thinking of falsifying the thought of Origen in
seeing there a rather energetic affirmation—which is rarely
the case [24]—of the efficacy of the Eucharist in erasing sin.

---

24. See H. Urs von Balthasar (*Parole et Mystère chez Origène*, Paris,
1957, pp. 58-64), who analyzes very finely the process of the allegorical

But to benefit from it, it is necessary to be pure: "In the case of the bread of the Lord, accordingly, there is advantage to him who uses it, when with undefiled mind and pure conscience he partakes of the bread" (*In Matt. comment.*, 11, 14; *AN*, vol. IX, p. 443). The example of Judas inspires in Origen the following remarks: "As soon as Judas had finished his portion of the Meal, Satan entered into him. When the Savior had said to him: 'Do quickly what you are about,' and when Judas had received his portion, he left. Therefore, it would not be absurd to affirm here that he who eats unworthily the bread of the Lord or drinks his chalice unworthily eats and drinks to his judgment. In the bread and the cup there is an excellent virtue operating for the good in him whose disposition is good, for condemnation in him whose disposition is bad. Thus the portion given by Jesus was of the same kind as that which he gave to the other Apostles in saying: 'Take, eat.' But in them it was operative for salvation, in Judas for condemnation so that after his portion of the Meal, Satan entered into him" (*Comment. in Joan.*, 32, 24, [16]; ed. E. Preuschen, *G.C.S.*, 4, p. 467).

The ecclesial perspective flourishes in this doubtless authentic fragment: "When your soul suffers, burdened with the sufferings of sin, you are sure, you are disregarding hell, you are defying the tortures of the eternal fire and you are lying to yourself. Do you disregard the judgment of God on those who make fun of him and the Church who is warning you? You are not afraid of communing with the body of Christ when you approach the Eucharist (*communicare non times Corpus Christi accedens ad Eucharistiam*) as if you were clear and pure, as if there were nothing unworthy in you—in all that do you think you are fleeing God's judgment? Do you not remember what is written: 'There are among you the infirm and the sick, and several have fallen asleep'? Why some infirm?

explanation of the scriptural passages treating the Eucharist. See also P. Batifol, *Études d'Histoire et de Théologie positive*, 10me édit., Paris, 1930, pp. 269-274.

Because they do not judge or examine themselves, nor do they understand what it is to commune with the Church (*communicare Ecclesiae*), nor yet what it is to be admitted to so many and such excellent sacraments" (*In Psalm.*, 37, hom. 2, 6; *P.G.*, 13, 1386).[25]

Origen considers sin, all sin, a breaking with the Church, whence the sense he gives to public penance and public reconciliation.[26] The Eucharist purifies, saves in washing away stains on the condition however that he who approaches it be in communion with the Church.

At the other extremity of the Alexandrian tradition, with Cyril of Alexandria, this time in connection with a more profound Christology, the certitude of the medicinal value of the Eucharist goes hand in hand with the certitude of the sanctifying value (of which we shall speak in the following chapter). For the bread of the *Eulogia* * can bring us the marvelous gift of immortality (this is why the Lord offers it to us) only if, at the same time, it delivers us from the infirmities of sin. Cyril finds some striking images to express his thought: "Impure silver, if melted with lead, becomes entirely purified by the fact that the lead takes on all the impurities of the melted

----

25. "One must then say that one enters in an inconsiderate fashion into the sanctuary of the Church who, having done a sinful deed and not caring about the stain that is in him, accepts to pray on the bread of the Eucharist. Such an action profanes the sanctuary and produces stain" (*Selecta* in Ezech., 7, 22; P.G., 13, 793); "In a moment he will enter into the nuptial banquet he will eat the flesh of the lamb, he will drink the drink of salvation. Let no one enter this banquet with soiled clothing. Wisdom has given the same precept in another place: 'At all times let your clothing be clean.' For your clothing was washed once when you received the grace of baptism, your body was purified, you were ridden of all stain from the flesh and the spirit. What God has purified, do not soil" (*In Exod.*, Hom. 11, 7; *Sources chrèt.*, p. 243.)

26. Thus *In Judices*, Hom. 2, 5; P. G., 12, 961. *In Numeros*, Hom. 10, 1-2. In the Origenian concept of Penance see E.F. Latko, *Origens Concept of Penance*, Quebec 1949 (especially pp. 80-86); K. Rahner, *Doctrine d'Origène sur la Pénitence*, *in Rec. de Sc. Rel.*, 1950, pp. 47-97, 252-286, 422-456.

metal. It is a similar work which the Lord accomplishes in us. When we were impure he blended corporally and spiritually with us and thus made the impurities which were in us disappear. He takes away our sins in order that by him and because of him we may become pure and brilliant" (*De Ador. in Spir. et Ver.*, 3; *P.G.*, 68, 297D; trans.).[27] It is this work of the incarnation which in some way becomes part of us by the mediation of the Eucharistic body of Jesus. It purifies us from the vein of all our miseries, a little like the Lord himself who, during his earthly life by the simple contact of his flesh, purified the sick of their fever and led them back to health: "There he is entering Peter's house where a woman is in bed with a burning fever. When as God he would have been able to say: 'Abandon your evil and arise,' he did not act this way. But showing that his flesh, which was the flesh of God, was efficacious for curing, he touched her hand; and Scripture says that at the same time the fever left her. But we also receive Jesus. May he enter into us also, may we hold him in our spirit and in our heart, for he will then extinguish the flame of sinful passion, he will excite us, giving us good spiritual health in order that we might serve him and accomplish what pleases him. . . . Consider again the usefulness that there is in touching his holy flesh. . . . For when by mere words or by a simple acquiescence he could accomplish miracles, he laid his hands on the sick in order to teach us something necessary. For we had to, yes, absolutely, learn that this sacred flesh bore in it the energy of the power of the Logos, that which he had made his own in infusing in it the power which is fitting for God. May Jesus enter into contact with us, or rather may we enter into contact with him, by the mystical *Eulogia,*

---

27. It is a question of the incarnation as such, and we recognize the Alexandrian Christology. Nevertheless the image is applied also to the Eucharist. Compare with this text: "If we desire eternal life in a lively way, and if we want to have in us Him who gives immortality, etc. . . . Christ when he is in us curbs in our members the chewing law of the flesh, revives piety toward God, and extinguishes passions" (*In Joan*, IV, 2; *P.G.*, 73, 584-585; trans.).

in order that he might deliver us also from the infirmities of the soul, from the inroads of the tyranny of the demons" (*Comment. in Lucam*, IV, 38; *P.G.*, 72, 52A-C).[28]

However, the effect of this remedy varies according to the state of the sinner who receives it. If it purifies, calms, and relieves the soul enfeebled by sin, it strengthens and excites the man already disengaged from the drosses of evil: "Those who are still subject to some ills hidden in the soul, can partake of the *Eulogie* of Christ, but differently from the saints who receive it for growth in holiness, the strengthening of the will, energy to persevere in virtue. Whereas they are partakers in the fashion proper to the sick: for the removal of vice, the abandonment of sin, the mortification of the passions, the recuperation of spiritual health. For since, according to the Scriptures, Christ is the new Creature, we also receive him into ourselves in order that by his sacred flesh and blood, we might be, by him and in him, restored to a new life, that we depose the old man who, according to the Scriptures, is corrupted at the will of his own erroneous desires" (*De Ador. in Spir. et ver.*, 12; *P.G.*, 68, 793B-C).[29]

Sometimes even, instead of curing, contact with the body of Christ aggravates the sickness and becomes the occasion of death: "If you destroy the idols made by men and adore God, says Scripture, and decry the ways of the unfaithful, then 'I will bless your bread and your wine and your water.' These words of Scripture are mystical and profound. Indeed, par-

---

28. "It is not according to our own good works, but as Scripture tells us according to his great mercy that we are made participants of so great a goodness. When he had delivered us by cleansing us of our sins and clothing us with the grace of adoption, he offered himself to us in an admirable viaticum, led himself up for our good as an immaculate host and as the lamb at the slaughter, making us participants in the life-giving *Eulogie*, which is his holy flesh and blood" (*De Ador. in Spir. et ver.*, 7; P.G., 68, 501; trans.). See also *In Joan.*, IV, 2 (Comment. de 6, 54; P.G., 73, 577).

29. The context is very interesting here, for Cyril leans on the Old Testament, showing that in Jesus the realities of the Old Testament find their completion.

ticipation in the mysteries of Christ and the grace of holy baptism serve as a spiritual blessing to those who are sincere with God. Whereas to those who are not sincere, inclined to apostasy, the partaking of the spiritual Eulogie will be rage and condemnation and the source of all evils. It seems to me that this is what Paul, that wise man, says: 'Whoever eats and drinks unworthily the body and blood of Christ eats and drinks his own condemnation and does not discern the body. Let the man prove himself therefore and then eat this bread and drink of this cup.' For those who really love God, this participation in the holy mysteries will truly be a blessing; they will be delivered from their infirmities in order not to succumb freely to this sickness which wounds and leads to indolence..."(*De Ador. in Spir. et ver.*, 6; *P.G.*, 68, 416D-417A).[30]

What then are the conditions required to be able to approach the Lord's Meal fruitfully? Baptism first,[31] then an authentic belonging (not purely nominal) to the Church: "It is with holy souls whom he fits to partake of this holy nourishment, in the body of Christ; strangers are not permitted to come to the Eulogie. As strangers it is necessary to consider both the infidel or unbaptized, and those who are broken by a contrary opinion, and those who are in disagreement with the sentiments of the saints, and those who, by perversity, are separated from authentic doctrine" (*De Ador. in Spir. et ver.*, 11; *P.G.* 68, 761D).[32] It would not be necessary however, to take pretext of the purity required and of the desirable piety of heart to abstain from the nourishment of immortality. Each faithful, be he the least fervent, should receive the bread of the Ευλογια: "If we desire with all our heart eternal life and want to have in us him who gives immortality, let us not

---

30. See *De Ador. in Spir. et ver.*, 12; *P.G.* 68, 797.

31. Cyril comes back often on this necessity of Baptism.

32. An allusion is certainly made here to the Eucharistic eating. We must interpret this text with regard to its whole context and to the exegetical method followed by Cyril in this work: see in the institutions of the Old Covenant prefigurations of the cult of the New Law.

imitate the negligence of those who refuse to receive the *Eulogia*,
let us not be mistaken with the special pretexts of piety which
the devil cleverly invents to lose us. But, you say, it is written:
'He who eats this bread and drinks this cup unworthily eats
and drinks to his condemnation.' I have examined myself
and known myself to be unworthy. To him who speaks this
way, I answer: 'When will you be worthy? When will you
present yourself before Christ? If your faults prevent you from
approaching, and even if you ought never cease falling ('Who
knows his offences?' says the Psalmist), will you remain without ever having partaken of the sanctification which gives
eternal life?' Resolve then to live better and in a more honest
fashion, then partake of the *Eulogia* believing that it possesses
the power of guarding you not only against death but even
against sickness. For Christ, when he is in us, curbs in our
members the corrosive law of the flesh, revives piety toward
God, extinguishes passions, seeking less to impute to us the
sins in which we find ourselves than to cure us as sick men.
As the good shepherd who gives his life for his sheep, he binds
up him who is wounded and raises up him who has fallen"
(*In Joan.*, IV, 2, comment. de 6, 57; *P.G.*, 73, 585).[33]

These extracts chosen from among several, show the richness of Cyril's Eucharistic theology and also his optimism
on the salvific efficacy of this sacrament. Because it is the body
of the divine Logos, this Logos who is blended in Jesus in
humanity as such (we are at Alexandria and the accent on
the salvific value of the incarnation in itself need not surprise

---

33. "Can they understand it, these baptized who have received divine
grace but who, by neglecting to come into the churches, by their slowness to
approach the *Eulogie* of Christ, exclude themselves, whatever may be their
badly understood pretexts of piety which they invoke in order not to
commune, form eternal life by refusing to be given life? In spite of its
appearance of pious respect this abstention turns to their wickedness and
ruin. Rather let them recall courage in all the strength of their soul to be
delivered from their sins, let them do their best to lead a right life, and
then let them approach the life-giving comunion with confidence" (*In Joan.*,
III, 6, comment. de 6, 35; *P.G.* 73, 527 A B).

us), the Eucharist bears a mysterious power. It permits to deify man, to lead him to partake of the immortality of God. But because he whom it must thus transform is buried in sin, it must snatch him out of it, remove his blot, cure him of his wounds, strengthen him. All that is accomplished at the same time that he is deified.

Cyril's theological outlook probes the very depths of the Eucharistic mystery: this union of man with Christ is accompanied, always in the same act, by the union of the faithful to his brothers, and our theologian is very categorical on this point too: "To melt us into unity with God and our brothers, who by body and soul differ from one another and to blend us in some way with one another, the only Son, Wisdom and Counsel of the Father, invented a wondrous way. By a single body, his own, he sanctifies the faithful in the mystical communion, making them one body with him and among themselves. Who would be able hereafter to separate and deprive of the physical union that they have among them those who are bound together in unity with Christ by partaking of his holy and one body? If we all partake of a single bread we all form a single bread. Christ cannot be divided; therefore, the Church is called the Body of Christ and we its members according to St. Paul. All united to the one Christ by his holy body, all receiving it, one and indivisible, in our own bodies we are members of this one body and we must consider our members as belonging to him more than to us" (*In Joan.*, XI, 11, comment. de 17, 21; *P.G.*, 74 560).

Already then the Eucharist seems to us fully the sacrament of Salvation, at least for the first moment of the Salvific dynamism of which we were speaking above. It saves the faithful in making him escape from the slavery of sin in Christ the Lord. But that is in union with all his Christian brothers in the bosom of the Church Pilgrim. In short, the activity of the Bread of the *Eulogia* * is conceived like the construction of this Church Pilgrim, the church on earth, which has already passed into the world of God but is still exposed to sin. It is the Church of weak sinners who must ceaselessly be released from their miseries, but who still possess in them a germ of the living divine life. We have without doubt here the key which permits us to seize upon the subjective dispositions required, according to Cyril, for a fruitful participation in the table of the Lord. It is not necessary to be pure from all sin (Cyril seems even to affirm the impossibility of absolute sanctity for man), but it is necessary "to be of the Church," to possess in oneself the Spirit of the new Life bursting from the paschal Christ. Commenting on the appearance to Mary, in the evening of the resurrection, Cyril writes: "The uncircumcized, that is the impure, must not touch the sacred body of the Lord, but those only whom spiritual circumcision has purified. The circumcision of the heart is effected in the Spirit according to Paul, but this spiritual circumcision takes place only when the Spirit dwells in us by faith and Holy Baptism. Was it not fitting then that Mary who had not yet received the Spirit be pushed out of contact with the sacred body? . . . The holy churches have taken example from this. For we keep away from the holy table, we who already believe in the divinity of Christ and profess the faith, the catechumens who have not yet been given the Holy Spirit. For he does not dwell in those who have not received baptism. When they have become partakers of the Holy Spirit, then nothing will be able to prevent them from touching our Savior Christ. This is why the ministers of the Holy Mysteries say to those who want to partake of the Mystical *Eulogia*: 'Holy things for holy people,' showing thereby that the partaking of holy things is fitting only for those who have been sanctified in the Spirit" (*In Joan.*, XII, 1, comment. de 20, 17; *P.G.*, 74 696B-D).

For the Eucharist is the food exclusively of the Church, reserved for those who, become members of Christ by Baptism, are not consequently separated from the ecclesial communion.

It is in the same pastoral and doctrinal climate that we must situate the first three homilies on the Pasch of the Pseudo-

Chrysostom,[34] manifestly impregnated with the great themes of the Alexandrian theology. Here we find the same accent on the divinizing role of the spiritual flesh of the Eucharistic Christ (*Hom.* 2, 7, 11, 18), on the redemptive role (*Hom.* 2, 1-7), on the ecclesial dimension of Salvation that it effects (*Hom.* 1, 11-15). But the text to comment on imposes a certain insistance on the prerequisite conditions of purity, and the third homily stops there: there are necessary Baptism, the stripping away of carnal habits ("as long as you do not strip yourself of carnal habits, you are an *allogène* and a stranger, and there is for you neither participation nor communion with the Holy One, the Christ who comes from heaven; for one must be heavenly to approach the heavenly, and no one can become heavenly without having rejected the earthly," *Hom.* 3, 6), and eagerness (*Hom.* 3, 12; *Hom.* 2, 17-18).

In Cappadocian theology Gregory of Nyssa is on that matter the witness *par excellence*. Certainly, as we will show, he insists on the divinizing role of the Eucharistic body of the divine Logos * who comes to sow in the flesh of the faithful a seed of immortality. But, in the very logic of his concept of the redemption, he associates this divinizing function with the destruction of sin. Here we find again the term *pharmakon* to designate the marvelous food which the Lord offers to us: "For as they who owing to some act of treachery have taken poison, allay its deady influence by means of some other drug (for it is necessary that the antidote should enter the human vitals in the same way as the deadly poison, in order to secure, through them, that the effect of the remedy may be distributed through the entire system), in like manner we, who have tasted the solvent of our nature, necessarily need something that may combine what has been so dissolved, so that such an

---

34. They have been edited, commented on and translated into French by P. Nautin, *Trois homélies dans la tradition d'Origène*, Paris, 1953 (*Sources chrétiennes*). M. Nautin shows, in leaning solidly on the Christology of the author, the appurtenance of these homilies to the theological current represented by Athanasius, Apollinarus, Cyril.

antidote entering within us may, by its own counter-influence, undo the mischief introduced into the body by the poison. What, then, is this remedy to be? Nothing else than that very Body which has been shown to be superior to death, and has been the First-fruits of our life. For, in the manner that, as the Apostle says, a little leaven assimilates to itself the whole lump, so in like manner that body to which immortality has been given it by God, when it is in ours, translates and transmutes the whole into itself. For as by the admixture of a poisonous liquid with a wholesome one the whole draught is deprived of its deadly effect, so too the immortal Body, by being within that which receives it, changes the whole to its own nature" (*Disc. Cat.*, 37, 2-3; *NPN*, 2nd series, vol. V, pp. 504-505).

One will note the last phrase: the medicinal effect of the Eucharistic food is not separated in fact from its effect of divinization. Penetrating into the body of man, the Eucharist infiltrates, with the food (*ibid.*, 37, 7, 11-12), into the whole organism, to bring its own divine vigor which destroys sin and cures the consequences of this presence of poison. We have signaled above the theory of the twofold means of sanctification put forward by Gregory; we meet it again here. By faith, the soul blends with the author of Salvation and finds in this mixture at once cure and divinization; by the bread of the *Eulogia*, the body blends with the immortal body "which has been shown superior to death" and finds there at once cure and immortality.

However we must never take part without discernment in the meal to which Christ invites us. In the *De perfectione et qualem oporteat esse christianum*, Gregory makes his own the warnings of Paul to the community of Corinth, underlines also that in his burial Jesus was enveloped with an immaculate winding-sheet and enclosed in a new tomb which nothing had yet soiled: "The precept of the Apostle and the remark of the Evangelist, he concludes, incite us also to receive the holy body with a pure conscience; if that is soiled by the taint of some sin, we must wash it and purify it with the water of our tears" (*P.G.*, 46, 268-C).

The seventh homily of the Pseudo-Chrysostom[35] bears the same insistances. For it equally, the purifying value of the passion of Christ holds an essential place in the economy of human Salvation: "The only Son of God, willing, in agreement with his Father, to release man and snatch him out of the punishment which menaces him, conceives at once the moment and the mode of his aid; the moment on the one hand to intervene in time for cure, the mode on the other hand to render himself apt to effect the purifying restoration. . . . As the only Son of God wanted to procure to fallen man resurrection, to renew him, and by his own passion to recreate him in the original state, see what he does. Since he was himself the creator of the first man, he had to be also, after his fall, his healer for the redressment of all nature" (ed. P. Nautin, *Sources chrèt.*, 26-27, pp. 134-136). The ritual celebration of the Eucharist permits the faithful of the New Covenant to participate in this Pasch and to receive its benefits, one of which is that of cure: "The Savior, having arrived at his passion, gives bread and a cup as an imitation of the most excellent sacrifice, accomplishing his own body and blood by an ineffable epiclesis which orders the Pasch in these figures. . . . In manifesting the Pasch *par excellence*, the Savior presented it as a safeguard against the evils which menace us, against devils, idolatry and any kind of stain, and made our nature free to recover blessedness; since, arrived at the time of his passion, he prescribed that we also in imitation of him do that in the symbols that he has given us, saying: 'Do this in memory of me;' it is with reason that each year, having arrived at the same anniversary after the equinox, for all our salvation, to get rid of the evils and to take part in the heavenly graces imitating the Savior, we accomplish the Pasch in the most brillant burst in the universe" (*ibid.*, 39-40, pp. 148-150; trans.).

---

35. Edited, commented on, translated into French also by P. Nautin, *Homélies pascales, III, Une homélie anatolienne sur la date de Pâques en l'an 387*, Paris, 1957 (*Sources chrétiennes.*)

THE SCHOOL OF ANTIOCH

The Alexandrian tradition attaches a great importance to the Eucharist-pardon relationship. How much of this applies to Antioch? The interest borne to this salvific dimension of the Eucharistic meal is no less there, and the same scriptural texts impose themselves on the pastors.

It is thus that John Chrysostom, in face of abuse, of a certain laxity, of a certain lightness in his Christians, it seems, finds in his language, as an orator, realistic expressions to recall the purity of conscience required of whoever approaches the altar: "A great number of us, I know, are accustomed to throng about the sacred table on the occasion of this solemnity (the baptism of our Lord). I have often said to you, in place of seeing in the presence of a feast a sufficient reason to communicate, it would be necessary first to purify one's conscience and only afterward touch the august sacrifice. He who is impure and soiled does not merit participation, even on a feast day, in this divine and awesome flesh. But he who is pure and who has erased all his prevarications by sincere repentance deserves to participate in the divine Mysteries, whether you are celebrating a feast or not, and to enjoy God's gifts forever. Since certain of the faithful, I do not know how, are deceived on this point, and some, whose consciences are filled with a mass of sins, as soon as they see a feast arrive, fascinated in some way, approach these holy mysteries upon which, in similar dispositions, they would not even be able to cast their eyes, know well that we repel those whose unworthiness is known to us. But as for those whose unworthiness escapes us, we abandon them to God who reads into the soul of each right up to his most secret thoughts" (*De Baptismo Christi et Epiphania*, 4; *P.G.*, 49, 369-370).

He comes back ceaselessly on this point: "Let there be no Judas among us; let no one advance who is infected with the poison of iniquity. This sacrifice is a true spiritual food. Just as bodily nourishment aggravates sickness if the stomach which receives it is filled with bad substances—not by its own nature but because of the bad state of the stomach itself—thus this spiritual nourishment, when it is received into a soul full of perversity, only makes its condition worse and more deplorable —because of this same perversity" (*De Prod. Judae*, Hom. 1, 6; *P.G.*, 49, 380-381).[36]

However, he well knows the marvelous purifying power of this blood of the table of Christ: "If only he sees you come back from the feast of the Lord, he (the devil), as one who would see a lion with his mouth spitting fire, will flee away more quickly than the wind. And if you show him your tongue touched by the precious blood, he will not be able to hold his stand; if you show him your purpled mouth, he will retreat as quickly as a wretched animal" (*Huit Catechèses baptismales*, Cat. 3, 12; ed. A Wenger, *Sources chrèt.*, p. 158). Elsewhere, he underlines that this Eucharistic blood is "the blood which annulled the note of our sins, the blood which purified our soul, which effaced every sin, which triumphed over powers and principalities" (*Hom. de Coemeterio et Cruce*, 3; *P.G.*, 49, 398).

There exists then not contradiction between, on the one hand, this certitude of the redemptive efficacy of the blood of Christ given in the Eucharistic cup and, on the other, these exigencies of purity: "For like as ye did that, He saith, in remembrance of the miracles in Egypt, so do this likewise in remembrance of me. That was shed for the preservation of the firstborn, this for the remission of the sins of the whole world. For, 'This,' saith He, 'is my blood, which is shed for the remission of sins.'...Wherefore it is needful in all respects to be vigilant, for indeed no small punishment is appointed to them that partake unworthily. Consider how indignant thou art against the traitor, against them that crucified Him. Look therefore, lest thou also thyself become guilty of the body and blood of Christ. They slaughtered the all-holy body, but

---

36. See also *Hom. in Ephes.*, 3, 4-5; P.G., 62, 28-30; J. Bareille, t. 18, pp. 200-203

thou receivest it in a filthy soul after such great benefits" (*Hom. in Mat.*, 82, 1, 5; *P.G.*, 58, 739, 743; J. Bareille, t. XIII, pp. 137, 145; *NPN*, 1st series, vol. X, pp. 492-495). We touch here upon what seems to be for John Chrysostom the principle of the solution: "For 'I keep the passover,' He saith, 'with my disciples.' This table is the same as that, and hath nothing less. For it is not so that Christ wrought that, and man this, but He doth this too. This is that open chamber, where they were then" (*ibid.*, 5; *NPN*, 1st series, vol. X, p. 496). To be able to participate fruitfully in the Lord Christ's meal and thus to perceive the grace of pardon, it is necessary to be in the attitude of the true disciples, not in that of Judas. Then it is necessary to adhere with all one's heart to Christ, to tender all one's forces to the realization of his will, to belong by the depth of one's life not to the world with its lusts and lightnesses. An attitude of truth and rightness. Otherwise one comes as a traitor to sit at the liturgical table whose mysterious reality meets exactly that of the table of the upper room in the night of the passion. The Eucharist is the true festival meal of Christ with his disciples. Then, "For a festival is therefore appointed, not that we may behave ourselves unseemly, not that we may accumulate sins, but rather that we may blot out those which exist" (*Hom. in J ad Cor.*, 27, 5; *NPN*, 1st series, vol. XII, p. 162).

But of all oriental tradition it is without doubt Theodore of Mopsuestia who brings us, on this point still, the most important witness. We find with him a balanced view, supple, cleared of any all too unilateral tightness, attentive to the diverse aspects of the mystery. In the next chapter we shall show the depth of his considerations on the divinizing role of the Eucharist, but those take their whole bearing only when situated in the climate which his theology of the purifying function of the consecrated species is going to reveal to us.

In his *Second Homily on the Mass*, speaking of the communion rites, he relies on the prophet Isaias to profess a great optimism: "If then it is without taking care that we sin, it will be hard for us to approach the holy mysteries; if, with zeal we do good and with horror of evil we repent sincerely of the sins we commit (we who being sinners have been cited for penance in view of life and of universal salvation by the sole mercy of him who has called us) certainly we will have the gift of the remission of sins by the reception of the Holy Mysteries, according to the word of our Lord Christ, since even by the words of blessed Isaias it is possible to learn it. . . . There were on the altar (in the vision of Isaias) burning coals, the revelation of the mystery which should be transmitted to us. First this coal was black and cold; but when fire approached it, it became luminous and warm. The food of the sacred mysteries also should be something similar, for what is offered is common bread and wine, but by the coming of the Holy Spirit it is changed into body and blood; it is thus that it is transformed into the power of a spiritual and immortal food. . . . In the same way certainly that this Seraphim approached, purified and relieved all the prophet's sins, thus we also must believe that in communion with the Holy Mysteries our debts are absolutely covered if we repent, suffer and have compunction in our heart for our sins. . . . But it is the bishop who will give you the Mysteries in his hand, saying: 'The Body of Christ. . . .' He takes them with his hand so that we receive them with confidence in his hands. Not only do we have no fear of their greatness, but we even have confidence because of grace. If in fact the burning coal which was offered in the hand of the Seraphim, absolutely released sins in approaching the lips and did not consume according to nature, even more (when you see the bishop give you from his hands with great assurance this gift, because of the grace of the Spirit which is in him in view of this ministry) you must have confidence and receive with great hope" (*Hom. Cat.*, XVI, 2e sur la Messe, 35-38; ed. Tonneau-Devreesse, pp. 591-595).

Theodore expresses then energetically his faith in the purifying role of the body of Christ given in the Mysteries. But he does not conceive this role as purely mechanical; the faithful must have what we would call contrition for his sins.

Moreover, he does not ignore the words of Paul and the demand for purity that they express. That leads him to distinguish clearly two states of sin: "It is not the sins which by human weakness come to us which merit keeping us from communion with the Sacred Mysteries. In fact in the same way as those who are accustomed to sin must not approach this communion without fear, thus, for those who take care of their salvation it is fitting to approach to receive the Sacred Mysteries, considering that, the same as to sustain this life we necessarily take nourishment, the same also for future subsistence it is a spiritual food which the economy realized by Christ our Lord will procure for us by a divine gift. It is fitting then that we should not keep ourselves from it absolutely, and that we should not approach it with negligence, but that we apply ourselves to good will all our strength. Having applied ourselves, let us throng to the communion, knowing well that if we deliver our life to a complete lack of care, sinning without fear, doing whatever no matter how, without any care for the good, it is for our condemnation that we eat and drink this nourishment which is too high for words. But if we take care of our life and if we rush to do good, if we reflect about it all the while in our heart, sins will not injure us at all which happen without our thinking, by weakness. But on the contrary, it is not simply mediocre succor that we draw from the reception of the Mysteries. The body and blood of our Lord and the grace of the Holy Spirit which will be given to us will procure for us a tendency toward good works, will fortify our dispositions, will repel vain calculations and will also extinguish sins absolutely—if yet it is not voluntarily that we have acted, but that they have assailed us without our thinking and that by the weakness of our nature and without desiring it, we have fallen, but that we have felt a great sorrow for them and with a lively contrition we pray to God for these sins which we have committed. Doubtless indeed, the communion in the Holy Mysteries will give us the remission of such sins since our Lord himself has said clearly: 'This is my body which was broken for you to the remission of sins,' and: 'This is my blood which was shed for you to the remission of sins,' and: 'I have come not to call the righteous but the sinners to penitence' " (*Hom. Cat.*, XVI, 2e sur la Messe, 33-35; ed. Tonneau-Devreesse, pp. 587-593).

There exist then two categories of sin. Certainly, our common daily sins, committed more by weakness than by inner malice, do not take away from us the access to the Lord's table. On the contrary, they ought to incite us to come often and with the confidence of finding there remission as well as strength not to commit them again. On the contrary of John Chrysostom, Theodore, instead of insisting on the requisite conditions of purity, prefers to urge his faithful to frequent communion. And we must note that he binds this medicinal action of the Eucharistic body and blood to the presence of the Holy Spirit. But there are other sins which Theodore calls "the great sins" (*ibid.*, 39; p. 597), which render us unworthy of participation in the Mysteries and demand a preliminary recourse to the remedy of ecclesial penance.[37]

What are then concretely these great sins? First, it seems, there is a certain state of indifference, a complete lack of care

---

37. "Since you know that — that it is in his great sollicitude for us that God gave us the grace of penitence and showed us the remedy of contrition and that, as physicians of sin, he has established bishops in order that by their mediation we receive treatment here below and remission for sin and be delivered from the sentence to come — it is therefore with great confidence that we must approach bishops and reveal our sins to them who, with all sollicitude, compassion and love ... offer treatment to the guilty without letting that be known which they must not reveal but keeping to themselves what has taken place — as they sit there, true and benevolent fathers, who are obligated to remember the shame of their sons and to impose on their bodies what will cure them" (*Hom. Cat.*, XVI, 2e sur la Messe, 44; trans. Tonneau-Devreesse, p. 603; trans.). This text, joined to several affirmations of John Chrysostom (thus in the *Huit Catechèses baptismales*, Cat. 6, 23; edit. A. Wenger, p. 226) poses a difficult problem: is it already a question of our sacrament of confession which would then be required in the case of a great sin? Theodore is more explicit and a bit clearer than John Chrysostom in this sense.

and concern for the things of faith, the fact of not preoccupying oneself with the demands of the Christian condition (*ibid.*, 33; p. 587; 34, p. 589), of "sinning without belief," of "persevering in the same sins" (*ibid.*, 39, p. 597), in short of "rejecting the law" of the Christian life.[38] But there are also certain major transgressions in important points on the "Christian law," in contradiction with the very name of Christian. A type of this case is the incest of which Paul speaks to the Corinthians and on which he elaborates a whole doctrine of medicinal penance (*ibid.*, 42-43, pp. 599-603), recalling that "if there is any one who is called brother and is adulterous, greedy, idolatrous, drunken, insulting, stealing, with such an individual one does not even take bread." For such are equal to a break with the Church. Penance permits correction and cure under the care of the bishops, and to whomever refuses this remedy, appertenance to the Church must be refused: "As for the brothers in the faith, by means of this amendment, if they want to receive it, they receive remission of their sins and are freed from the menace of punishment for the world to come. Consequently, as it appears that there are people who do not accept the amendment which is offered to them, the Apostle says: 'Take out the bad from the midst of you,' as one would say: 'Let him be excluded from among you, absolutely;' a word similar to what our Lord says: 'If he does not hear the Church, let him be esteemed by you as a pagan and a publican' " (*Hom. Cat.*, XVI, 2e sur la Messe, 43; Tonneau-Devreesse, p. 603). We possess a fragment of the commentary of Theodore on I Cor., 11, 33-34 where the same doctrine is met,[39] however with a strong insistence on

---

38. The term *nomos*, used here, appears very often in the Catecheses of Theodore, and there it always signifies "law" (whether natural or human), "institution," "norm of conduct" (see the index given by Tonneau-Devreesse, *op. cit.*, p. 614).

39. K. Staab, *Pauluskommentare aus der Griechischen Kirche*, Munster, 1933, p. 189.

the note of optimism: "I would affirm without hesitation that someone having committed the great sins, but having decided to abandon evil and to give himself over to virtue according to the precepts of Christ, will participate in the Mysteries, well persuaded that he will receive there the remission of all his sins." How, in fact, would the sacrament of the death of Christ not bring us the goods that this death acquired for us, in particular that of pardon? (*ibid.*)

One sees by these few citations at once the realism and the balance of the thought of Theodore of Mopsuestia. The bread of the resurrection (whose effect of divinization and of immortality he has so magnificently put in relief) is also the bread of redemption, of pardon, of the first stage of salvific dynamism. Under the signs of the death of Christ, the virtue of it attains to sinful man whose heart is right and fundamentally attached to Christ in spite of its weaknesses. Thus, the Eucharist grows and intensifies the fraternal communion of all the members of Christ while washing the Church from the sin of its members and removing from it all stain: "When then it is of the same body of our Lord that we all are nourished and it is communion with him that we take by means of this food, it is the one body of Christ that we all become" (*Hom. Cat.*, XVI, 2e sur la Messe, 24; Tonneau-Devreesse, p. 571). But to be able to benefit from this marvelous efficacy, it is necessary to possess in oneself the Holy Spirit, who integrates into the Church.[40] Baptism is the source of this incorporation: "He gave us in Holy Baptism a new birth and by that made of us his own body, his own flesh, his progeny" (*ibid.*, 25, p. 575). Penance gives back to him who lost it the living presence of the Spirit. For not only is the Eucharistic mystery celebrated only in the Church, it distributes equally its effects only in the Church. All this occurs in the interior of the Body of Christ.

If we were to extend the investigation, to question Ephraim

---

40. "Become a single body by the sole virtue of the Holy Spirit, all the faithful are called to the one hope to come" (*Hom. Cat.*, X 18, p. 273).

of Syria [41] and Theodoret of Cyr,[42] we would find the same
constants that John Damascene in the eighth century crystalized
in the following formula which imposed itself on the Latin

---

41. "Moses, the chosen man, went up on Sinai in order to prefigure
your mysteries; he built a temple tabernacle and covered it with silk veils;
the Spouse has covered you with a robe of glory and has tinted your lips with
his life-giving blood; night and day chant the praise of him who has exalted
your horn over all the earth ... by his coming he has chased from you the
vile victims of sacrifices and has posed in you as a trophy his living body
and the chalice of his blood; he has invited your sons to eat of it in order that
by him their sons might be pardoned" (*Hymn. de Instaur. Eccles.*, II, 2, 5;
Th. J. Lamy, *Sancti Ephraem Syri hymni et sermones*, t. 3, Malines, 1889, pp.
966-968). "Receive this bread, eat it in faith without hesitation because it is
my body, and he who eats in faith takes within him the fire of his Spirit
whereas if someone would eat it in doubt, it is no more than mere bread for
him. He who eats with faith this holy bread in my name will be saved pure
if he is pure, will be acquitted if he is a sinner ... The manna that the
Israelites ate in the desert and that they did not honor, the manna which fell
from heaven and which they collected, was the figure of this spiritual bread
which you receive now. Take, eat, all of you; in this bread you eat my body,
true source of pardon; I am the bread of life" (*Sermo In Hebd. Sancta*, 4, 4;
Lamy, t. I, pp. 414-415).

42. "It is not to another part of the body but to the mouth that the
Seraphim applies the coal. What is accomplished then shows the sin of
Isaias. He has indeed gone up to the altar with impunity; and the Seraphim,
although drawing his name from the fire and exercising a divine office,
seizes the coal with tongs and not with bare hands. And applying it to the
mouth of the prophet, he signifies the liberation of the prophet's sin. By that
is decreed, designated as a type, the enjoyment of our own gifts, the liberation
from our sins by the body and the blood of the Lord" (*In Is.* 6, 6; *P.G.*, 31,
268; trans.; to be read in parallel with the texts of Theodore of Mopsuestia
cited above). "Also, whoever eats the bread or drinks the chalice of the Lord
unworthily will be guilty of the body and blood of the Lord: here Paul is
fighting those whom ambition was torturing, and also him who had
fornicated, and with them who had eaten without discernment the meats
offered to idols; but also those of us who dare to receive the Holy Mysteries
with a heavy conscience. He says guilty of the body of Christ and of his blood.
That signifies that, as Judas who delivered him over, the Jews who insulted
him, thus those who received his most holy body in stained hands and bear it
to a criminal mouth dishonor it" (*Interpret. Epist. I ad Cor.*, 11, 27; *P.G.*, 82,
318). See also *Hist. Eccles*, 5, 17; *P.G.*, 82 1232C-D.

Middle Ages: "So the bread of the table and the wine and water are supernaturally changed by the invocation and presence of the Holy Spirit into the body and blood of Christ, and are not two but one and the same. Wherefore to those who partake worthily with faith, it is for the remission of sins and for life everlasting and for the safe-guarding of soul and body; but to those who partake unworthily without faith, it is for chastisement and punishment, just as also the death of the Lord became to those who believe life and incorruption for the enjoyment of eternal blessedness, while to those who do not believe and to the murderers of the Lord it is for everlasting chastisement and punishment" (*De fide orthodoxa*, 4, 13; *NPN*, 2nd series, vol. IX, p. 83). There is no possible doubt that the oriental tradition on the one hand is unanimous in recognizing a marvelous medicinal power of the Eucharist with regard to the sins of those who receive it with a right heart, contrite and loyal to the Church. On the other hand it maintains with firmness that to eat and drink the body and blood of the Lord without these dispositions amounts to eating and drinking one's own condemnation. To participate fruitfully in the Holy Mysteries, it is necessary to be filled with the Spirit which welds together the members of the Church.

THE LITURGICAL PRAYER OF THE EAST

We will not then be astonished to see these two certainties transpire in the liturgical prayer of the Eastern Churches, and it will permit us to seize anew on this consciousness which the assembly of the faithful has in living, with each Eucharistic celebration, an intense mystery of purification. Before the communion rite they ardently ask the Lord to purify their hearts in order to render them worthy of his table; in the very rite of communion they proclaim their faith in the redemptive role of the food which they receive. But if we read attentively all the prescribed texts of the various rituals, we will see quickly that of these two purifications the second is without doubt the most important and the most profound.

It is thus that the Clementine Liturgy of Book VIII of the Apostolic Constitutions, in the very heart of the epiclesis,* asks: "Send down upon this sacrifice Thine Holy Spirit, the Witness of the Lord Jesus' sufferings, that He may show this bread to be the body of Thy Christ, and the cup to be the blood of Thy Christ, that those who are partakers thereof may be strengthened for piety, may obtain the remission of their sins, may be delivered from the devil and his deceit, may be filled with the Holy Spirit, may be made worthy of Thy Christ, and may obtain eternal life upon Thy reconciliation to them, O Lord Almighty" (*Const. Apost.*, VIII, 12, 39; *AN*, vol. VII, p.489). In the prayers which follow the communion, it is expressed in this very compact formula: "Now we have received the precious body and the precious blood of Christ, let us give thanks to Him who has thought us worthy to partake of these His holy mysteries; and let us beseech Him that it may not be to us for condemnation, but for salvation, to the advantage of soul and body, to the preservation of piety, to the remission of sin, and to the life of the world to come" (VIII, 14, 2; *AN*, vol. VII, p. 491; see also VIII, 5, 2 of *Const. Apost.*).

In its turn the Liturgy of Saint James in its Greek text abounds in the same sense. The celebrant does not cease proclaiming his unworthiness and that of the people, imploring pardon of God in order to be able to approach worthily the Holy Mysteries: "God, have pity on me a sinner, for I have sinned against heaven and against you, and I am not even worthy of glancing at this holy and spiritual table on which your only Son, our Lord Jesus Christ is given to me mystically as a sacrifice, to me a sinner, soiled by every sin; by him I offer to you this supplication in order that your Spirit the Paraclete be sent to me, that he strengthen me and make me worthy of this liturgy" (Mercier, *P.O.*, 26, p. 160; Brightman, *op. cit.*, p. 31; trans.); "God and Lord of all, by your love of man, make us who are unworthy worthy in this hour of being united among ourselves by the bond of peace and love, without fraud

or hypocrisy" (Mercier, p. 182; Brightman, p. 43; trans.);
"God who, in your great and ineffable love for man, have
sent your only Son into the world in order to gather in the
stray sheep, do not look away from us at the moment we
offer you this awesome, unbloody sacrifice. Indeed, it is not
in our righteousness that we trust but in your good mercy. . . .
Therefore, we pray and invoke your goodness that this Mystery
accomplished in view of our salvation be not for the punishment of your people but for the pardon of sins, for the renewal of souls and bodies" (Mercier, p. 192; Brightman, p.
46); "We are at the point of offering to you this awesome and
unbloody sacrifice for our sins and the ignorances of the people;
send in us, O God, your good grace, sanctify our souls and
our bodies and our spirits, convert our thoughts to those of
piety, in order that we be able to offer you mercy and peace,
the sacrifice of praise" (Mercier, p. 196; Brightman, p. 48);
"Remit, erase, pardon, O God, our offenses that we have
committed voluntarily and those that we have committed in-
voluntarily, those that we have committed in full knowledge,
those that we have committed without knowing it" (Mercier,
p. 222; Brightman, p. 58). At the moment of the communion
this consciousness of unworthiness of the sinner is expressed
in a magnificent prayer: "Christ, Lord, our God, heavenly
bread, nourishment of the whole world, I have sinned against
heaven and against you; I am not worthy to participate in the
communion of your Holy and Immaculate Mysteries. But in
your ineffable goodness and patience make me worthy of
partaking, not for my judgment and without confusion, of
your most holy body and your precious blood, for the remission of my sins and eternal life" (Mercier, p. 232; Brightman,
p. 63).

We cannot insist better on the necessity of a pure conscience to approach the altar in order to offer the sacrifice of
Jesus and to be nourished with the food of Salvation (for never
are these two aspects, sacrifice and communion, separated
here). But the same Liturgy sings with as much lyricism the
marvelous effects of the Eucharistic bread on the sinful soul

which is judged worthy of being nourished by it. The prayer of *epiclesis* * asks that the Spirit sanctify and transform the bread and wine "in order that they procure to all those who partake the remission of sins and eternal life, sanctification of soul and body, fruitfulness in good works, strengthening of your holy, catholic and apostolic Church founded on the rock of faith, in order that the gates of hell prevail not against it, delivering it from all heresies and scandals of fomenters of iniquity and from all enemies ranged against it, right up to the consummation of the ages" (Mercier, p. 206; Brightman, p. 54; trans.). The formula for the distribution of communion is the following: "The holy body of our Lord and God and Savior, Jesus Christ, is distributed to his faithful for the re-mission of sins and life eternal" (Mercier, p. 234; trans.).[43] Finally, the prayers after the communion and the admonitions of the deacon come back on this theme: "We give you thanks, Christ our God, who have made us worthy of partaking of your body and blood for the remission of our sins and life eternal" (Mercier, p. 236; Brightman, p. 64; trans.); "We who have just partaken of the communion of the saints, immaculate and life-giving Mysteries in remission of our sins, let us pray: Glory to you; glory to you; glory to you, Christ the King, only-begotten Logos of the Father, who have made us worthy, we your sinful and unworthy servants, to enjoy your immaculate Mysteries for the remission of our sins and life eternal; glory to you" (Mercier, p. 236; Brightman, p. 65; trans.).[44]

---

43. This text is lacking in Brightman. It is interesting to signal here the realism of the contemporary rite: "The purifying embers of the body and blood of Christ our God are given to me, a weak slave and sinner, for the remission of faults and the pardon of sins in this world and in the other ... By your living and life-giving blood shed on the cross, may my faults be remitted and my sins pardoned" (*Petit Paroissien des Liturgies orientales*, Harissa, 1941, pp. 256-257; trans.).

44. An investigation into the Syrian Anaphora of Saint James as it is edited by O. Heiming (*In Anaphorae Syriacae quotquot in codicibus adhuc repertae sunt*, vol. II, fasc. 2, Rome, 1953), reveals to us the same insistences. Let us note this beautiful prayer of the epiclesis: "Let him make of this bread the life-giving body, the salutary body, the heavenly body, the body

The Nestorian Liturgy also is full of allusions in this sense. Witness this magnificent prayer of preparation to the proclamation of the *Anaphora*: * "Glory be to you who find the lost; glory be to you who assemble the dispersed; glory be to you who reconcile the separated; glory be to you who lead the wanderers back to the knowledge of truth; glory be to you, O my Lord, who have called me into your goodness in spite of my wretchedness and have reconciled me with you to make me a known member in the great Body of your holy Catholic Church, in order that I might be able to offer you this life-giving and holy and agreeable sacrifice, the memorial of the passion, death, burial and resurrection of our Lord and Savior Jesus Christ in whom you have placed all your kindness and by whom you have decreed to erase the sins of the whole human race.... Yes, our Lord and our God, do not consider the multitude of our sins, do not hold the weight of our iniquities in horror, but rather by your ineffable goodness accept this sacrifice at our hands and endow it with the power to erase our innumerable sins" (Brightman, pp. 271, 273).

---

liberating our souls and bodies, the body of the Lord and God our Savior Jesus Christ for the remission of sins and the eternal life of those who receive it.... Of the mixture which this chalice contains let him make the blood of the New Covenant, the salutary blood, the life-giving blood, the heavenly blood, the blood of the Lord and God our Savior Jesus Christ for the remission of sins and the eternal life of those who receive it" (*op. cit.*, pp. 151-153). This accent on the purifying dimension still strongly encroaches upon the present Liturgy of Saint James as it is presented in the *Petit Paroissien des Liturgies orientales*. Let us cite these texts of the rites preparatory to the comunion: "By this consummation of your body may bad desires be made distant from me; by this drinking of your chalice of life may the passions of my flesh be extinguished; may I become worthy of the remission of my faults and the pardon of my sins, O our Lord and our God, for eternity" (*op. cit.*, p. 225); "Bless this assembly who adore you and who receive your body and your precious blood for the remission of sins, the pardon of sins and the recovery of innocence before you" (p. 258). And the one after the celebration: "May the holy body and the blood of propitiation which I have received from you be for the pardon of my faults, the remission of my sins and my assurance before this awesome tribunal of our Lord and God forever" (p. 266).

The rites of the fraction and of the communion return unceasingly on these values of pardon: "Change, O God, the odor of our corruption and stain into the pleasant savor of your sweet love, purify us of all taint of sin. O good Shepherd who, having come to look for us, have led us from our separation and have accepted our return. In your goodness and mercy pardon my offenses and my sins, both those that I know and those of which I am ignorant" (Brightman, p. 289); "Let us receive the gift of eternal Life. Let us receive it with an overflowing love and humble will. Let us associate in the Mysteries of the Church in pure prayer and with ardent piety; returning from our separation and bewailing our sins in confident penitance, let us ask God, the Lord of all things, for mercy and pardon, and let us pardon our neighbor his offences. . . . Let us receive the holy things and be sanctified in the Holy Spirit: Lord, pardon the sins and transgressions of your servants. In union and peace of spirit let us receive the communion of the Holy Mysteries, in peace toward one another: Lord, pardon the sins and transgressions of your servants. May they be to us, Lord, pledge of the resurrection of the body, salvation of souls and of life without end" (Brightman, pp. 294-295).

The formula of holy communion is remarkable again here: "The body of our Lord is given to . . . for the pardon of his offenses, the precious blood is given to . . . for the pardon of his offenses, for the spiritual feast of eternal life" (Brightman, p. 298), says the celebrant, while the choir sings: "Reinforce, Lord, the hands which are extended and have received holy things for the pardon of offences" (p. 300). There follows this very beautiful prayer: "May Christ, our God, our Lord, our King, our Savior, our Life-giver, he who pardons our sins, who in his grace and mercy has made us worthy of receiving his precious body and blood which sanctify all things, accord us the state of being true in our thoughts, our words, our bearing, and our actions. And, O my Lord, may these first-fruits which we have received and which we receive procure the pardon of our offences, the remission of our sins and the great hope of the resurrection of the dead and the new life in the

Kingdom of Heaven with all those who have pleased you, of your grace and mercy, forever. Amen." (Brightman, p. 302)

All the elements which we have found above are in this Liturgy: the prerequisite purity, the ecclesial dimension of sin and of Salvation, the definitive gift of pardon and of remission to those who approach the altar worthily, all in inseparable connection with the hope of future glory.

Still in the Antiochan liturgical group, if we question the Byzantine Churches, they also proclaim their faith in the pre-requisite holiness to celebrate the Liturgy and in the purifying effect of the Eucharistic food. In the Liturgy of John Chrysostom, the Eucharistic synaxis is opened by a prayer in which the priest asks: "We pray you, who are good and the friend of men, to cast your eyes on our request, to purify our souls and bodies from all taint of the flesh and spirit and to give us a place before your holy altar without reproach and without condemnation. . . . Give to them who always serve you with fear and love the privilege of participating without reproach and without condemnation in your Holy Mysteries and of being judged worthy of your Heavenly Kingdom" (Mercenier-Paris, *op. cit.*, p. 231; Brightman, p. 317; trans.; for the text of the ninth century; p. 376 for the modern text). But he asks that the Holy Spirit make of the bread and wine the body and blood of Christ "in the way that they will become for those who partake the purification of their soul, the remission of their sins, the communion of the Holy Spirit, the fulness of the Kingdom of Heaven, confidence before you and not their judgment and condemnation" (Mercenier-Paris, p. 241; Bright-man, pp. 330, 387; trans.). Before communicating, he repeats: "Deign to have us participate in the awful Mysteries of this holy and spiritual table with a pure conscience for the remission of our sins, the pardon of our faults, the communion of the Holy Spirit, the inheritance of the Heavenly Kingdom, con-fidence before you and not judgment and condemnation" (Mercenier-Paris, p. 244; Brightman, pp. 338, 390).

It is necessary, above all, at the core of this Byzantine Liturgy, to note the ritual of the communion. The deacon begins by proclaiming: "Here am I who approach Christ, our immortal King and God. Give me, O Lord, the precious and most holy body of our Lord God and Savior Jesus Christ for the remission of my sins and life eternal," then the priest gives him a portion of the Eucharistic species saying: "To the deacon ... is given the precious body, holy and immaculate, of our Lord God and Savior Jesus Christ for the remission of his sins and life eternal." This is the formula that the priest also applies to himself after having humbly asked: "I pray you to have pity on me and to pardon my voluntary and involuntary faults, committed in word and deed, knowingly and unwittingly; judge me worthy to participate without condemnation in your immaculate Mysteries for the remission of my sins and eternal life ... may the communion in your Holy Mysteries turn not to my judgment nor to my condemnation but to the health of my soul and body." This is repeated for the communion of the chalice. When the deacon has drunk of the cup, the priest says to him: "May what has touched your lips release your iniquity, purify you from sin." And they give the faithful the bread and wine with a similar formula (Mercenier-Paris, pp. 247-249; Brightman, pp. 394-395).

The office of the Holy Communion in this same Byzantine rite explains this aspect very well. In the preparatory prayers they ask: "O Christ, allow me to pour out tears which erase the stains of my heart in order that with a purified conscience I might approach with faith and fear, Lord, the communion of your divine gifts. May your immaculate body and your divine blood be profitable to me for the remission of my sins, for the communion of the Holy Spirit, for eternal life, and to take from me grief and tribulation, O Friend of mankind" (Mercenier-Paris, p. 290; trans.); "Deliver me from the heavy burden of my sins, you who take away the sins of the world and cure the ills of men, you who call and comfort those who are suffering and who are burdened, you have not come to call the just but rather sinners to penitence; purify me from all stain of body and spirit, teach me to do holy works, animated by your spirit of fear. Then, having the good witness of my conscience and receiving a portion of your sacred gifts, I shall be united to your body and blood, I shall have you living and dwelling in me with the Father and your Holy Spirit. Yes, Lord Jesus Christ, my God, may this participation in your venerable Mysteries be not my judgment nor my condemnation and may I not become sick in soul or body by partaking unworthily; but allow me to receive forever up to my last breath this portion of your holy gifts without deserving condemnation" (pp. 297-298; trans.).[45]

The prayers of thanksgiving insist (and magnificently so) on the gift of total remission received with the consecrated bread and wine: "You who have given me voluntarily your flesh as food, you who are a fire which consumes the unworthy, do not burn me, O my Creator, but rather permeate among my members in all my joints, in my loins, in my heart. Consume the thorns of my sins, purify my soul, sanctify my heart, fortify my legs and my bones, illumine my five senses, establish me whole in your fear" (p. 309).

It is useless to insist further. We would be able to add to our dossier many other texts of the oriental liturgical traditions: the present Maronite Liturgy;[46] the Liturgies of the Alexandrian

---

45. "I know, Lord, that I am not worthy to receive your precious blood and your holy body; I am subject to sin, I eat and drink my own codemnation not discerning your body and blood, you who are my Christ and my God. But confident in your mercy I approach you who have said: He who eats my body and drinks my blood dwells in me and I in him. Therefore, have pity on me, my God, do not dishonor me, sinner that I am, but act with me according to your mercy. May these holy species cure, purify, illumine, guard, save and sanctify my soul and my body; may they chase from me all bad thoughts and actions; may they deliver me from any diabolic action which is being exercised in my spirit and by that on my senses . . . may they be to me a sure defence before your awesome tribunal; may they be for me neither my judgment nor my condemnation" (*op. cit.*, pp. 298-299).

46. "Have pity on us, Lord, and send from heaven your Holy Spirit, the author of life, in order that he brood over this sacrifice and make it a life-giving body for the pardon of our faults, for our purification and our sanctification" (*Petit Paroissien, p.* 317); "May these Holy Mysteries of life be for the remission of sins, the pardon of faults, the health of the soul and body, the force of our consciousness" (p. 318); "Have, Lord, our

group such as the Liturgy of Saint Mark; [47]but they would bring us nothing new. In the East the faithful people assembled for the Eucharist believe in the marvelous power of the consecrated food with regard to sin, and they have the lively consciousness of accomplishing thereby a step into the mystery of Salvation, a step which, snatching them out of their misery, makes them nearer to the Kingdom of the heavens. But they also believe in the necessity of a certain purity of heart to benefit from this marvel of divine mercy; is this not the sense of the recitation of the Pater [48] and the formula "holy things for the holy" which serves as an invitation to communion? The great texts of Matthew and of Paul, whose contents we explained above, have lost nothing of their force all along the centuries in the East.

---

bodies sanctified by the reception of your holy body, may our souls be calmed by your blood which purifies, and may that be for the pardon of our sins and faults" (p. 355; trans.); "May the body of our Lord Jesus Christ be given to me for the pardon of my sins and my faults and for eternal life; may my sins be erased by your life-giving blood, Lord Jesus, Word of God, come to save us" (p. 336; trans.), etc. .

47. See Brightman, *op. cit.*, p. 113-143. The text of the epiclesis is again strongly marked by this dimension: "(may this bread and this wine) become for all of us who partake of it the means of faith, of sobriety, of moderation, of sanctification, of renewal of the life of the body and spirit, of the portion of the happiness of eternal life and immortality, of the praise of your most holy name, of the pardon of sins" (p. 134). It would be equally necessary to study here the very rich liturgy of the Coptic Church which one finds translated by C. Bezold in C.A. Swainson, *The Greek Liturgies*, Cambridge, 1884, pp. 349-395. Let us make up here, in the line of I Cor. 11, 27-29, the following passage: "If there is someone here who is pure, he can eat of the sacrifice; but he who is not pure, in whose heart there exists rancor, who has bad thoughts of impurity, must not participate for he must not be consumed by the fire of the Divinity. I am innocent of your blood and of all your irreverences with regard to the body and the blood of Christ; I do not have to answer about what you will receive from him; I am innocent of your offence, and your sins will fall back on your own head if you do not take part in the sacrifice in a state of purity" (p. 394).

48. On this recitation of the Pater, see A.J. Jungmann, *Missarum Sollemnia,* trad. franc., t. III, Paris, 1954, pp. 200-218. Saint Augustine

THE WESTERN TRADITION

Is all this the same in the West? We will present here as witnesses only some of the most illustrious Fathers, but their affirmations are truly a common heritage of all the Churches they represent.

Ambrose of Milan

Let us not stop at Tertullian, at Cyprian who, if he insists with force on the purity demanded of whosoever approach the Lord's table, does not however ignore that the Eucharist is the food of the weak.[49] Let us immediately question Ambrose

---

underlines strongly in this recitation of the Pater before the communion the profound sense of the request "forgive us our trespasses" (see the texts cited by Jungmann, *op. cit.*, p. 207); these words erase our sins of fragility. This concept of the role of the Pater is certainly equally present in the oriental liturgies. See the prayer which prepares for its recitation in the Anaphora of Timothy of Alexandria (*Anaphorae Syriacae*, vol. I, fasc. 1, Rome, 1939, pp. 41-43): "Allow that this food and this drink of sanctity be not for our judgment or our condemnation ... Therefore, God, allow us by thy holy name to be far from all thoughts which are not pleasing to thee, allow us to chase away by this holy name all thought of death ... "

49. "Against the law of the Gospel, against your deferential request with regard to me, before any penitence, before the confession of the greatest and most serious of faults, before the laying-on-hands by the bishop and clergy for reconciliation, they are not afraid of offering the sacrifice for them and of giving them the Eucharist, that is to say of profaning the sacred body of the Lord ... The *lapsi* indeed are excusable on this point. Who would not make haste to pass from death to life? Who would not hurry to recover health? But it is the duty of the leaders to stick to the rule" (*Epist.*, 15, 2, 1; trans. L. Bayard, t. I, p. 43-44; trans.; see *Epist.*, 16, 2, 1-3, pp. 446-447). "Now it is not for the infirm but for the strong that peace is necessary; it is not to the dying but to the living that communion must be given. In this way those who excite and propel to combat will not remain without arms and discoveries, but will be protected by the body and blood of Christ; since the Eucharist is a defense to those who receive it, those whom we want to see defended against the adversary will be furnished with the Lord's food" (*Epist.*, 57, 2, 2; L. Bayard, t. II, pp. 155-156 trans.).

of Milan, the privileged witness of Western sacramental faith
and practice. For him, the Eucharistic bread and wine bear
in them a mysterious redemptive power which extinguishes sin
and cures its wounds.

It is thus that in the De Sacramentis, the paschal catechesis
of which (according to the surest contemporary critical opinion)
he is truly the author,[50] he writes: "Before the words of Christ,
the chalice is full of wine and water; when the words of
Christ have been added, the blood is effected, which redeemed
the people. . . . Great and venerable indeed is the fact that
manna rained upon the Jews from heaven. But understand!
What is greater, manna from heaven or the body of Christ?
Surely the body of Christ, who is the Author of heaven. Then,
he who ate the manna died; he who has eaten this body
will effect for himself remission of sins and "shall not die
forever.". . . So, as often as your receive, what does the Apostle
say to you? As often as we receive, we proclaim the death of
the Lord. If (we announce) the death of the Lord, we proclaim
the remission of sins. If, as often as blood is shed, it is shed for
the remission of sins, I ought always to accept Him, that He may
always dismiss my sins. I, who always sin, should always have a
remedy" (De Sacr., IV, 5, 23-6, 28; FC, vol, 44, pp. 305-306).

Is it necessary to underline the profound accord between
this very rich text and the theology of the Eastern Fathers?
Saint Ambrose often returns to the point: "Then do you
hear that, as often as the sacrifice is offered, the death of the
Lord, the resurrection of the Lord, the elevation of the Lord,
is signified, and the remission of sins, and do you not take this
bread of life daily? He who has a wound requires medicine.
The fact that we are under sin is a wound; the medicine is
the heavenly and venerable sacrament" (V, 4, 25; CF, vol.
44, p. 317), he affirms in commenting on the little phrase of
the Pater noster: "Give us this day our daily bread." However, if the neophytes can thus be nourished by the celestial

---

50. See B. Botte, *Ambroise de Milan, Des Sacrements, des Mystères,
Explication du symbole*, 2e édit., Paris 1961, pp. 7-21.

remedy, it is because, beforehand in the baptismal bath, they have been purified: "He sees that you are clean of all sin, because transgressions have been wiped away. Thus He judges you worthy of the heavenly sacraments, and thus invites you to the heavenly banquet. 'Let Him kiss me with the kiss of His mouth.' Yet on account of the following—both the condition of man and the Church—your soul sees that it is cleansed of all sins, that it is worthy so as to be able to approach the altar of Christ—for what is the altar of Christ but a form of the body of the Church—it sees the marvelous sacraments . . ." (V, 2, 617; *FC*, vol. 44, p. 311; see IV, 1, 4, p. 102; IV, 2, 7, pp. 104-105).

The exegetical works of Ambrose betray the same view: on the one hand the Eucharistic communion brings a grace of remission of sins, on the other hand only the pure should participate in it, even when it is no longer a question of the reception of the Eucharist on the day of Christian initiation. The first aspect is underlined in texts like these: "I am the living bread come down from heaven; he who will eat this bread will live eternally. That means that (in the rest of the speech) he is not concerned with temporal life or with the death of this life. Even if someone has died of this latter, if he has received my bread, he will live forever. He receives it, who examines himself, and he who receives me will not perish from the death of a sinner; for this bread is the remission of sins" (*De Patriarchis*, 9, 39; *P.L.*, 14, 686; trans.); "Then keep yourself ready, in order to receive your protection, to eat the body of the Lord Jesus in which is found the remission of sins, the exigency of divine reconciliation and divine protection" (*Expos. in Psalm.* 118, sermo 8, 48, *P.L.*, 15, 1384; trans.; see also *ibid.*, sermo 15, 28; *P.L.*, 15, 1420; sermo 18, 28, *P.L.*, 15, 1462; *De Cain et Abel*, I, 5, 19, *P.L.*, 14, 345; etc.). The necessity of an anterior purification comes out of affirmations like this one: "The Apostle teaches us to keep apart from any brother who acts in a disorderly fashion; let us pierce him with the spiritual sword of the Word of God. Let us not make any acception of persons, but let us dispel from the altar of Christ any who is impure in order that he might reform himself, correct his sins, and thereby deserve to return to the sacraments of Christ" (*De Helia et Jejunio*, 12, 82; *P.L.*, 14, 727). Besides, a long allegorical chapter of the commentary on Luke seems to speak of the Eucharistic food, distinct from the Word of God, given only to those whom the Word has already cured: "It was in order, after having cured them of their grievous wounds, that he delivered them from hunger by spiritual food. Thus no one receives Christ's nourishment if he has not first been cured, and those who are invited to the feast are already cured by the invitation. . . . A mysterious order is observed everywhere: first the remission from sins brings a remedy to the wounds, then the food of the heavenly table is multiplied. Moreover, this crowd is not yet nourished with the most substantial food; the hearts which fast from solid faith cannot be nourished by the body and blood of Christ: "I had you drink some milk," it is said, "not food: you were not yet capable of it, and even now you are not." The five loaves of bread correspond to the milk; solid food is the body of Christ, the generous drink is the blood of the Lord. It is not at first that we eat everything, nor that we drink everything. "Drink first this," it is said. There is a first thing and a second and a third. There are first the five loaves of bread, in the second place the seven, in the third the very body of Christ" (*Exp. Ev. sc. Luc.*, 6, 69-71).

Augustine

But it is Augustine who represents on this point in the Western tradition, analogously, what Theodore of Mopsuestia represented in the East: the pastor-theologian, attentive at once to the immediate pastoral context and to the inviolable implications of the revealed foundation. There results a balanced doctrine, perhaps lacking at times a logical framework, but always marked on the edges by the spirit of finesse. His Letter 54, in which he answers certain questions of Janvier, is for our problem a key document. Janvier is worried: some fast on Saturdays, others not; some communicate daily with the body and blood of Christ, others are content to do it on certain days only. What attitude should he adopt? These are, answers Augustine, observances leaving complete liberty to the faithful: let him conform to the practice of the Church to which he belongs, according to the example and the advice given to Augustine by Ambrose himself. But in the passage Augustine informs us on the two opinions relative to the communion which were current at this time: "Someone will say that the Eucharist is not to be received every day. You ask: 'Why?' 'Because,' he says, 'those days are to be chosen on which a man lives with greater purity and self-restraint, so as to approach so great a sacrament worthily. "For he that eateth ... unworthily, eateth and drinketh judgment to himself.'" Another, on the other hand, says: 'Not at all, if the wound of sin and the onset of disease are so great that such remedies are to be postponed, then everyone should be debarred from the altar by the authority of the bishop, in order to do penance and to be reconciled by the same authority; for, this is to receive unworthily, if one receives at a time when he ought to do penance; but he should not deprive himself of Communion or restore it to himself at his own wish and will. But if his sins are not so great that a man is judged fit for excommunication, he ought not to cut himself off from the daily remedy of the Lord's Body." With good reason, perhaps, does someone break off the quarrel by exhorting them to remain, first of all, in the peace of Christ. Let each one do what he thinks he ought to do according to his faith and devotion. Let neither of them dishonor the Body and Blood of the Lord, but vie with each other in honoring this life-giving sacrament. For, there was no quarrel between Zachaeus and the centurion, nor did one set himself above the other when one, rejoicing received the Lord into his house, and the other said: 'I am not worthy that Thou shouldst enter under my roof.' Both honored the Savior in diverse and even contrary manners; both were weighted down with sins; both found mercy. There is force in the comparison of the manna: as among the ancient people it tasted to each one according to what he liked, so in the heart of each Christian is that sacrament by which the world is brought into subjection. This one honors Him by not daring to receive the sacrament daily, that one by not daring to let a day go by without receiving it. But, that food is not to be despised, as the manna was not be disliked. Thus, the Apostle says it is unworthily received by those who do not distinguish it from other food, and do not render it the veneration eminently due; therefore, when he says: 'he eateth and drinketh judgment to himself,' he adds: 'not discerning the Body.' This is very clear if all that passage of the first Epistle to the Corinthians is carefully read" (*Epist.*, 54, 4; *FC*, vol. 12, pp. 254-256).

The Eucharist cures, it is a food for sinners (wretched ones like Zachaeus and the centurion of the Gospel). However, certain grave sins (the great sins), of the type which demand public penance imposed by the bishop, are momentarily preventing its use, until the public reconciliation with the Church: sickness has such a virulence that it necessitates first general cares without which the power of the remedy would be dissolved. For before caring for the wounds and contusions, even dangerous ones, of someone who has drowned, it is necessary first to think of restoring his breath. . . . Besides, he who receives this food-remedy must, if he wants to prove its salvific effect, do it in spirit of faith and profound respect, for is not the body of Christ present, itself the vanquisher of sin forever? These are the fixed norms for Augustine. As to the divers forms which inspire this respect of the body of Christ, let each one consult his own conscience and the custom of his Church. With certain ones this respect will lead to receive the Eucharist bread only when in a quite particular state of inner sanctity because they put the accent on the disproportion between their sinful condition and the holiness of the Lord (their attitude is that of the centurion). With others on the contrary, like Zachaeus, this respect will push them to receive as often as possible (without paying too much heed to their wretched state) the body of the Savior in order that he might complete his purifying work in them, for they are dazzled by faith in the redeeming power of the Eucharistic bread. In the two cases, however, the Eucharist acts as a remedy to the profit of the faithful. Even when the respect commands a rarer recourse to its virtue, the Christian, then fervent and desirous of receiving his Lord to make himself alive by him, tries, under the power of this desire, to put his moral life in harmony with the demands of purity proclaimed by the Gospel, and the effective reception of the sacrament will achieve this process of redemption.

Many other affirmations of Augustine, so many that it would be fastidious to take them up one after the other, go in the same sense. We ought in any case to take a look at certain passages of the *Tractatus* 26 *on Saint John*, less because of their contents than because of their insertion into a context profoundly marked by the ecclesial dimension of the Eucharistic communion. They teach us that Augustine never separates this purifying effect from his great vision of the Eucharist as the builder of the Church. The case of Judas inspires in him the following remarks: "How many do receive at the altar and die, and die indeed by receiving? Whence the apostle saith, "Eateth and drinketh judgment to himself." For it is not the mouthful given by the Lord that was the poison to Judas. And yet he took it; and when he took it, the enemy entered into him: not because he received an evil thing, but because he being evil received a good thing in an evil way. See ye then, brethren, that ye eat the heavenly bread in a spiritual sense (*spiritualiter*); bring innocence to the altar. Though your sins are daily, at least let them not be deadly (*peccata etsi sunt quotidiana vel non sint mortifera*). Before ye approach the altar, consider well what ye are to say: "Forgive us our debts, even as we forgive our debtors." Thou forgivest, it shall be forgiven thee: approach in peace, it is bread, not poison." (*In Joan. Evang.*, tr. XXVI, 11; *NPN*, 1st series, vol. VII, p. 171).

But further on, still in the same immediate context, Augustine is going to make precise that: "This it is, therefore, for a man to eat that meat and to drink that drink, to dwell in Christ, and to have Christ dwelling in him. Consequently, he that dwelleth not in Christ, and in whom Christ dwelleth not, doubtless neither eateth His flesh (*spiritualiter*) nor drinketh His blood (although he may crush the sacrament of the body and blood of Christ carnally and visibly with his teeth), but rather doth he eat and drink the sacrament of so great a thing to his own judgment, because he, being unclean, has presumed to come to the sacraments of Christ, which no man taketh worthily except he that is pure" (*ibid.*, XXVI, 18; *NPN*, 1st series, vol. VII, p. 173). Is not to dwell in Christ to dwell in the Church? And then to be worthy of the Lord's table, is it not, in fact, simply to be a living and true member of the ecclesial Body of Jesus? Augustine makes the bond explicit: "It is for this that the Apostle Paul, expounding this bread, says: 'One bread,' saith he, 'we being many are one body.' O mystery of piety! O sign of unity! O bond of charity! He that would live has where to live, has whence to live. Let him draw near, let him believe; let him be embodied, that he may be made to live (*incorporetur ut vivificetur*). Let him not shrink from the compact of members; let him not be a rotten member that deserves to be cut off; let him not be a deformed member whereof to be ashamed; let him be a fair, fit, and sound member; let him cleave to the body, live for God by God: now let him labor on earth, that hereafter he may reign in heaven" (*ibid.*, XXVI, 13; *NPN*, 1st series, vol. VII, p. 172).

Because it is the sign of the Church as well as its nourishment, the Eucharist can produce its fruit only in him who, in the very depths of himself, is of the Church, a living member of the Body of Christ. This is why only those reborn in the baptismal bath receive it (a remark which Augustine makes often) or those whom some very grave sin has not separated from the ecclesial Body: the saving virtue of the Head can normally reach only those who are in some way welded to him.

In short, for the Latins, quite like their Eastern brothers, the Eucharist exercises a mysterious action on the sins of those who receive it: as a remedy, it cures and strengthens; as an antipoison, it chases sin. But that at the very moment when, uniting men with the Father and to each other in Christ the Lord, it builds up the Church in its deepest reality as the communion of Life.

We are here face to face with this first step of Salvation of which we were speaking in the first chapter. Nevertheless, all cannot receive it for their pardon, and certain ones commit, in approaching it, a sin which condemns them. For, sacrament *par excellence* of the Church, it bears fruit only in those who, by their baptism and the righteousness of their Christian life, belong to the Body of Christ as living members in spite of their sins of weakness, as poor and wretched sinners who have not lost love, however, and thereby live as welded to the Head. Therefore, this holy mystery is present and active only in the Church, in the most pregnant sense of the expression.

The Western Liturgy

The Christian of the West, accustomed to live the Liturgy, will have easily recognized in all that we have just said some of the major themes of every Eucharistic celebration in the Latin rites.

In the Roman Liturgy the celebrant, before offering the sacrifice (inseparable in its very dynamism from the communion which achieves it) implores ceaselessly his pardon (*Aufer a nobis; Oramus te Domine per merita sanctorum tuorum; Per evangelica dicta deleantur nostra delicta; In Spiritu humilitatis et in animo contrito; Lavabo*). But this imploring doubles in fervor at the moment of the communion rites because he does not want to be exposed to the condemnation recalled by Paul, and often his prayer ceases to be private in order to become that of the whole liturgical assembly: *Pater noster; Libera nos; Agnus Dei; Domine non sum dignus.* Remarkable is the *Perceptio corporis tui*: "Let not the sharing of your Body, O Lord Jesus Christ, which I unworthy make bold to receive, become my judgment and condemnation. But through your goodness may it be my safeguard and a healing remedy both of soul and body."

We recognize there the consciousness of the necessity for a very great purity in order to approach the altar. But the other dimension, that of the Eucharistic bread and wine as a source of pardon for those who receive them worthily, traverses equally this whole Roman Liturgy. First the sacrifice is offered "for [the] . . . countless sins, offences, and failings" of the priest and holy people who surround him (*Suscipe sancte Pater*), for "the atonement of their sins for the salvation and safety in which they hope" (Memento of the living), in order that the ecclesial family be "save[d] from everlasting doom" (*Hanc igitur*). As for the communion of the body and blood the celebrant asks: "By this your most holy Body and Blood deliver me from all my sins and from all evils" (*Domine Jesu Christe*), he presents to the faithful the consecrated host saying: "Behold the Lamb of God, behold him who takes away the sins of the world," and in the two prayers of the ablutions one finds the following expressions: "that from a temporal gift it may become for us an eternal remedy," "grant that there remain no stain of wickedness in me whom these pure and holy sacraments have refreshed."

It is especially the postcommunions which put in relief this action of the Eucharistic food on sin. The documents are so numerous that one cannot dream of citing them all. But the few texts which follow will suffice to show that this dimension of the Eucharistic mystery, far from being purely lateral, indeed accidental, to the balance of Christian faith in the Eucharist, is on the contrary at its essential core: "Grant that the holy gifts that you have given us may atone for our wickedness and help us on to the celebrations to come" (3rd Advent); "may the receiving of your holy Sacrament revive us. May it cleanse us of our former evil ways (*a vetustate purgatos*) and enable us to take part in the fellowship of your saving mysteries" (Ember Friday in Winter); "may this Communion, O Lord,

cleanse us from sin (*purget a crimine*)...may it also make all
of us sharers, in a heavenly remedy" (Circumcision); "may the
partaking of your Sacrament cleanse us from our hidden sins
(*et a nostris mundemur occultis*) and save us from the deceits
of the enemy" (Ember Wednesday in Lent); "through the
working of this Sacrament may our sins be cleansed away
(*vitia nostra purgentur*)" (Ember Friday in Lent); "may your
holy Sacrament cure our vices (*vitia nostra curentur*) and give
us your everlasting medicine" (Ember Saturday in Lent); "we
pray that all those to whom you grant a share in so great a
mystery may be freed from all guilt and danger (*a cunctis
reatibus et periculis absolve*)" (3rd Sunday in Lent); "we
who have been cleansed by this holy Sacrament ask that we
may gain both pardon and grace (*sacris mysteriis expiati, et
veniam consequamur et gratiam*)" (Tuesday after 3rd Lent);
"may the heavenly meal which we have eaten make us holy.
May it cleanse us from all error (*a cunctis erroribus expiatos*)
and make us worthy of your heavenly promises" (Wednesday
after 3rd Lent); "may the receiving of this Sacrament cleanse
us from sin (*mundet a crimine*) and show us to the kingdom
of heaven" (Friday after 3rd Lent); "do not let these heavenly
gifts bring unfavorable judgment on those for whom you have
given it as a remedy (*quae fidelibus tuis ad remedium profixisti*)"
(Thursday after 4th Lent); "we pray that our sharing in this
Sacrament may cleanse us from our own sins (*a propriis reatibus
indesinenter expediat*) and keep us safe from all harm" (Friday
after 4th Lent); "we ask that our sharing in this saving sacrament may both cleanse and heal us (*et purificationem nobis
tribuat et medelam*)" (Monday in Passion Week); "we who have
had our oldness cleansed away (*ad omni vetustate purgatos*)
ask that the holy reception of your sacrament may transform
us into a new creature" (Wednesday in Easter Week); "behold
your people. Mercifully forgive the earthly faults (*a temporalibus
culpis absolve*) of those whom you have graciously renewed
with the heavenly sacrament" (Friday in Easter Week); "that
by these gifts which we have received in faith we may be
purified from sin (*purgemur a vitiis*) and saved from all

dangers" (4th Easter); "may we be purified by these holy mysteries (*mysteria sumpta purificent*) which we have received; may we be defended by their power" (4th Pentecost); "may your healing power mercifully free us from our evil desires, (*tua medicinalis operatio a nostris perversitatibus clementer expediat*)" (7th Pentecost); "may your sacraments always cleanse and guard us (*purificent nos semper et muniant*). May they guide us to the attainment of eternal salvation" (14th Pentecost); "we ask you graciously to cleanse our minds and to refresh us (*purifica mentes nostras benignus et renova*)" (16th Pentecost); "we pray that through the holy sacraments which we have received, you will grant that the gift of their healing power will cure all that is evil in us (*quidquid in nostra mente vitiosum est, ipsorum medicationis dono curetur*)" (Last Sunday after Pentecost); "cleanse us by the Sacrament which we have received: ... that this holy Communion may bring upon us not guilt to our damnation but pardon to our salvation; that it may cleanse the guilty and confirm the feeble, that it may strengthen us against every danger in this world, and obtain for thy faithful people both living and dead the remission of all their sins" (prayer for the living and the dead).

Such formulas, so compact that one always hesitates to translate them, go back very far into the history of the Latin liturgy. We find their comments and expressions in the most ancient prayers of the sacramentaries. That proves their traditional value.[51]

---

51. On the prayers of the Sacramentaries, see E. Janot, *L'Eucharistie dans les sacramentaires occidentaux*, in *Rech. de Sc. Rel.*, 1927, pp. 5-24 (especially 18-19). As typical examples let us cite the postcommunion of the Vigil of Christmas in the Gelasian: *"Concede nobis quaesumus ut sacramenta quae sumpsimus, quidquid in nostra mente viciosum est, ipsius medicationes dono curetur"* (edit. L.C. Mohlberg, *Liber Sacramentorum Romanae Ecclesiae Ordinis anni circuli*, Rome, 1960, p. 9); that of Tuesday of the fourth week of Lent: *"Caelestia dona capientibus quaesumus, Domine, non ad judicium pervenire faciaris, quod fidelibus tuis ad remedium providisti"* (p. 37); and the following: *"Sit nobis quaesumus Domine medicina mentibus et corporibus, quod de sanctis altaris tuis benedictione percepimus, ut nullis*

The theological synthesis of Thomas Aquinas

We understand then why Saint Thomas, so attentive to the traditional foundation, is questioned rather lengthily on the effects of the Eucharist in the heart of sinful man. His response gathers all the views that we have up to here encountered, but tries to put them in place definitively, thanks to the great principles of his sacramental theology.

For him the Eucharist possesses in itself the power of remitting all sins without exception, be they the most enormous (III, 79, 3) since it is the sacrament of the passion of Christ "the source and cause of the remission of all sin." But it cannot always exercise this virtue, because of the bad dispositions of the communicant. It is not a question here, in fact, of an efficient capacity which is mechanical and magical (Saint Thomas accords more to human liberty than some presentations of his thought would let us believe): the faithful must enter freely into the movement of grace. Is not the Eucharist the sacrament of the new Covenant? A Covenant demands a free engagement of two parties. Saint Thomas is going to explain himself. The *"res"* of the Eucharistic eating is, he says, love in its two dimensions of union with the Father and of union with the brethren in Jesus. Then, the faithful who puts in

---

adversitatibus perfruamur, qui tenti remedii participatione munimur" (p. 197); *"sacrosancti corporis et sanguinis Domini nostri Jesu Christi refectione vegetati, supplices te rogamus, omnipotens Deus, ut hoc remedio singulare ab omnium peccatorum nos contagione purifices et a periculorum munias incursione cunctorum"* (p. 215); *"Vivificet nos quaesumus Domine participatio tua sancta misteriis et pariter nobis expiationem tribuat et munimen"* (p. 215); *"Concede nobis Domine quaesumus, ut sacramenta quae sumpsimus, quidquid in nostra mente vulneratum est ipsius miserationis dono curetur"* (p. 133). From the Leonine Sacramentary let us cite, according to the edition of L.C. Mohlberg, *Sacramentarium veronense*, Rome, 1956, the following texts: *"Ab omni nos Domine quaesumus vetustate purgatos, sacramenti veneranda perceptio in novam transferat creaturam"* (p. 7); *"Sacris caelestibus Domine vitia nostra purgentur, ut muneribus tuis possimus semper aptari"* (p. 25); *"Quaesumus omnipotens Deus ut qui nostris fatigamur offensis, sacris mysteriis expiemur"* (p. 49).

himself no obstacle to this gift of love can receive it. In the body and blood of his Son, God delivers to man all his agape; * he introduces him into his friendship with the reciprocal relations which it necessarily implies: God, in Jesus, loves man and man, in Jesus, loves God. But as love is properly that which extinguishes sin, the well disposed faithful receives thus, in this movement of the love of God which is awakened in him, the pardon of his venial sins and even of the grave sins of which he is not conscious or to which he is not attached. On the other hand, he who, in a state of grave sin, holds to his sin, refuses evidently by the very fact to let himself be invaded by the friendship of Christ. This seems so since he refuses to break with what shrivels him up egotistically and proudly and breaks all dialogue with his God. And God violates no liberty . . . then, into this man who is obstinate in his sin the source of pardon cannot pass (III, 79, 3).

Moreover, the Eucharistic sign itself shows this very well to whoever can read it in faith. The body of Christ is given under the sign of food. Man is fed only if he is still alive. How then would the sinner who is deprived of grace, therefore of the new Life, be able to profit in some fashion from the food of the Lord's table? Besides, if, in spite of his state of entrenchment in sin, he should approach this meal, he commits a sacrilege because he is lying gravely against the truth of the sacrament. That is the great impurity which merits condemnation and makes him sacrilegious, a liar. In fact, the Eucharist has as its effect the *Corpus Christi mysticum quod est societas sanctorum,* the ecclesial Body of Jesus. Only he who is incorporated into Christ and wants to intensify this incorporation receives it, or he who in the very depths of himself desires appurtenance to the Church. Mortal sin consists precisely in a refusal of Christ himself, in a refusal to belong to his members (III, 80, 4). It is, then, to mock the Eucharist, to communicate when, in fact, one refuses the love of Christ and of his members. For that amounts to picking up the food which "makes the Church" when, in the most intimate recesses of oneself, one scorns the Church. We see the beautiful balance of this

Thomist thesis, also how it gathers up all the traditional values that we have cleared up to here. It could not be shown better how the whole Eucharistic mystery is lived not only in an exterior ecclesial context but especially in a heart really belonging to the Church. Only the faithful in such a state receives pardon from his sins by the eating of the consecrated bread. And Saint Thomas says in conclusion that this sacrament cannot, then, effect the remission of sins in him who receives it with the consciousness of having committed a grave sin not yet pardoned by recourse to ecclesiastical Penance.

But it can happen that a faithful, not sufficiently contrite for grave sins (and therefore not yet pardoned since for Saint Thomas only contrition can obtain pardon), but who does not know it, approaching the Eucharistic bread with devotion and reverence, receive at the same time, with the love of Christ, the pardon of all his sins.[52] In a very balanced text of commentary on I Cor. II (lect. 7; ed. CAI, n° 690), after having recalled that contrition, joined to the desire of recoursing to confession and of completing satisfaction, gives remission from guilt and eternal pain, but that only confession and satisfaction inspired by contrition completely remit pain and reconcile one with the other members of the Church, Saint Thomas makes a clarifying remark. He admits that, in the case of necessity (thus when someone does not have the means of presenting himself at confession), contrition suffices in order that one can commune sacramentally with the Eucharistic body of Christ. However, he adds that ordinarily it is necessary before communing to confess one's grave sins and to accomplish satisfactory pain.[53] And, as no man can have the certitude of being truly contrite, in the exceptional case envisaged, a habitual sign of contrition suffices: the Eucharistic bread will be able, by the love that it will infuse, to make simple attrition give

---

52. III, 79, 3, corpus, ad 1; III, 80, 4, ad 5.

53. "*In necessitate, puta quando aliquis copiam confessionis habere non potest, sufficit contritio ad sumptionem sacramenti; regulariter autem debet confessio praecedere cum aliqua satisfactione.*"

place to an authentic contrition, and thus erase all sin (III, 80, 4, ad 5).[54] This is a solution dictated by a very fine theology (how far we are from the puzzling distinctions of the casuists and of the mean considerations of the moralists!) and where the great optimism of living Tradition about the redemptive value of the Eucharistic body and blood vibrates to the fullest.

The Council of Trent

The Council of Trent in its 13th session finds, in the list of errors to examine, an article which did not exist in the catalog established in 1547 and was denounced by the Jesuit Laynez. It is expressed thus: "The Eucharist was instituted solely for the remission of sins." Laynez underlines that, contrary to that proposition, the Eucharist is, for the Orthodox faith, the sacrament of refection, not that of remission.[55]

Then, in the second chapter of the decree *De SS. Eucharistia*, we see appear at the end of the discussions of the theologians and the Fathers of the Council the following nuance: "Christ willed that this sacrament be received as the spiritual food of souls, by which be maintained and fortified those who live of his own life, the life of him who said: "He who eats me shall live also by me;" that it be received also as the antidote by which we would be delivered from our daily sins and preserved from mortal sins" (Denz., 875).[56] The slightly abrupt text of canon 5 of the same sessions reads, without this precious precision: "If someone upholds either that the *principal* fruit of the

---

54. "*Potest contingere sine culpa ejus (quod aliquis non habeat conscientiam sui peccati); puta cum doluit de peccato sed non est sufficienter contritus. In tali casu non peccat sumendo Corpus Christi, quia homo per certitudinem scire non potest utrum sit vere contritus. Sufficit enim si in se signa contritionis inveniat, puta si doleat de praeteritis et proponat cavere de futuris*" (III, 80, 4, ad 5).

55. *Concilium Tridentinum*, t. V, p. 934. Ed. Goerresgesellschaft (Ehses)·

56. "*Tanquam antidotum quo liberemur a culpis quotidianis et a peccatis mortalibus praeservemur.*"

Eucharist is the remission of sins, or that it produces no other effects, let him be anathema" (Denz., 887). So, the purifying role of the Eucharistic bread is officially proclaimed by the magisterium of the Church and inserted in its place among the major effects of this sacrament. This appears right along with the effect of consolidation of the Body of Christ in unity and with the effect of food of hope for the People of God en marche. For the second chapter is completed thus: "He has further willed that this sacrament be the pledge of our future glory and of eternal happiness; finally that it be the symbol of unity of this one Body of which he is himself Head and to which he willed that we live united and attached by the bond of faith, of hope, and of love, in a very close manner, in order that we might proclaim all the same profession of faith and that among us there might not exist any schisms" (Denz., 875).[57]

This will not prevent the Council from recalling, in the same session and still in reaction against certain doctrines of the Reformers:[58] "If someone upholds that faith alone is a sufficient preparation for the reception of the sacrament of the most holy Eucharist, let him be anathema" (Denz., 893). Chapter 7, in fact, treats lengthily of this necessary preparation. We will have to come back on its contents. It will suffice us for the moment to cite its essential passages:

"If one should participate in the sacred functions only if he be holy, the more the holiness and the divinity of this heavenly sacrament appears clearly to the Christian, the more diligently he must watch that he approach only with great reverence and holiness, especially when we read these words of fear of the Apostle: "Whoever eats and drinks unworthily eats and drinks of his own condemnation, not discerning the

57. *"Pignus praeterea id esse voluit futurae nostrae gloriae et perpetuae felicitatis, adeoque symbolum unius illius corporis, cujusque ipse caput existit, cuique nos, tanquam membra, arctissima fidei, spei et caritatis connexione adstrictos esse voluit, ut idipsum omnes diceremus, nec essent in nobis schismata."*

58. See Denz., 755.

body of the Lord." Also, he who wants to commune must remember this precept: "Let a man examine himself."

"The custom of the Church shows that this necessary examination consists in that no one who is conscious of having committed a mortal sin, however contrite he may seem to be, must approach the Holy Eucharist without having first made use of sacramental confession. The Holy Council prescribes that this must be observed perpetually by all Christians, even by priests in obligation to celebrate on account of their office, provided that they do not lack a confessor. If in an urgent necessity it should happen that a priest celebrates without having first confessed, let him make his confession as soon after as possible" (Denz., 880).

And Canon 11 continues thus after the anathema which we have just recorded:

"To prevent that so great a sacrament be received unworthily and to death and condemnation, the Holy Council prescribes and declares that those whose conscience is charged with mortal sin, however contrite they may think themselves to be, be held to go beforehand to sacramental confession if they have a confessor at their disposal. If anyone dare teach, preach or affirm with obstinance the contrary, or to defend the contrary in public dispute, let him be excommunicated by the very deed" (Denz., 893).[59]

The present code of canon Law, in canons 807 and 856, takes up these disciplinary laws. But whereas the Council of Trent seemed to limit to the celebrating priest the faculty of communicating with a mortal sin on his conscience, not confessed through the lack of a confessor, but regretted in contrition, canon 856 enlarges this possibility to the simple faithful in "case of necessity."

This long survey of the living Tradition of the Church has brought us face to face with a too universally attested truth,

---

59. See the very nuanced commentary of A. Michel in Hefele-Leclercq, *Histoire des conciles*, t. 10, pars 1, Paris, 1938, pp. 282-283. We are now preparing a long study on the story and the meaning of these texts.

and one which has been too often inscribed in the totality of the major documents for us not to consider it essential to the fundamentals of faith concerning the Eucharist. The Eucharist builds up the Church not only in strengthening the union of the faithful with the Father and among themselves in Christ, but—and at the same moment—in snatching them progressively from the world of sin. This is an altogether dynamic dimension of its ecclesial efficacy. It is, in the strict sense, the sacrament of the Church Pilgrim, already saved in the initial act of baptism, but however yet to be saved; the Church of this earth in the state of passage from this world of sin to the world of God: from Eucharist to Eucharist, the Church accomplishes its Pasch toward the definitive Kingdom and makes ever looser the bonds by which its members still adhere to the dark universe of evil.

THE EUCHARIST DELIVERS THE CHURCH FROM SIN

It is necessary for us now to reflect on these foundations and to try to clear from them some essential implications for an integral theology of the relationship between the Eucharist and the Church.

A Liturgical Assembly of Sinners

At the starting point of the whole Eucharistic celebration, there is the Church. On this point all Tradition is in accord. The Eucharist is not, chronologically, the first sacrament; it comes at the end of Christian initiation and demands that all participants have at least received baptism. The unbaptised catechumens, even though already in a certain fashion in the bosom of Mother Church, cannot, properly speaking, take part in the Eucharistic Liturgy nor receive the consecrated food. And the formula of invitation to communion, "holy things for holy people," can be explained as "holy things for the baptized" (and "for the baptized who are worthy of them"). The Eucharistic celebration presupposes then an already constituted ecclesial community. It is hardly difficult to discover why.

First in the plan of *sacramentum tantum*,* of the signs themselves. It is, we said above, a festival meal, the memorial of the last meal of Christ with his own. To such a meal one does not invite just any one. Biblical tradition had attached a very special value to the participation in the sacred meal, more particularly to the paschal meal of which the Last Supper of the Lord is at once the completion and the surpassing: "No stranger will be able to take part . . . neither the guest, nor the hired servant shall take part" (Ex. 12, 43-45). Certainly the Church, the People of the New Covenant, break the barriers, dissolve any nasty smell of segregation, but that is perfect and total only within itself. As the people of God, it is drawn from the world, holy, "a chosen race, a royal priesthood, a holy people, a people chosen to announce the praises of him who called you from the darkness to his eternal light" (I Peter 2, 9), "children of God without blemish in the midst of a depraved and perverse generation" (Phil. 2, 15). Then the Lord's meal can unite only those who, having received the Word of God, "are no longer strangers or guests" but are become by baptism "fellow citizens of the saints, of the household of God" (Ephes. 2, 19). To whoever is not yet part of the Church in this full and explicit manner or has been rejected from it, access to this table of the festival meal is forbidden.

Moreover, the food which is given here does not serve the natural life, but the new eternal life, announced in the Gospel and which begins to gush forth in the faithful (normally) only in the instant of their new birth. To profit from the mysterious power of this bread and wine, it is necessary then to be already reborn "in the water and the Spirit" of baptism "for the remission of sins" (Acts 2, 38).

If now we are situated in the plan of the *res et sacramentum*,* we shall discover another reason for this necessary participation to the Church by Baptism in order to be able to take part in the Lord's meal. The Eucharist, we have already often noted, has the value of a sacrificial meal (always in the accomplishment of the paschal meal). In Christ, the faithful assembled offer to the Father, sacramentally but truly, the sacrifice of the death of Christ the Servant, and, in return in these signs themselves, receive, in order to share them, the goods that in Christ the Father offers to them. Thus the communion of Life is established between God and men. But, to be able truly and fully to offer to the Father the sacrifice of the paschal Christ, it is necessary to be passed mysteriously into him "by a death like to his own" (Rom. 6, 5). Baptism alone can inaugurate this passage into Jesus, in the ordinary economy of the Christian mystery. Let us distrust here again a dissociation, theologically unacceptable, between the ascendant movement of the sacrificial offering and the descendant movement of the gift of the body and blood of the risen Jesus. The offering to men by the Father and in Jesus of the bread and wine, changed into the body and blood of the *Kurios* * is situated at the end of a dynamism in which the ecclesial community, in Jesus, offered to the Father, under the sign of this changed bread and this wine, the human sacrifice of Jesus, sacramentally re-presented, concentrating in him the sacrifice of all men. Because he accepts this sacrifice, the Father in return charges this human offering with his own divine gifts: these goods thus become in the strongest sense of the term, communional goods. We have already underlined the fact that there is not sacrifice and communion, but sacrifice-of-communion, the communion taking its sense only at the end of the sacrificial offering. We see by that how the faithful can participate authentically in the Lord's meal—and therefore eat the body "delivered for sins," drink the blood "of the remission of sins"—only once really incorporated into Christ the Head. In fact, this incorporation alone, in the strictest sense of the term in Pauline language, permits him to accomplish the first moment of the Eucharistic dynamism, the offering in Christ of the paschal sacrifice. The Eucharist presupposes, necessarily therefore, the ecclesial community created in the baptismal bath by the connected action of water and the Spirit. In this sense it admits only the saints.

However, this ecclesial community, although cleansed in the water of purification, endowed with the Holy Spirit, the breath of the new Life, risen in the most profound part of its being, still belongs to this world. Its members remain in sin. If the baptismal gift has plunged each of them into the mystery of the life of the Kingdom, this was an initial act at the head of a series. One must now enter freely into the first gift respond generously to the call of the Lord with all his demands: the new Life, far from destroying his liberty, leads him, on the contrary, to surpass himself. But the forces of evil are not yet extinguished in hearts. Like the *Qahal* (assembly of the People) of the desert, the *Ekklesia tou Theou* is going to undergo the harsh test of temptation which will be its daily lot until the entry into the celestial Jerusalem at the Parousia. And this test, for still enfeebled men, is welded by checks, by sins. Sins against God first. The communion of Life begun by baptismal grace has a tendency to dislocate itself under the incessant renascent flames of original egoism: man feels himself tempted to life "for himself" and no longer "for God" as the risen Christ (Rom. 6, 10-11). Sins against his brothers follow. Lukewarm in his love of God, the baptized is seen inclined no longer to discover in his neighbor a brother to love as God loves him and to serve as Christ who gave himself for him (John 13, 13-15). On the contrary, inclined to judge all by reference to his own self, he tends to use him or to repel him according to his own interests. In a word, sin wants to release, to disengage the communion of Life with the Father and the brethren in Jesus which constitutes the very essence of the Church.

Besides, if, from generation to generation, the Church grows with new members, it takes them as they are, with all their human richness but also with all their natural weaknesses, all the limits of their original milieu. Because it is Catholic it must be able little by little to purify all these values, to skim off their defects in order to transfigure them into the risen Jesus. Not to destroy them, but to make them pass into the new world of Salvation.

Finally, if on this earth the Kingdom of God must sweep him away from the kingdom of darkness, this battle is not being played abstractly: it is being played in the daily life of each member of Christ: "If you belonged to the world, the world would know you for its own and love you; it is because you do not belong to the world, because I have singled you out from the midst of the world, that the world hates you" (John 15, 18-19). The decisive battle is won in the paschal act of Christ, but (to take up the example which Oscar Cullmann gives) the fight is pursued in the daily acts of each faithful until the great victory of the Parousia. Such is the concrete situation of the Church Pilgrim. It is not a situation of peaceful repose, but of continual passage from the world of sin to the world of God, with the certitude, however, of the definitive victory already given in *arrhes*.* In short, it is an essentially paschal situation. Incessantly, *hic et nunc*, although purified radically in the baptismal bath and saved in the " once for all " of this sacramental event, the Church needs redemption, Salvation. It is necessary that the redemption inaugurated at baptism be pursued and deepened. The water of baptism made a "new Creature," launched into the adventure of a new life of heavy demands. It will be absolutely necessary, henceforth, to maintain in it this purity of the new creature in spite of the assaults of evil and the weakness of human nature, to make it progress, to uproot it more and more from the world of sin in which it must however dwell up to the Parousia as "leaven in the dough." In a word, to render it more and more holy, more "of God," without thereby drawing it away from the world. We see that it is no longer a question of the violent act of a birth into a new world by deliverance from a totally different previous life; it is a question rather of the continual deepening of the new Life by a more and more complete passage into the baptismal foundation. By the immersion-emersion the Christian received in him, at the same time as grace, the dynamism proper to this, which is a paschal dynamism. In the risen Christ, of whom he possesses in himself the virtue by a mysterious identification, he must, by totally engaging his own liberty, accomplish the passage, simply inaugurated at baptism, from this world to the world of God, to penetrate more and more into the reality which he has become. But that must be made always in the Church.

The Eucharistic Purification of the People of God

Here the Eucharist plays its role to the full. It bears in it the blood of the Covenant, shed to the remission of sins, but accepted by the Father, therefore, the blood of the communion of Life merited in the sacrificial death and restored in the resurrection. It is quite at once inseparably the "sacrificial blood" and the "blood of the risen Lord." In the Jewish Passover meal the faithful, through the sign of the food, participated in the liberating event. Here the Christian, by eating the bread and drinking the wine which have been changed into the body and blood of Jesus, also participates in the event of the definitive Pasch, but in the totality of this event, in all its aspects, in its very essence as the passage from the world of sin to the world of the divine heritage. Because the body and blood of the sacrifice are given to him, the marvellous efficacy of the death of Christ joins him: for in the bread and wine he receives the real body and blood of Jesus the Servant, the body and blood in which Jesus suffered and offered his sacrifice of redemption from sin, the body and blood born of Mary, which the glory of the resurrection leaves essentially identical to what they were on this earth, as we said in the preceding chapter. But he receives them in the act of their oblation. Then he is pardoned from his sins. But because this body and blood are those of the risen Christ, the bearers of all the eschatological goods that the Father reserves for men (since they are also the body and blood of the *accepted sacrifice*), these goods, of which he already possesses the *arrhes** since baptism, are rooted further into him and his communion of Life with the Father and the brethren is revived and grows. The participation in the Eucharist truly effects in him a Pasch, a participation in the pasch of Christ, rendered sacramentally present. He passes a little more into the new Covenant, characterized precisely by a pardon from sin and the definitive gift of the communion of life.

Pardon from sins, we say. There is, however, more than a simple pardon of sins committed in the past, and the action of the Eucharistic bread on evil goes much deeper. It reaches down to their very roots which are, in fact, pride and egoism. The communion of Life breaks the barriers of egoism in projecting man into the world of love which is an opening to God and to others. More than past acts, the Eucharist chases little by little from the heart of the baptized a climate of sin, this climate that the death of Christ has destroyed and which is identified precisely with the World in the sense that Saint John understands it. Thus, the contact with the sacramental body of his Lord progressively makes the Christian the conqueror of evil. The Eucharist erases his sin, repairs the breaches which he has opened in the communion of Life, kills in him the sting of original egoism. All these effects living Tradition attributes to the nourishment of the Lord's meal. By the saving action of this sacred food, the members of the Church Pilgrim pursue their Exodus getting nearer, not only temporally but also qualitatively, to the celestial Jerusalem, that which has no more spot nor wrinkle, which bursts with sanctity, and of which each bears in himself the germ.

But they thus approach it within the Church. For this paschal effect of destruction of sin (first step of Salvation) the Eucharist accomplishes in the very moment when it unites man with the Father and with his brothers in Jesus the Lord; at the precise moment when it renders him more of the Church.

Essentially, the *res tantum*, the major effect of the Eucharist, consists in love extended in its two dimensions, that of union with God and that of union with the brethren. In the sharing of a same bread, the faithful all receive numerically one Life, that of the risen Jesus, come from a single source, the Father, by elements consecrated in a prayer numerically one, that of the whole liturgical assembly and of its single president. By that—the documents of Tradition abound on this point—they become one Body of Christ. But as we have

just shown, they are sinners, still of this world and fighting with temptation and with evil. And we have already
noted that sin, by its very law, aims at separating and
breaking the bonds, at destroying communion and, thereby,
the Church. Under any form that one envisages, sin distends
and tears apart the Body of Christ, at once in union with the
Father and in union with the brethren. One understands then
how, in pardoning it, and yet more deeply in destroying progressively its root in the Christian, the Eucharist overflows the
limits of the individual and attains the whole Church in the
depth of its mystery. It permits it to strengthen and to repair the
bonds of charity and unity in Christ.

It is not then a negligible or secondary effect. The Eucharist
intensifies in the Church the communion of Life and love; but
because it is a sacrament, a reality homologous with the present
economy of the Christian mystery, it can thus edify the eternal
Church only through the sinful condition, and by taking it
into account. Theology has neglected too much, it seems to
us, this very concrete dimension of the Christian situation and
has often interpreted the axiom: "The Eucharist builds up the
Church" in a somewhat idealistic fashion, as if each communicant met immediately the glorious Church of the end of
time. Certainly he meets it but through its present incarnation
in this time of Salvation history, in the Church heavily *en
marche* toward the heavenly Jerusalem. The Church on earth,
what we call here the　Church Pilgrim, is paschal not simply
because it bursts from the Pasch of Christ, from the transfixed
side of the exalted Jesus, but because from the event of the
Pasch of the Lord to the event of the Parousia of the Son
of Man, it passes with difficulty and sometimes sorrowfully,
but in the certainty of the hope of which it possesses the token,
in the wake of Christ, from this world to the world of the
Father, from the world of slavery and sin to the world of
freedom and glory. Its bread along the way, its *"viaticum,"*
must adapt itself to this exodus situation, must deepen its
acquisition from day to day, but in clearing from it little by
little the original taint and its　charms. The communion of

Life grows in the Church, transforms it into a living and homogeneous Body, closely welded to its Head, even plants in it the germ of the resurrection as the *arrhes** of the eschatological heritage but only (and necessarily) in delivering it more and more from attachments of sin, in liberating it. Which represents the first moment of Salvation.

In short, the Eucharist is truly the Paschal food of the Church, at once the joyous entry of the People of the Covenant into the Promised Land, and the break with the land of trial. It is the meal of a People *en marche* who still need redemption. ... It is the preparation for the messianic banquet of the glorious and eternally purified Church, which will be nourished with the goods of the Father, in an intense and unbreakable *Koinonia.** The Eucharistic meal already effects this communion * of men and God and, to intensify it and maintain it, extinguishes sins. Without this action on sin the Eucharist would not truly build up the Church eternal in the Church Pilgrim.

Eucharistic Purification and the Sacrament of Penance

One question cannot be missed: if the Eucharist has, face to face with sin, the efficacy which we have just recognized, what is the utility of the sacrament of Penance? Does it not duplicate the use of the Eucharist? Would not an intimate contrition for his sins, a detachment from evil, that the Eucharistic bread would bring to perfection, suffice for the sinner?

Let us say immediately that the problem is posed differently if it is a question of public Penance or of private Penance. In the ancient public Penance, the Church ex-communicates the sinner, suppresses ecclesial communion up to the day of his public and solemn absolution. Then, the principles which we have elucidated concerning Baptism are quite valid. No longer belonging (temporarily) to the Church, the sinner can no longer associate himself with the public and ecclesial oblation of the Paschal sacrifice, nor partake of its fruit. Since the eating of the body of Christ is the sign of living appurtenance with the Church, we cannot see how it would admit to its table him whom it excludes publicly from its bosom.

The case of so-called private sacramental Penance is much more complex. And the Tradition of the Church, as it is expressed by a Theodore of Mopsuestia or by an Augustine, then at the Council of Trent, obliges us to distinguish between grave sins ("mortal sins," "great sins") and venial sins ("light sins," "daily sins"). By its nature, grave sin does not escape the redemptive power of the Eucharist, the virtue of the Pasch of Christ, the expiation and redemption which is sufficient for all the sins of the world. It escapes, we read above with Saint Thomas, only by reason of the obstacle which is present in the guilty one. If, in fact, he does not have contrition for the sin he committed, the sinner still holds unto it and is, thus, opposed still freely to friendship with Christ. Christ violates no one, does not pardon him who does not desire pardon. This is a profound mark of respect for the liberty of man. It is quite a different matter when the sinner has real contrition for his sin. Certainly, the legislation of the Church, vigorously sanctioned by the Council of Trent, demands that each Christian who feels his conscience charged with a grave sin, whatever be the contrition with which he believes himself animated, must not approach the Holy Eucharist without having previously confessed sacramentally (Denz., 880, 893), and the code of Canon Law (can. 807, 856) insists on this point. But the Fathers of Trent refuse to say this is a question of an ecclesiastical precept or, on the contrary, of a demand of divine law. And we know that many leading theologians have upheld that, of itself, perfect contrition was sufficient and that the obligation of confession depended only on the wise and prudent will of Mater Ecclesia. We have cited above a text of Saint Thomas who admits that in case of necessity, where the impossibility of recourse to confession exists, contrition suffices, although regularly it is still necessary to have recourse to sacramental Penance. This is a view that the code of Canon Law itself confirms. We have equally noted how it can happen that a faithful who has confessed, but has not yet received his pardon through the lack of contrition, presents himself in good faith at the Holy Table "in a state of sin." Then, if he does it with piety and reverence, in receiving the body of Christ, he obtains a sufficient amount of love that his sin be erased (III, 79, 3, c, ad 1). In such a case, the Eucharist operates its effect in a guilty heart, having nevertheless made actions which would normally lead it back to charity. It happens the same way when the sinner forgets that he has gravely offended God (III, 80, 4, ad 5).

Only he who is knowingly still attached to his sin and, therefore, still in a state of refusal of the communion of Life with the Father and the brethren in Jesus, is then *de se*, still unworthy of the Eucharist (and, therefore, cannot receive the effect of pardon) when he comes to ask for the bread of love, the sign and cause of the Ecclesial Body. It is an unworthiness which springs from an actual lie. A man manifests, on the exterior, an intention which is not his own, demands socially an effect which on the inside he refuses, eats the nourishment which perfects the Church while he pretends to remain separated from the Head and members. It is not then a question so much of a "vessel soiled" by exterior sins (on which a whole predication has so much insisted) than of actual scorn which shows that one "discerns not the body." It seems to us, after having carefully examined the documents of living Tradition, that of itself such is the only obstacle to the medicinal action of the Eucharist. God cures only him who wants it. So this man must have found again the friendship of his Lord, or at least (for no one knows whether he is truly contrite, whether he truly has love, repeats Saint Thomas in III, 80, 4, ad 5), must have gone through the normal actions which lead to it.

In a law inspired by the wisest prudence and the concern for the salvation of each man (the experience of John Chrysostom has shown us the conformity to the law of this prudence), the Church has prescribed that the faithful who is gravely guilty must confess before communicating, and this is the surest means of assuring himself of the presence of love in him. Not to submit oneself to this law would amount to refusing the authority of the Church at the very moment when one wants to reassert his belonging to it, which is an evident contradiction. Let us not forget however that confession with out contrition is not sufficient to erase sin (at least for Thomist theology: "sin is remitted only through contrition;" Quodl. IV, art. 10, sec. c.; "actual sin . . . cannot be remitted without an actual movement of contrition": In IV Sent., d. 21, 1, 2, q^a 1). On the other hand, contrition accompanied by the desire to submit as soon as possible to the "power of the keys" can well erase all sin before the effective reception of the sacrament.[60] This necessity of recourse to the sacrament of Penance before participation in the Eucharist appears to us as the only consequence of an imperative precept of the Church that sees there the surest means to acquire the state of friendship. This explains the variations on this point in Tradition, according to the diverse regions and the degree of lack of care of the faithful.

As to venial sin, it is useless to slow up too much on that. Tradition is unanimous in recognizing that it poses no obstacle to the reception of the body and blood of the Lord.

In short, of itself, by the very nature of the internal law of this sacrament, the presence of the least parcel of authentic love not only renders one worthy to approach the Eucharist but powerfully incites one to go there. Recourse to sacramental Penance is, however, demanded by the Church, but solely in view of assuring this necessary presence of love, not on account of the other effects of absolution. We touch here on the

---

60. "Si antequam absolvatur habeat hoc sacramentum in voto, quando scilicet proponit se subjicere clavibus Ecclesiae, jam virtus clavium operatur in ipso et consequitur remissionem culpae" (Quodl., IV, art. 10); "nunquam potest esse vera contritio sine voto clavium Ecclesiae, quantumcumque sit dolor de peccato praeterito et propositum abstinendi in futurum; et ideo in contritione culpa remittitur" (ad 3). These are important texts on the connection between contrition and the desire to go to the sacrament. We know with what finesse this problem has been studied by H. Dondaine, L'attrition suffisante, Paris, 1943.

Church's exercise of maternal prudence and of her solicitude for her often too careless children.

But we still have not answered the question: in what can the role of the Eucharist with regard to sin be distinguished from that of sacramental Penance? It would be, so it seems to us, a mad theological method to be satisfied, in order to answer the question, with this level of effects. Since, by their nature as signs, the sacraments *"efficiunt hoc quod figurant,"* the signs themselves must reveal to us the proper modality of the work effected both by the Eucharist and by Penance in the life of faith of the Christian.

On this level of sign, the attitude of the baptized sinner appears to us very different in the case of sacramental Penance and in that of the Eucharist. We have shown above how, in the Eucharistic celebration, he came to deepen his very life as a member of the Church, to root him further into the communion of Life. United to his brothers in the liturgical assembly that is requisite to the Eucharistic action, he offered to the Father in Jesus the sacrifice of the New Covenant. Then, in communing with the body and blood of the *Kurios*, he received a deepening of his passage from a world of egoism and hatred to the divine world of disinterested love and peace. We have insisted on the fact that he drew away from it more than a pardon, a progressive uprooting from evil. In a word, it is a question, then, for the baptized, of an intensification of his vital belonging to the Body of Christ; this goes hand-in-hand with the weakening of all in him that is opposed to this belonging.

The sense of Penance is entirely another thing. It is still a question, certainly, of an action which is accomplished in the Church, but very differently. The sinner comes to the Church, which is endowed with the "power of the keys", as the prodigal child returns to the house of his father. He recognizes his sins (for he comes formally as a sinner), confesses them in taking consciousness of his infidelity in the face of the love of the Father in Jesus, of the little generosity which he puts in living his entrance into the communion of

Life. His heart is "broken" and "contrite"; he wants to renew and repair his relationship with God in so far as he can. Let us not forget that the matter of this sacrament (essential part of the sign) is something personal, the whole of the acts of the penitent sinner. These acts are detailed thus: first contrition, burning suffering for having offended God and the ardent desire to make up with him again; then the humble avowal of his sins inspired by this desire; finally the attempt (always maladroit and inadequate, but, moreover, always true if the contrition is sincere) to compensate by some special work the pain caused to the Father and to his brothers. Each of these acts has its value; not one may be neglected. Without doubt the pardon which the Church then accords comes from God, as the first movement of the heart provoking contrition. Nevertheless, the human activity comes into full play. Penance is the sacrament of man being converted to obtain his pardon from God; it is neither a simple demand for pardon nor an unilateral action of God. In the sacramental sign itself an authentic human activity and an efficacious capacity (not a simple whim) of return to the Lord are met along with a word from God which will effect pardon. Without the human activity there is no sacrament; and this activity must always possess the necessary elements in order that the sign that it constitutes be true: the sacrament of divine mercy is not to be confounded with an act of divine softness; God demands of man solid acts of love and repentance.

We see clearly then the difference between the pardon given in the Eucharist and the pardon obtained in Penance. In one case, as in response to the sacrificial movement of man, God increases his communion of Life which drives sin back. In the other, in conjunction with penitence and the rejection of sin by the human heart, God absolves. Then, the grace of the Eucharist and the grace of Penance, far from concurring, should normally coexist. The faithful, guilty of simple venial sins, who comes to the confessional after a fervent communion has without doubt received in his communion the pardon for his sins. However, the gesture that he makes is full of meaning and is not futile: even if his sins are pardoned, he must still feel himself a poor sinner, pained at having offended God, desirous of repairing. The obligation of satisfaction remains, even after pardon; and normally it belongs to the confessor to impose it not mechanically but in proportion to the accused sins (when will we think over the present pastoral application of Penance in light of these ideas? . . .). If this penitent does not find pardon in his recourse (since he already has it) to the sacrament, he finds, however, an authentic grace of conversion that was not given him in the Eucharist, and the sign which he has accomplished completes in him, in connection with the word of the minister, the purification of all the remains of sin. In the inverse sense, the faithful pardoned by the sacrament of Penance receives in the Eucharistic bread a salvific force which destroys in him the most secret roots of sin and permits him to integrate this redemption with that of the whole Church on earth.

The Eucharist is revealed now to us as a sacrament which is marvelously adapted to the condition of the Church Pilgrim as the sacrament of the first step of the Salvation of the Church *en marche*. If of an immense crowd of baptized already incorporated into Christ "by water and the Spirit" it must little by little make a coherent People, realizing better and better the ideal of the glorious Church, it does this in taking into account its sinful condition. The Eucharist tightens the Communion of Life, but in the very moment it snatches men from the empire of evil. Thus, it is truly the nourishment of the People of God in its earthly stage: an already saved People, already the bearer in *arrhes* * of the goods of the Promise, but also a People of sinners who are still heavily attached to this world and its calls.

In the dynamism of Christ's Pasch this Sacrament makes the Church *pass* little by little, adhere more to the goods of the resurrection, detaching itself more from the bonds of sin. This happens not in a single stroke, no longer in projecting it out of the world. But on the contrary, since it is the bread of love, in making it assume human values more and more in order to

transform them (without destroying them) into Christ the
Lord. By itself it can even purify these values, rid them of their
worthless elements through contact with the glorious body. The
Bread of the *Koinonia*,* is truly the bread which maintains
the earthly Church in its Paschal state, in the awaiting of the
great epiphany on the day of the *Parousia*.*

CHAPTER IV

THE EUCHARIST AND THE SECOND MOMENT
OF THE SALVATION OF THE CHURCH

The mystery of Salvation does not stop at this moment of the rooting-up, of the breaking of the bonds of slavery. It is achieved in a projection of man into the very bosom of the world of the resurrection, the new world inaugurated in the Lord Jesus.

This projection towards an end implies for the intermediary stages between the starting point of the dynamism and the ultimate point of arrival, a situation of tension. The Eucharist, which appeared to us in the preceding chapter as the food of the redemption and the purification of the Church *en marche* toward the Parousia,* is going to appear to us now as the sacrament of ecclesial hope, the food which from stage to stage intensifies and strengthens (in rendering it more and more alive) the tension of the People of God toward the decisive entrance into the communion * with the goods of the Father in the Day of the Son of Man. This is a novel aspect, and traditional also as we shall see, of faith in the Eucharist.

THE EUCHARIST AND ECCLESIAL RESURRECTION OF SCRIPTURE

This truth is affirmed by Scripture itself in the narratives of the institution. Christ, we have seen, does not create his Eucharist *ex nihilo* in the evening of the Last Supper. He makes it the end point in which is accomplished the Old Testament rite of the paschal meal.

The Jewish Passover Meal

The Passover Meal was already considered as the sacrament in which the hope of the People was revitalized and nourished. In fact, through the rites of the eating of the lamb, of the unleavened bread, of bitter herbs, in the exalting climate of benediction and thanksgiving, in which this celebration was completed, the whole people of Israel relived the marvel of the past. This was not an empty memorial, in words or ritual; it was not a mere doctrinal reminder of an historical occurrence; it was not just a prayer of thanksgiving prompted by the memory of a great event. This was an actualization of the Passover, by means of which, *hic et nunc*, the People participated in the event, but in order to let themselves be impregnated with its power and dynamism. The instructions of the *Mishna* are very revealing on this point: "Each one is held to consider himself from generation to generation as if he himself had gone out of Egypt" (that is, had been at once delivered from the slavery of Pharaoh and cast forward into the great adventure of the conquest of the Promised Land) "For it is written: In that day (when you celebrate the going out of Egypt), tell this to your son: it is because the Lord has intervened for me when I went out of Egypt. Therefore, we owe him thanks, praise, blessing, glory, homage, veneration and adoration. He does for us and our Fathers all these marvels; he led us from slavery to liberty, from pain to joy, from affliction to jubilation, from darkness to the great light, from servitude to redemption. Let us sing before him: Alleluia" (*Mishna*, Pesahim 10, 5).[1] For this Passover meal has for Israel the value of a *Zikkaron*, of a memorial.[*]

---

1. See the commentaries of the *Talmud babylonien, Seder Mo'ed, Pesahim,* chap. 10, 116b-117b, trans. H. Freedman (under the direction of Rabbi Dr. I. Epstein), t. II, pp. 595-604.

2. M. Thurian, *L'Eucharistie, Mémorial du Seigneur,* Neuchâtel-Paris 1959; F.J. Leenhardt, *Le sacrement de la Sainte Cène,* Neuchâtel-Paris, 1948, pp. 9-48; H. Haag, art. *Pâque,* in *Suppl. Dict. de la Bible,* t. VI, col. 1140-1141, Paris, 1960; P. Benoit, *Les récits de l'institution et leur portée,* in *Lum. et Vie,* 31, 1957, pp. 49-76 (especially 51-54), taken up in *Exégèse et*

This notion of *Zikkaron* (memorial*) counts among the richest of the theology of Israel. [2] It implies a certain objective presence of that of which one makes "memory." In the case of the passover, it is a *Zikkaron* because on account of the historical event, this "memory" is oriented toward three directions: we find there "the triple *anamnesis*, the triple memorial of a typical past deliverance, of an actual deliverance by the sacramental act of the passover meal, and of a salvation to come at the day of the Messiah. And, if one gives thanks for the past which has become present by the sacrament, one prays God to accomplish his salvation in sending the Messiah. The deliverance of the past becomes a token of that which is to come, perfect and definitive." [3] We see that the Passover does not consider the participation of the faithful in the past event as a point of arrival of which he ought to be satisfied, but on the contrary as an opening toward the future: the fact of reliving, *hic et nunc*, the glorious past, the sign *par excellence* of the *hesed we emet* (mercy and fidelity *) of the God of the Covenant, instills further the motif of hoping for the final deliverance at the so much awaited day of the glorious intervention of the Messiah. Does it not concern the same God and the same Promise, and the same People and the same history? In reliving the deliverance liturgically, the redemption from Egyptian slavery—the token of the great eschatological * deliverance of which, at least for the contemporary Judaism of Jesus' time we perceive more and more the completely spiritual dimension of the deliverance from sin—one reminds God that he made a Promise,[4] and, in confidence, one prays him to

théologie, t. I, Paris, 1961, pp. 210-239; P.E. Bonnard, art. *Pâque*, in *Vocabulaire de théologie biblique*, Paris 1962, pp. 734-736.

3. M. Thurian, *op. cit.*, p. 36-37.

4. On the various significations of the verb *Zakar* and of its derivatives, see M. Thurian, *op. cit.*, pp. 27-33. The verb *Zakar* signifies first to think of something as already past and therefore, as already known (Ps. 77, 12-13), then to remind oneself of a duty or a decision (Gen. 9, 15-16) or a situation, then to remember something in favor of someone (Neh. 5, 19), to remind someone of something (Is. 43, 25-26), to cite a name and in particular that of God (Ps. 45, 18), to recall oneself to God by a sacrifice.

execute it. It seems that in the last centuries of Judaism the accent on this eschatological dimension of the passover rite has gone on being accentuated, and that, on the other hand, among all the major festivals of Israel, the Passover has more specially concentrated on this value of hope.[5] Certain details of the celebration, in particular the cups, acquire then a very special Messianic significance: one sometimes fills a cup for Elias because one hopes that the Messiah will appear in the course of a Passover night.[6]

At the very moment when the Passover night celebrates and actualizes the deliverance, it nourishes hope. The negative dimension of a break with the difficult situation of slavery exceeds itself not simply in the positive dimension of possession of an already marvelous inheritance but still more in the hope of an increase of this inheritance itself by an even more radical redemption from all that oppresses. Nevertheless it is necessary immediately to make precise that this hope is not first an individual hope. It is the People, as such, who relives the past event in the rite and reminds God of his promise. For the historical Passover, of which—through the sacramentality of the meal —one becomes the beneficiary, concerned not so much the individual as the Qahal (the People *), and through that the individual. The eschatological deliverance which one awaits will unfold in an identical climate: the eschatology of Israel is clearly collective, and if, little by little, it breaks through faith in a personal salvation, that is not conceived in opposition to the salvation of the People as such or tangentially to it, but in profound harmony with it. [7] Then, when it celebrates in the joy of the festival of the liberation of the People, after the Exile, Israel turns itself towards the future and dreams, in making it a memorial to God—of the marvelous restoration of the past

---

5. The basic study here is: A. Strobel, *Die Passa-Erwartung als urchristliches Problem in Luc XVII, 20s.,* in *Zeitschr. für die neutestamentl. Wissensch.,* 1958, pp. 157-196 (especially 164-171).

6. For a rapid but suggestive treatment see F.J. Leenhardt, *op. cit.,* (pp. 20-21).

7. The whole theology of the "remnants" would have to be discussed here.

which subtends its hope. We know in fact how Jewish thought binds this so much awaited future with the historical facts of the past, especially with the marvels of the Exodus; the march into the desert conceived this time as a triumphal promenade into an enchanting land (Is. 41, 18-20), in the midst of an overflowing joy (Is. 51, 9-11), under the immediate leadership of Yahweh (Is. 52, 12) who will renew, but more marvelously in favor of his People the miracles formerly accomplished for the generation of the desert (Is. 43, 16-21; 48, 21; 52, 12; etc.). We easily understand then that the *Zikkaron* (memorial*) of the past collective marvel is exceeded in a collective hope.

But this strengthening of collective hope is accomplished by the eating of the meal, through it one could say, by the "sacramental" food which is destined to make the People commune with all the realism of the historical event: the unleavened bread recalling the promptness of the obedience of the Fathers, the bitter herbs recalling the sorrow of slavery, the passover lamb recalling the response of God, as the *Mishna* makes precise (Pesahim 10, 5). It is not then a question of simply contemporary values, or super-imposed values, but of values closely overlapping one another.

In deepening its participation in the historical salvific event of the liberation of Israel, at the same time the faithful sees his certitude of the future accomplishment of the Promise deepened. The more he enters into the historical experience of the People (fruit of the faithfulness of the love of Yahweh), the more he feels that he can lean on the Word of God without fear of deception. All that transpires under the cover of an unique act, the sacramental eating of the Passover meal.

The Narratives of the Institution

When in the Last Supper Christ makes this passover rite complete in bringing forth the Eucharist which will become the *Zikkaron* * of his own Pasch, it is clear that he assumes equally this dimension of hope to transpose it in the whole context of the new Covenant that we brought out in the preceding chapter. Besides, certain expressions of the synoptic tradition confirm this point for us. Luke puts on the lips of Christ, at the beginning of the passover meal, the following words: "I have longed and longed to share this paschal meal with you before my passion; I tell you, I shall not eat it again, till it finds its fulfilment in the kingdom of God. And he took a cup, and blessed it, and said, Take this and share it among you; I tell you, I shall not drink of the fruit of the vine again, till the kingdom of God come" (Luke 22, 15-18). Matthew and Mark, representatives of the other liturgical tradition concerning the Last Supper, use an analogous expression (Matt. 26, 29; Mark 14, 24). What we have just said of the paschal meal permits us to grasp the importance of this declaration of Jesus in such a moment. He expresses here, in dependence on the theme of the messianic meal, the tension of his new Pasch toward the Kingdom. Quite as Israel renewed its hope through the paschal meal, the new Israel will nourish its hope by the memorial of the new Pasch on which the New Covenant will depend: "Do this for a commemoration of me . . . this cup is the New Testament, in my blood which is to be shed for you." (Luke 22, 19-20). To give to these words of Christ all their strength, certain exegetes speak of a "vow of abstinence":[8] in thus engaging himself solemnly and somewhat emphatically[9] on not eating the Passover again and on not drinking the cup again till the definitive manifestation of the Kingdom, Jesus would express in concrete fashion his ardent supplication to the

---

8. See in particular J. Jeremias, *The Eucharistic Words of Jesus,* trans. A. Ehrhardt, Oxford, 1955, pp. 165-172; G. Dix, *The Shape of the Liturgy,* Westminster, 1944, p. 54. Jeremias is the immediate source of M. Thurian, op. cit., pp. 208-217.

9. J. Jeremias (*op. cit.,* pp. 165-167) emphasizes how this emphasis is grammatically expressed by the use of *ou mè* (Luke 22, 16, 18; Mark 14, 25; Matt. 26, 29) which in New Testament Greek is used to express an irrevocable promise when it is joined to the emphatic and solemn word, amen (Mark 14, 25). Besides, Luke, at the beginning of verse 22, uses the participle *gar* which affects the sense of the verb "to drink:" it is not a question of the formal expression ("I resolve not to drink again").

Father for this manifestation. This would then be much more than a verbal promise, but a concrete engagement which gives to the disciples the unshakable assurance of the accomplishment.[10] However solid this interpretation is, one thing is deduced with certitude from these texts: the next Pasch which will take Jesus in the midst of his own will be the messianic Pasch of the true People of the new Covenant, in which will be drunk the new wine (Mark 14, 25) of the new Creation; precisely the very thing that Israel was awaiting from passover meal to passover meal. But from now till then, Jesus will not be content with giving his Church the order of re-enacting his gesture "in commemoration of him;" he gives it also, in this gesture, the marvelous food through which, communicating with his own historical Pasch, and the liberating event, it will nourish its hope.[11] Here again it is not then a question of an awaiting without dynamism, but of a confident awaiting, upheld in this confidence. By the partaking of his body and his blood, which seal the new Covenant and realize the hope of Israel, the faithful will take on the dynamism necessary to arrive at the definitive completion of this Pasch in the Day of the Son of Man, the Day in which the Church will be forever introduced into the Kingdom of resurrection and glory (Matt. 25, 31-46).

The thought of Paul

Paul, when he affirms in I Cor. 11, 26: "Every time that you eat this bread or drink this cup you herald the Lord's death till he come again," goes in the same sense. And the richness of the context will permit us to reveal in a better way still the ecclesial dimension of this hope. The exegetes, in fact,

10. See M. Thurian, *op. cit.*, pp. 213-214.

11. On the obvious sense of the words of Christ see P. Benoit, *Le récit de la Cène dans Luc 22, 15-20*, in *R.B.*, 1939, pp. 357- 393; *Les récits de l'institution et leur portée*, in *Lum. et Vie*, 31, 1957, pp. 49-76.

remark on the grammatical construction of the phrase [12] in which the verb is a prospective subjunctive and includes an element of finality.[13] It would be necessary to translate "till the goal be attained: his coming again" (compare with I Cor. 15, 25; Apoc. 2, 25); it is not then a question of a simple flat statement ("we celebrate till the day he comes") but of an affirmation translating the climate of waiting, of ardent supplication for the coming of the Lord in glory, which—after meeting it in the rite of the Jewish Passover—we have revealed in the words of Jesus at the Last Supper. And thus is implied the connection between the Eucharist and this coming: the Church celebrates the first in a state of tension toward the second, in a climate of eschatological finalization. Several scholars note the bond between this "till his coming again" of Paul and the liturgical *maranatha.** [14]

This amounts to saying that, in the celebration of the "memorial" of the death of the Lord, the Church nourishes its hope in rendering more alive its tension toward the eschatological * completion of the mystery in which *hic et nunc* it participates. We emphasize, the Church; for all this is accomplished collectively, as the whole context from which this little phrase is extracted and those that we have studied in the preceding chapter show. If Paul recalls to the Corinthians the sense of the Eucharistic celebration, it is because he wants to react against an individualism and an egoism such as have come to profane the very mystery of the memorial * of the death of Jesus. So much the more that for him the Church, in all the realism of its unity, is built up precisely by reference to the Eucharistic body of the risen Jesus. By the Eucharist, in fact, the risen body of the Lord nourishes and transforms the body

---

12. J. Jeremias, *op. cit.*, p. 164-165.

13. "*Achri ou elthe* is not simply a definition of time, but *elthe* is a prospective subjunctive in which, as appears from the omission of *an*, an element of finality is contained" (J. Jeremias, *op. cit.*, 164).

14. J. Jeremias, *op. cit.*, p. 164.

of sinful man in order to integrate him more and more into his own mystery of resurrection.[15] This diffusion of Christ the Head into his members is what in fact constitutes the Church the Body of Christ: "The one bread makes us one body, though we are many in number; the same bread is shared by all" (I Cor. 10, 17). The Church is edified then in this lifegiving contact with the glorious Lord. We grasp the importance of this remark for our subject. When, in the Eucharistic synaxis, the faithful "heralds the death of the Lord till he come," it is not a question there of a future without attachment with the present. For already—in the participation of all in the same Eucharistic bread—this future, the object of hope, is realized: the Church, whose glory will burst at the return of the Son of Man, is perfected in living contact with him who, already transfigured himself, will transfigure it in this time to come (Phil. 3, 21; Col. 3, 1-4). Already, moreover, and by this contact, it receives in it the *arrhes* * of this final glory; already it is associated with the messianic banquet because already the Kingdom of God exists. But, however, it still awaits what it enjoys to be manifested definitively in its fulness. If, in fact, in the depths of itself, it is already risen, seated with Christ in the heavens (Eph. 2, 6; Col. 212), it remains, nevertheless, still of this world of death, as we said above. Then, the eating of the body of Christ stirs up its hope. It truly takes part in the "meal of the *Kurios*" glorious and glorifying, but in a situation of tension which seeks to be resolved. The more it communicates with the mystery of glory, the more its desire of the definitive possession of this glory is revived.

We speak of the Church. Is it to say that the faithful would be dissolved then in the whole? Certainly not, and the theology

15. L. Cerfaux, *Le Christ dans la théologie de S. Paul*, Paris, 1954, pp. 264-266; 320-322; *La théologie de l'Eglise suivant S. Paul*, Paris, 1948, pp. 201-218, 243-259, 276-280; P. Benoit, *Corps, Tête et Plérome dans les épitres de la captivité*, in R.B., 1956, pp. 5-44 (taken up in *Exégèse et Théologie*, t. 2, Paris, 1961, pp. 107-153).

of Paul has nothing of a collectivism which would scorn the individual. But since contact with the Eucharist welds the faithful to Christ the Head and by that, to all his brothers, his personal hope is necessarily inscribed on the interior of the whole, therefore, at the core of ecclesial hope. United to the risen Christ, he is, by the very fact, passed into the Church as a member of the Body of Christ. He becomes then jointly dependent of the whole (in remaining himself, with his personal destiny and his personal hope). And we understand then that he can only have hope when rooted in the hope of the Church, in sinking his personal hope into the great eschatological awaiting of the whole Body. There is no contradiction between ecclesial collective hope and individual hope, but rather a harmonious subordination. The Eucharistic bread cannot nourish the faithful without *ipso facto* inscribing him more profoundly into the dynamism of the great ecclesial hope.

The VIth chapter of John

With John, in a completely different theological context, we meet the same values. And his sixth chapter will become for living Tradition the point of reliance of all serious reflection on this point.

Right away John situates us in a full eschatological * context. Christ has just multiplied the bread, and this sign awakens in the Jews the memory of the manna of the desert. In the Judaism of Jesus' time, they attached a messianic significance to the manna. They awaited, as sign of the end of time, a renewal of this miracle of the desert, to such a point that the *Apocalypse of Baruch* (doubtless nearly contemporary with the Gospel according to John) can write: "In those days the treasures of manna shall fall again from heaven; in those days they will eat it because then it will be the time of the end" (Bar. 29, 8).[16] We understand then that the messianic hope

---

16. See the texts assembled in H.L. Strack-P. Billerbeck *Kommenter z. N.T. aus Talmud und Midrash*, t. II, Munich, 1924, pp. 481-482; t. IV, pars

of the witnesses of the "sign" accomplished by Jesus was awakened by this. Besides, John takes care to note: "The Passover, the feast of the Jews, was near" (6, 4). We know in a rather sure way that, during this liturgical time, the description of the deliverance from Egypt and of the march to the desert occupied the choice place.[17] The words of Jesus find in this fact a new resonance which plunges them into the climate of collective hope described above.

We do not want to discuss here the delicate problem which continues to divide the exegetes: is the central theme of this VIth chapter of John faith or the Eucharistic eating?[18] Let us say simply that it seems useless to us to want to break off here between faith and sacrament. The whole discourse has a Eucharistic finality and John seems to write it in thinking of the liturgical experience of the Christian community to which he destines his Gospel,[19] for let us remember the Johannine

---

2, Munich, 1928, p. 954. See also in B.F. Westcott, *The Gospel according to St John*, ed. 1881, p. 101, note 21, texts of Philon of Alexandria.

17. This has been put to light and exploited by B. Gartner, *John VI and the Jewish Passover*, in *Conjectanea neotestamentica*, Uppsala, 1959. See especially pp. 14-20 which transcribe documents of primary interest for our subject.

18. Among the most interesting studies on this problem, let us cite A. Feuillet, *Les thèmes bibliques majeurs du discours sur le pain de vie*, in *N.R. Théol.*, 1960, pp. 803-822, 928-939, 1040-1062 (taken up in *Études johanniques*, Desclée de B., 1962, pp. 47-129); E. J. Kilmartin, *Liturgical influence in John VI*, in *Cath. Bibl. Quart*, 1960, pp. 183-191; D. Mollat, *Le chapître VI de saint Jean*, in *Lum. et Vie*, 31, 1957, p. 107-118; X. Leon-Dufour, *Le mystère du pain de vie*, in *Rech. de Sc. Re.*, 1958, pp. 581-523; P.J. Temple, *The Eucharist in John VI*, in *Cath. Bibl. Quart.*, 1947, pp. 442-452; and among the old commentaries which remain on this classic point, M.-J. Lagrange, 8e ed., Paris, 1947, pp. 160-196; B.F. Westcott, *op. cit.*, pp. 95-115; Scott, *The Fourth Gospel, its Purpose and Theology*, Edinburgh, 1906, pp. 126-140. See equally Y. M.-J. Congar, *Les deux formes du Pain de Vie*, in *Sacerdoce et Laïcat*, Paris, 1962, pp. 23-159.

19. We are aware of the thesis of O. Cullmann, *Les sacrements dans l'Evangile johannique*, Paris 1951, more especially on pages 62-69. C.H. Dodd, more reserved as to the place to accord the sacramental mystery in the theology of John, sees there, nevertheless, an important explanation. He

concept of the reception of Christ: one receives Jesus only by faith. He is the authentic and unique nourishment of this: "Who believes in me shall never be thirsty" (6, 35). By faith, the believer receives Christ not only because he would possess then a vague statement of truths, but because he meets the person of Christ itself. And thus, the dynamism of faith, instead of being opposed to the sacramental eating of the body of Christ, leads there normally. Besides, whatever be the value of this interpretation,[20] one seems today definitively in agreement in affirming that the last section of the discourse concerns directly the Eucharist.[21] We can thus rely on this section for our reflexion (John 6, 51 b, 58). John puts on the lips of Christ the following words: "This bread which I am to give is my flesh, given for the life of the world. . . . Believe me when I tell you this; you can have no life in yourselves, unless you eat the flesh of the Son of Man, and drink his blood. The man who eats my flesh and drinks my blood enjoys eternal life, and I will raise him up at the last day. My flesh is real

---

writes: "In considering the background, however, we must give full weight to the use of water and of bread and wine in the primitive Christian sacraments. It was this which made these symbols inevitable ones for the evangelist, whatever enrichment of content they may have received from diverse sources. He was not chosen to speak directly about the sacraments, but for the Christian reader the allusions are inescapable. Not only the symbolism of water and bread of life has its roots here, but also the vine-symbolism" (*The Interpretation of the Fourth Gospel*, Cambridge, 1953, p. 138). He goes even to say that the words, "I am the vine," "I am the bread," were intended to express the mysterious part of truth contained in the affirmation "this is my body" (*ibid.*, pp. 138-139). On this same problem, see E.J. Kilmartin, *op. cit.*, and R.E. Brown, *The Johannine Sacramentary reconsidered* in *Theol. Stud.*, 1962, pp. 183-206.

20. We are not inventing it since many exegetes are oriented today in this line already present with the Fathers.

21. "It is uncontestable, and now almost uncontested, that the last part of the discourse describes the Eucharistic sacrament. So uncontestable that certain ones among the exegetes who constrain so clear and insistent a teaching with St. John — thus Bultmann — do not hesitate to attribute this section to an editor, careful to align the fourth Gospel on the common sacramental teaching of the Church" (D. Mollat, *op. cit.*, p. 107).

food, my blood is real drink. He who eats my flesh, and drinks my blood, lives continually in me, and I in him. As I live because of the Father, the living Father who has sent me, so he who eats me will live, in his turn, because of me. Such is the bread which has come down from heaven; it is not as it was with your fathers, who ate manna and died none the less; the man who eats this bread will live eternally."

Put back into the paschal context that we have just underlined, these affirmations seem to us to signify what follows. During the Exodus, a marvelous bread upheld the march of Israel toward the Promised Land. Nevertheless this earthly bread could not "remain in life eternal" (6, 27). Jesus gives to his own (also *en marche* towards the Promised Kingdom) "the bread come from heaven," alone capable of procuring to the world the Life eternal in the mystery of the resurrection of the last day: "the man who eats this bread will live eternally" (6, 58 to approach 6, 27, 33). That is so because this bread is in fact himself (6, 35, 48, 51), his flesh and his blood "given for the Life of the world" (6, 51). Even more, in this flesh and blood thus given, the whole plan of the Father realized in Jesus comes to meet the faithful: "as I live because of the Father, the living Father who has sent me, so he who eats me will live, in his turn, because of me" (6, 57). Will not Jesus say later: "I have come so that they may have life, and have it more abundantly" (10, 10)? In the life-giving flesh and blood for eternal Life, that toward which all the history of Salvation was marching, the hope of which the liturgical "remembrance" of the Passover revived the fervor, is already attained by the faithful. The Eucharist appears, therefore, essentially as a food bearing promise of resurrection. Not a purely verbal promise, but already real: he who eats this bread draws upon the source of eternal life (6, 58). In other terms, Christ presents us here with the Eucharist as the bread of Salvation, this Salvation which John conceives always as essentially the "gift of Life:" "God so loved the world, that he gave up his only-begotten Son, so that those who believe in him may not perish, but have eternal life." (3, 16), a revelation to which the following affirmations, which clarify it, make a ready echo: "The man who eats my flesh and drinks my blood enjoys eternal life, and I will raise him up at the last day" (6, 54), "the man who eats this bread will live eternally" (6, 60). All the hope of the Gospel (the Good News of Salvation) is concentrated in the Eucharist.[22]

"He who eats my flesh, and drinks my blood, lives continually in me, and I in him" (6, 56) bears out our text. This theme of the "dwelling in Jesus," which we have presented in the first chapter, introduces us into the ecclesial aspect of this hope drawn up in the bread of Life. And this verse of the VIth chapter situates us in the vast perspectives which will open in the XVth chapter, the allegory of the vine. The goal of the mission of Christ, presented above as a goal of Salvation, can quite as well be expressed in terms of "dwelling:" he wants to make "Dwell in him," those who will receive him. But because he himself dwells in his Father, in him the faithful meet the Father: "That they too may be one in us, as thou Father, art in me, and I in thee ... that they should all be one, as we are one; that while thou art in me, I may be in them, and so they may be perfectly made one" (17, 21-23); "If a man has any love for me, he will be true to my word; and then he will win my Father's love, and we will both come to him, and make our continual abode with him" (14, 23). We recognize there the mystery of the Church as the communion of Life in its vertical dimension of unity of men with the Father in Jesus. To pass into this communion of Life there is a condition, repeats Jesus: believe in him in an active fashion: "my words live on in you" (15, 7), "keep my commandments" (15, 10). But is not the supreme commandment expressed thus:: "Love one another" (15, 16-17)? Then, there is no dwelling in Jesus without the

---

22. This has been put to light vividly by E. Ruckstuhl, *Die literarische Einheit des Johannes evangelium*, Fribourg, 1951, p. 249. In the same line, and indicating its dependance with regard to this author, P. Mollat writes: "The Eucharist appears as the living sacrament of the lifegiving will of the Father with regard to men in his Son" (*op cit.*, p. 116).

love of our brothers, without the horizontal communion. This clarifies magnificently our little verse from chapter VI: "He who eats my flesh, and drinks my blood, lives continually in me, and I in him." Adhesion to the word of Christ leads, we have said, to the eating of the bread of eternal Life, the food of hope, the nourishment of resurrection. However, this nourishment will be able to produce this effect of Life in the faithful only if it opens him in the same instant to the love of his brothers. He marches full of hope toward "the resurrection in the last day," only if bound to them whom he meets in dwelling in Jesus. As the manna of the desert had nourished all the People who had gone out of Egypt in awaiting the Promised Land, the Eucharist nourishes the hope of all the Church which is held toward the day when all those whom the Father has given to Christ will share with him, definitively, the inheritance of glory (17, 24). That, however, will occur at the end of a long process of continual purification, of daily redemption of which this same Eucharist will have been the instrument.

Scripture, then, presents us the bread of the Eucharist truly as the salvific nourishment of the Church in all the richness of the notion of Salvation that we revealed in the first chapter. It is the edification of the Body of Christ, but by a continual purification from sin and a progressive strengthening of hope. That is what the nourishment of the Lord accomplishes. It bears three effects radically inseparable the one from the other, meeting in the notion of the Church Pilgrim, that is the paschal Church, the Church in the state of passage from this world to the Father in Jesus. The Eucharist builds up the Church in rendering more and more alive its tension toward the definitive manifestation of its mystery at the Day of the Son of Man, in rendering it more and more risen, therefore, at once snatched from the world of evil and passed into God. It nourishes the hope of the faithful by rooting him more and more profoundly into the communion of Life with the Father and the brothers in Jesus, and for that in freeing him more and more from the radical vice of egoism.

THE EUCHARIST AS THE NOURISHMENT OF HOPE
IN TRADITION

This optimistic vision of the Eucharist as the nourishment of hope passes also into the living Tradition of the Church. This view is not content to skirt the faith in the purifying function of this same bread, but on the contrary meets with it to design the marvelous quality of this sacrament: the bread of Salvation of the Church Pilgrim. Some more vigorous witnesses, in the major moments of dogmatic reflexion, are going to permit us to catch this consciousness that the Church has of the efficacy of the Lord's meal in its march full of hope to the Parousia. *

The first witnesses

Studying the role of the Eucharist on sin, we slowed up a bit on the thought of Ignatius of Antioch. In the very texts that we analyzed then, Ignatius makes echo to the words of Jesus reported by John. On the point of completing his letter to the Ephesians he writes:

"Come together in common, one and all without exception in Charity, in one faith and in one Jesus Christ, who is of the race of David according to the flesh, the son of man and Son of God, so that with undivided mind you may obey the bishop and the priests, and break one Bread which is the medicine of immortality and the antidote against death, enabling us to live forever in Jesus Christ." (Eph. 20, 2; *CF*, vol. I, p. 95).

We see the balance of this beautiful Eucharistic text.[23] We meet there all the elements that our scriptural investigation revealed to us. The Eucharist makes the unity of the Church

---

23. See the commentary of J.B. Lightfoot, *Apostolic Fathers*, Part 2, vol. 2, London, 1889, p. 87: *"Ena arton klontes,* the reference will be to the *agape,* but more especially to the eucharistic bread, in which the *agape* culminated and which was the chief bond of Christian union." On the whole of the thought concerning the Eucharist, read P. Camelot, *Ignace d'Antioche, Lettres:* Sources chrét., Paris, 1951, pp. 52-55.

("breaking one bread"), this unity which is drawn only in the one Lord Jesus. But, while forging this communion, it cures man of his wounds in order to lead him to the immortal life of glory. For this unity, by its very dynamism, tends to a definitive union with Christ ("our common hope": *Ephes.*, 21, 2) and wants "to find Jesus Christ" (*Rom.*, 5, 3) forever. The ecclesial communion, as realized on this earth, cannot be satisfied with its state; it calls for a surpassing, that of glory. The Eucharist, the remedy of immortality, poses already as a spring-board toward this surpassing: "Desire within me has been nailed to the cross and a flame of material longing is left. Only the living water speaks within me saying: Hasten to the Father. I have no taste for the food that perishes nor for the pleasures of this life. I want the bread of God which is the flesh of Christ, who was the seed of David; and for drink I desire His blood which is love that cannot be destroyed." (*Rom.* 7, 2-3; *CF*, vol. I, p. 111).[24] Why this action of the Eucharistic bread? Because the Eucharist "is the flesh of our Savior Jesus Christ, the flesh which suffered for our sins which the Father, in His graciousness, raised from the dead. And so denying the gift of God, these men perish in their disputatiousness. It were better for them to love [25] and so to rise again." (*Smyrn.*, 7, 1; Lightfoot, 6; *CF*, vol. I, p. 121). If Saint Ignatius attributes to the Eucharist this marvelous value of bread of immortality, it is because it contains the risen body of the Savior. Let us not, however, stiffen his

---

24. On this passage and on *Trall.*, 8, 1, P. Camelot writes: "There is not to wonder if such passages have a properly Eucharistic significance; they only recall, under images borrowed from the usages of the Eucharistic liturgy, that the first object of faith and love of the Christian is the reality of the flesh and blood of Christ, and that in this faith he finds life .... Still less moreover would it be necessary to interpret these texts in the sense of a purely symbolic signification of the Eucharistic elements .... These quite spiritual reports of faith and love, between the Christian and Christ, are expressed by Eucharistic images and symbols, which suppose the realism of Eucharistic faith; the symbolism does not exclude the realism, it supposes it and finds in it its foundation" (*op. cit.*, pp. 54-55; see J.B. Lightfoot, *op. cit,.* p. 226).

25. See our note 1, of the preceding chapter.

thought. It is not easy to grasp whether the accent bears on the fact that it is a question of the risen flesh or more simply on the fact that it is a question of the authentic flesh of Christ, that which historically has died and arisen for our Salvation. We see the nuance and its importance: the immediate context (battle against the Docetes) goes especially in the sense of the second alternative.

In the spring of living Tradition, the optimism of Irenaeus of Lyon attains on this point perhaps its summit. And in book IV of the *Adversus Haereses* we meet, in a passage which has posed heavy problems to Theology,[26] a capital affirmation:

"Then, again, how can they say that the flesh, which is nourished with the body of the Lord and with His blood, goes to corruption, and does not partake of life? Let them, therefore, either alter their opinion, or cease from offering the things just mentioned. But our opinion is in accordance with the Eucharist, and the Eucharist in turn establishes our opinion. For we offer to Him His own, announcing consistently the fellowship and union of the flesh and Spirit.[27] For as the bread, which is produced from the earth, when it receives the invocation of God (*invocationem Dei*), is no longer common bread, but the Eucharist, consisting of two realities, earthly and heavenly; so also our bodies, when they receive the Eucharist, are no longer corruptible, having the hope of the resurrection to eternity" (*Adv. Haer.*, IV, 18, 5; *AN*, vol. I, p. 486).

Just then as the ordinary bread, once it has received the divine *epiclesis*,* becomes the Eucharist, our corruptible bodies,

---

26. See H.D. Simonin, *A propos d'un texte eucharistique de S. Irénée*, in *R.S.P.T.*, 1934, pp. 281-292; D. Van den Eynde *Eucharistia ex duabus rebus constans*, in Anton., 1940, pp. 13-28; J. Betz, *Die Eucharistie in der Zeit der griechischen Väter*, t. I, 1, Fribourg, 1955, pp. 213-214, 272-273.

27. We possess the Greek text of this passage; Harvey reproduces it on p. 205. The Latin bears here: "*Offerimus enim ei quae sunt ejus, congruenter communicationem et unitatem praedicantes resurrectionem carnis et Spiritus,*" The Greek bears: "*Homologountes sarkos kai pneumatos egersin,*" but it may be that this Greek text is corrupt and that the Latin version represents the authentic thought of Ireneus (Harvey, *op. cit.*, p. 205, note 3).

once they have received this Eucharist, are no longer corruptible because henceforth they possess the token of the glorious resurrection. Further on Irenaeus comes back more clearly on this idea:

"When, therefore, the mingled cup and the manufactured bread receives the Word of God, and the Eucharist of the blood and the body of Christ is made, from which things the substance of our flesh is increased and supported, how can they affirm that the flesh is incapable of receiving the gift of God, which is life eternal, which (flesh) is nourished from the body and blood of the Lord, and is a member of Him?—even as the blessed Paul declares in his Epistle to the Ephesians, that 'we are members of His body, of His flesh, and of His bones.' He does not speak these words of some spiritual and invisible man, for a spirit has not bones nor flesh; but (he refers to) that dispensation (by which the Lord became) an actual man, consisting of flesh, and nerves, and bones—that (flesh) which is nourished by the cup which is His blood, receives increase from the bread which is His body. And just as a cutting from the vine planted in the ground fructifies in its season, or as a corn of wheat falling into the earth, and becoming decomposed rises with manifold increase by the Spirit of God, who contains all things, and then, through the wisdom of God, serves for the use of men, and having received the Word of God, becomes the Eucharist, which is the Body and Blood of Christ; so also our bodies, being nourished by all, and deposited in the earth, and suffering decomposition there, shall rise at their appointed time, the Word of God granting them resurrection to the glory of God, even the Father, who freely gives to this mortal immortality and to this corruptible incorruptibility, because the strength of God is made perfect in weakness" (*Adv. Haer.*, V, 5, 2-3; *AN*, vol. I, p. 528).

This is a very compact text, traversed by all the Christian optimism. Nourished by the Eucharist and buried in the earth to decompose, our bodies will become as the grain of wheat: their decomposition will be only a stage in view of a marvelous fruitbearing. After the rotting, our bodies will surge from the earth, "will rise" like a plant in spring, for the resurrection in which their present reality will be transfigured. And what will have been the germ of this transformation? The Eucharist of their earthly life. Resituated in their immediate context, these phrases take still more importance. Irenaeus binds them in fact to his presentation of the Word as *"fabricator mundi,"* which plunges us into the full heart of his Christology. For him, Salvation consists in a restoration of the communion * of man with immortality and incorruptibility (*Adv. Haer.*, III, 19, 1; Harvey, III, 20, 1). The realization of this work of restoration demands that the Word itself be made flesh because the universe, in the initial creation, came into existence by him: "God procures Salvation for the men who are in creation, thanks to the same Word by which he realized this creation" (III, 10, 1; Harvey, III, 11, 7). Thus the Eucharist gives immortality and incorruptibility because it results from the action of the Word of God (the ultimate source of immortality for creation) on the earthly nourishment. Through it and by it is effected the connection of man with the Word become flesh for the restoration of the image of God, "so that what we had lost in Adam—namely, to be according to the image and likeness of God—that we might recover in Christ Jesus" (III, 18, 1; *AN*, vol. I, p. 446). Thus has Irenaeus, at the beginning of this passage, underlined our union with the body of Christ, as members.

The Fathers of the School of Alexandria

At Alexandria Origen, in his commentary on Matthew's text of the institution, where (we noted in the preceding chapter) he emphasizes so vigorously the purifying function of the body and blood of Jesus, lets his faith pierce into the flight of hope that the faithful draws out equally in this nourishment: "Yes, the Lord will eat and drink this new paschal bread and wine in the Kingdom of God; and he will eat and drink with his disciples. In fact, just as he did not retain his equality with God as a thing to be clung to but humbled himself becoming obedient even unto death, so will he eat anew this bread and drink anew this fruit of the vine; and, because of his great goodness and love for man, he will eat and drink with his disciples when he returns the Kingdom to his God and Father. . . . For it is clear that in the Kingdom of God we will eat and drink the true food and that which thus builds up and maintains this most true of lives" (*In Matt. comment*, ser. 86; *P.G.*, 13, 1735; trans.). The Eucharistic nourishment must be surpassed when the regime of faith will surpass itself in the face to face vision; to the bread and wine which nourish the earthly life of the Christian will succeed the perfect knowledge of God in Jesus. We recognize the great theses of Origen and the difficult problem of their interpretation: do the body and blood of Jesus in the Eucharist represent here simply the teaching of Christ by which is nourished the souls of the faithful in the awaiting of the striking revelation of the *apocatastase*? Or does he truly discern the physical body and blood? To answer categorically seems to us impossible, but the context swarms with indications which push toward an admission that the realistic interpretation is certainly not radically excluded.[28]

Athanasius also, in texts which we have already studied and on which we shall not stop again, believes in the quality of

---

28. The following text informs us on the thought of the other privileged witness of the Alexandrian tradition at its point of origin — Clement of Alexandria: "And the blood of the Lord is twofold. For there is the blood of His flesh, by which we are redeemed from corruption; and the spiritual, that by which we are anointed. And to drink the blood of Jesus, is to become partaker of the Lord's immortality; the *Pneuma* being the energetic principle of the Logos, as blood is of flesh. Accordingly, as wine is blended with water, so is the *Pneuma* with man. And the one, the mixture of wine and water nourishes to faith; while the other, the *Pneuma* conducts to immortality. And the mixture of both — of the water and of the Logos — is called Eucharist, renewed and glorious grace; and they who by faith partake of it are sanctified both in body and soul. For the divine mixture, man, the Father's will has mystically compounded the *Pneuma* and the *Logos*" (Paedag. II, 2; *AN*, vol. II, pp. 242, 243); ed. O. Staelin, *G.C.S.*, t. I, pp. 168; one will find a study of this difficult text in P. Batiffol, *op. cit.*, pp. 258-216).

the bread of resurrection which possesses the nourishment of the Lord's table: "This is why he mentioned the Ascension of the Son of man into heaven: it was to snatch them away from the thought of the body and make them understand henceforth that the body of which he spoke is a heavenly food from on high and a spiritual nourishment given by him. He says in fact: 'The words which I have spoken to you are spirit and life;' which is the same as saying: what is shown and given for the salvation of one world is the flesh that I bear; but this very flesh with my blood I will give to you spiritually as food, in such a way that it be distributed spiritually to each one and become for all a safeguard in view of the resurrection of eternal life" (*Ad Serap.*, IV, 19).

In this text, and many others in the same sense,[29] Athanasius makes of the Eucharistic nourishment a celestial and spiritual food (that is to say, divine) bearer of a marvelous dynamism which leads him who eats it to the resurrection of eternal glory.

But at Alexandria, no one surpasses the great Cyril on this point. And we must slow up on his thought which represents without doubt an important stage in the evolution of the faith of the Church in the Eucharist.[30] And first to cite his commentary on the narrative of the institution:

"God had created all things for immortality, and at the beginning the world enjoyed salvation. But through the jealousy of the devil death entered the world when the tempter pushed man to sin and disobedience, thus making him fall under divine malediction. He said to him then: "You are dust, and you will

---

29. Each of the witnesses of Athanasius would merit being analyzed lengthily, for it is often difficult to see if he speaks there of the faith-nourishment or of the Eucharistic body. Sometimes the text seems ambiguous to us. Let us cite *Epist. heortast.*, 5, 1; 11, 14; 28 (P. G., 26, 1379-1380; 1412; 1433). The magnificent development of *Epist. heortast.*, 7, 5-8 (P. G., 1389-1397) seems to us to concern only the eating of Christ by faith. But perhaps for Athanasius the two eatings imply each other; certain passages of this letter let us believe it.

30. See J. Mahé, *L'Eucharistie d'après saint Cyrille d'Alexandrie*, in *Rev. d'Hist. Ecclés.*, 1907, pp. 677-696

return to dust...." How could man, henceforth dominated by death, find immortality? It was necessary that mortal flesh participate in the life-giving power of God. The life-giving power of God is the only-begotten Logos. Thus was he sent for us as a savior and a redeemer: he was made flesh. Not that he underwent some modification or change into what he was not, nor that he ceased to be the Logos. But born of a woman according to the flesh, he appropriated a body from her in order to implant himself in us by an indissoluble union, and thus to make us stronger than death or corruption. He reclothed our flesh in order to raise it up from the dead, thus to trace the way of return to incorruptibility for this flesh which was delivered from death; just as by a man came the resurrection from the dead, so all will die in Adam and be raised up in Christ. In uniting to himself flesh which is vowed to death, the Logos, God and life, delivered it from corruption and made it life-giving.... Moreover, it was necessary that he come in us divinely by the Holy Spirit, that he blend with our bodies by his sacred flesh and precious blood: which we have in the life-giving *Eulogia* as bread and wine. For, fearing that we would be repelled when we saw body and blood on the holy table of our churches, God, with regard to our weakness, communicates a force of life to the offerings and transforms them into the energy of his own body so that they be for us a life-giving communion and that the body of life be in us as a life-giving germ. Do not doubt it; it is the truth: the Lord has clearly said: "This is my body and this is my blood" (*Comm. in Luc.*, 22, 19; *P.G.*, 72, 908-912).

It has been necessary to cite nearly all this page of the commentary on Luke, for it situates the Eucharistic mystery perfectly in the core of the work of the Logos as Cyril conceives it.[31] Man must meet immortality and incorruptibility in participating of the life-giving power of God, which is the only-begotten Logos who became flesh for this end. By the

---

31. For the discussion of the realism of this text, see J. Mahé *op. cit.*, pp. 694-696.

Eucharist this life-giving flesh is blended with our own
to deposit in it the germ of immortality. This affirmation comes
back constantly under the pen of Cyril. We meet it for example
in his commentary on the Gospel according to Saint John:

"If what is corrupt is given life by the simple contact with
the holy flesh,[32] how would we not receive with more fruit the
lifegiving *Eulogia*—we who eat it? It will transform those who
have partaken of it into its own property, incorruptibility. Do not
be astonished, do not look, as the Jews did, for the reason why.
Instead think of water: by nature it is cold, but poured into a
container and brought near fire it nearly forgets its own nature
and passes into the energy of that which has conquered it. Thus
it is for us: although corruptible by the nature of our flesh, we
abandon our own weakness by blending with the true life and
we are restored to what is proper to this Eulogia, life. For it
was necessary not only that the soul be recreated by the Holy
Spirit in view of the newness of life, but also that our heavy and
earthly body be sanctified by a more tangible and homogeneous
participation, and that thus it be called to incorruptibility" (*In
Joan.*, 6, 54, lib. 4, cap. 2; *P.G.*, 73, 577-580, trans.).

We have shown in the second chapter how Cyril conceived
this process of sanctification. After having vivified and im-
mortalized the flesh of Christ, the Logos vivifies and immortalizes the flesh of the Christian who, by sacramental communion, is united to this divinized flesh.[33] But this divinization

---

32. Cyril has just brought in the example of the resurrection of
the young son of Naïm in order to show that "the Savior to raise
the dead did not operate solely with the word or in giving orders
unworthy of a God: he preferred to use his holy flesh as a cooperator
in order to show that it had become as a sole being with him, the
body being his own body and not that of another."

33. This idea is constant with Cyril. Let us cite the following passage:
"Let us repeat that the flesh does not help at all in sanctifying and
giving life to those who receive it, if we look only at its own
nature. But if we consider and if we believe that it is the
temple of the Logos, then we will understand that it can procure
holiness and life, not because of itself, but because of the Logos who
is united to it" (*P.G.*, 74, 528, trans.). "If we meditate on the mystery

of the faithful still *in via* does not have the value of final point: it awakes in him on the contrary an intense blast of hope which makes him tend with ardor but sureness toward the glorious resurrection:

"I will raise him up at the last day. He does not say: 'My body will raise him who eats it,' but: 'It is I who will raise him,' in order to show that he was one with his flesh. . . . Therefore, I who am in him by my flesh, he says, will raise up him at the last day who eats me. It is indeed impossible that he who is life by nature will not surpass corruption and halt death. Therefore, although death which by sin has invaded us submits the human body necessarily to corruption, because Christ is in us by his flesh, we will moreover truly arise: it is impossible and unthinkable that life does not enliven those in whom it will have been. As we hide a spark under a haystack in order to conserve the germ of fire, thus our Lord Jesus Christ by his flesh hides life in us and puts in us a germ of incorruptiblity which destroys all corruption which is in us" (*Jn Joan.*, 6, 55, lib. 4, cap. 2; *P.G.*, 73, 581, trans.).

The faithful who receives the *Eulogia* * is made one with Christ; he "becomes as melted and blended with him by the communion, so that he is in Christ and Christ in him . . . the smallest particle of the Eulogie secures then all of our body, saturates it with its own energy, so that Christ is in us and we in him" (*ibid.;* 584B).[34] It is an intimate union, which, although essentially different from the hypostatic union, exists

---

of the Incarnation and if we consider who it is that dwells in this flesh, we will understand without difficulty that it can give life but that by itself the flesh is no help" (*P.G.*, 73, 601, trans.) "The body of the Lord himself has been sanctified by the power of the Logos who was united to him, but it was made efficacious to this point that in the Eulogie it can communicate its own sanctification to us" (*P.G.*, 74, 528, trans.) etc.

34. This insistence of Cyril on the body no longer surprises us. We have seen above how for him (and for Gregory of Nyssa) the spirit sanctifies the human spirit and the Logos made flesh sanctifies the human flesh.

however for Cyril on a physical plane.[35] We will have remarked
how this effect of resurrection is associated explicitly in our
texts with the radical destruction of all corruption. It represents
the positive face of the marvelous efficacy of which pardon of
sins and their uprooting represented the negative face. Besides,
this union, in hope, with the flesh of Christ is not accomplished
in isolation; quite on the contrary, it goes hand in hand with
the deepening of the fraternal communion since "by one body,
his own, the only-begotten Son sanctifies the faithful in the
mystical communion, rendering them concorporal with him and
among them ... all united to the one Christ by his holy body,
receiving him all, one and indivisible, into our own bodies,
we are members of this sole body" (In Joan., 17, 21; P.G., 74,
560B, trans.).

Such is the marvelous efficacy of the Eulogia! * The human
flesh of Christ, become life-giving by its union with the power
of the Logos, is blended with our poor sinful and mortal flesh,
but to communicate to us his own life and thus destroy our sin
and deposit in us the germ of the resurrection.[36] Doing this, it
fuses us one to another in the unity of the Body of the Lord.
Our hope and our certitude of immortal Life is increased then
at the same time that our stains are erased and that our belonging to the Church is strengthened. These are radically inseparable
dimensions of the Eucharistic mystery and express all its richness. Let us recall that, with Cyril, we are face to
face with a Christology constructed on the Logos-flesh scheme:
the Eucharist is presented then as the place and the moment
where this descendant movement meets the individual.

It is the same theological climate that we meet in the three
first Easter Homilies of the Pseudo-Chrysostom, of which
M. P. Nautin has shown the appurtenance to the sphere of

---

35. This point has been well emphasized by J. Mahé, op. cit.,
pp. 685-686.
36. It is the flesh itself which is become lifegiving. It is not
simply the canal which would be content with letting it pass by
virtue of the Logos; see J. Mahé, op. cit., pp. 691-692.

influence of Alexandria [37]. We find there the same insistence
on the salvific value of the flesh sanctified by its union with the
Logos, the same connection between the union of the body of
the communicant with the bread of the *Eulogia* and the union
of his spirit with the Spirit of Christ, the same certitude that
the incarnation by that way attains its end to the profit of the
individual, especially the same confidence in the power at once
purifying and divinizing of the bread wich leads us to the Resurrection. For: "by the blood mercifully shed for us we receive the Holy Spirit, since the blood and the Spirit have been
joined in a single being, in order that by the blood which is
like our own we might be able to receive the Holy Spirit which
is not of our nature, and that by him we might ourselves close
the entry to death" (*Sur la Pâque*, II, 7; Nautin p. 82). Farther
on, in still more explicit terms, the text says:

"Those who do not present a body which is fit to blend
with his body make themselves guilty of an impiety toward the
Lord when he has given it to us in order that in blending us
with it we might blend with the Holy Spirit. In fact, the whole
reason that the Word of God is given in the body and was
made flesh, according to the words of the Gospel, is that, in
our lack of capacity to partake of him as the Word, we might
partake of him as flesh in appropriating our flesh to his spiritual
flesh, and our spirit to his Spirit, in the same way as making
possible, so that we become Christ-like in becoming temples
of the Spirit, what the Apostle says: "You are temples of God;"
and again: "Do you not know that your bodies are the temple
of the Holy Spirit in you, whom you receive from God." And
by this blending with the Spirit of Christ, bodies become things
to treat with holiness, to treat exactly as members of Christ.
... It is therefore through our preparation for the divine food
in this way and under such symbols that the Law has ruled
for our usefulness the prefiguration of that time. But it adds:

---

37. P. Nautin, *Homélies Pascales, II, Trois homélies dans la
tradition d'Origène: Sources chrét.*, Paris, 1953, pp. 26-41. See the
excellent study of pages 42-47.

'The head with the feet and the bowels,' thus giving us to understand by the head the beginning of the epiphany to men, that is the first parousia, and by the feet his end, that is the second parousia, without which it is not possible to believe in the first because this has not accomplished all that has been prophesied.... Therefore, bringing the two things together, Scripture said: "The head with the feet," that is the first parousia with the second, in order that you might receive the Lord when he is a Lamb led to the slaughter in shame, and that you might likewise see him as the King appearing in glory following the double prophecy of Isaias the prophet" (*Sur la Pâque*, II, 18-20: P. Nautin, pp. 90-94).

A whole theology of the incarnation and a whole pneumatology transpire here. By the Eucharistic bread we become the beneficiaries of the divinizing action of the Spirit of Christ shed on the world at the moment when the redemptive work of the Messiah arrived at its summit. But this work of the Messiah has not yet received its total fruition; thrown outside the world by men who led him to death, mocked him and overwhelmed him with their hate, the Son of man must come back glorious to judge the world, and introduce all of his own the Church, into the heritage. The spiritual nourishment of the Lord's table permits the faithful to live out this intermediate span of time, to penetrate more and more into the fruit of the first epiphany of the Messiah, in order to be able to be counted among those who will enjoy the glory of his return.

We can only admire the balance of this thought, the magnificent witness of the grandiose vision, radiating the saneness and optimism of a tradition that knows how to extract these vital truths from Scripture when it slows up on the contemplation of the great liturgical mystery which is at the heart of its life. We understand then the demands of purity which our preacher (as we said above) is carefully intent on justifying. We understand especially why at Alexandria the expression "Sanctification" designates spontaneously the Eucharistic communion.[38]

---

38. *Ibid.*, p. 125, note 66.

The Witness of the Church of Cappadocia

The *Catechetical Discourse* of Gregory of Nyssa, which we have already often cited, shows us that in Cappadocia one lives by the same certainty:

"But since the human being is a twofold creature, compounded of soul and body, it is necessary that the saved should lay hold of the Author of the new life through both their component parts. Accordingly, the soul being fused into Him through faith derives from that the means and occasion of salvation, for the act of union with the life implies a fellowship with the life. But the body comes into fellowship and blending with the Author of our Salvation in another way.[39]... What, then, is this remedy to be? Nothing else than that very Body which has been shown to be superior to death, and has been the First-fruits of our life. For, in the manner that, as the Apostle says, a little leaven assimilates to itself the whole lump, so in like manner that body to which immortality has been given it by God, when it is in ours, translates and transmutes the whole into itself. For as by the admixture of a poisonous liquid with a wholesome one the whole draught is deprived of its deadly effect, so too the immortal Body, by its union with that which receives it, changes the whole to its own nature. Yet in no other way can anything center within the body but by being transfused through the vitals by eating and drinking. It is, therefore, incumbent on the body to admit this life-producing power in the one way that constitution makes possible. And ... that Body only which was the receptacle of the Deity received this grace of immortality, and ... it has been shown that in no other way was it possible for our body to become immortal, but by participating in incorruption through its fellowship with that immortal Body...." (*Disc. Cat.*, 37, 1-4; *NPN*, 2nd series, vol. V, pp. 504-505).

---

39. See the note 34, p. 235.

Here emerges the patristic theology of the "inclusion of the humanity in Jesus." All the new Life, the life of incorruptibility and of immortality, is "concentrated" as it were in Jesus, the new Adam, the new homogeneous principle of the race, deified by the incarnation in him of the Logos, conqueror of death in his death and resurrection. But from him this new Life must be extended into all men (since he came for them), by a means adapted to their nature: the Eucharistic food, permits him to introduce himself into the body of sinners to cure them first, then to transform them into his own immortality. Gregory says:

"Since the God who was manifested infused Himself into perishable humanity for this purpose, viz. that by this communion with Deity mankind might at the same time be deified, for this end it is that, by dispensation of His grace. He disseminates Himself in every believer through that flesh, whose substance comes from bread and wine,[40] blending Himself with the bodies of believers, to secure that, by this union with the immortal, man, too, may be a sharer in incorruption. He gives these gifts by virtue of the benediction (*Eulogia*) through which He transforms the natural quality of these visible things to that immortal thing." (*Disc. Cat.* 37, 12; *NPN*, 2nd series, vol. v, p. 506). The Eucharist then sows in us through the divinized flesh introduced into our sinful flesh, the seed of immortality by which little by little we are completely transformed into the "proper substance" of the glorified humanity of Jesus. Thanks to it, on the one hand the plenitude of the new Adam is diffused, meeting concretely the individuals whom he contains mysteriously in him; on the other hand at the end of this diffusion it is still Jesus who appears. For the Eucharist

---

40. We know the great Christological problem which this text poses, and by implication the grave Eucharistic problem. But see P. Batiffol, *op. cit.*, 10e ed., pp. 405-407. Batiffol has changed on this point since the first edition of his work.

divinizes, immortalizes, but rebuilding and strictly uniting this new humanity: it makes all men's bodies, not only nominally but really, the bearers of the glorified flesh of the one principle of the new Life, Christ the Lord. Its marvelous power of "curing" is thus exceeded in divinization at the very moment when it edifies the Church.

The Fathers of the Antiochan School

But it is Theodore of Mopsuestia, representing the most illustrious of the Antiochan School, who seems to us to lead this point of faith to its maximum depth in a Christological context very different from that of the Fathers we just presented. This encounter of two traditions in their conclusions is not at all minimal for a theology attentive to grasping, under different modes of doctrinal explanation, the great stratifications of living Tradition. In the impossibility of presenting here all the important affirmations of Theodore, we limit ourselves to citing some of the more compact passages of his *Catechetical Homilies* on the Mass.

Why does Christ give us the bread to eat and the chalice to drink?

"Because it is by food and drink that we last in this life here below. But he called the bread "body" and the cup "blood" because the passion attains the body and crushes it and makes blood to shed; of these two (body and blood) by which the passion was accomplished, he makes the type of the food and drink in order to manifest the everlasting life of immortality; and it is in waiting to receive it that we partake of this sacrament by which we believe we have a strong hope of these gifts to come" (*Hom. Cat.*, XV, Ist on the Mass 9; Tonneau-Devreesse, pp. 473-475).

The body and the blood are not simply the nourishment of hope in this sense that, as signs of the paschal mystery in which "by the resurrection of the dead the body of Jesus received oneness with divine nature, became immortal and cause of immortality for others" (*ibid.*), they would recall to our faith the end toward which we tend. They already cause in us, under a mode adapted to our earthly condition, a mysterious tension, leaning on the reality of what they communicate truly, but aspiring to something even greater: they are "the body and blood of Christ into which the descent of the grace of the Holy Spirit transforms them" (*ibid.,* p. 477), capable of giving the gift of immortality to whoever eats them in faith:

"Being able to say: It is I who give life, (our Lord) forbore saying it, but said: 'I am the bread of life.' Since in fact the awaited immortality, of which the promise is given us here, is already in effect, present in the sacramental figures (*tupos*), by means of the bread and wine, that we are going to receive, he might very well therefore, call himself bread, himself and his body. . . . In fact, since in order to last in this life we take bread as food, which possesses nothing like life in its nature—but it is capable of maintaining life in us because God in his commandments gave it such a power—we are convinced necessarily by this not to doubt at all any longer that we shall also receive immortality in eating the sacramental bread since even though the bread does not of itself have such a nature, nevertheless once it has received the Holy Spirit and the grace which comes from him, it will be capable of leading those who eat it to the enjoyment of immortality" (*ibid.*, 12; p. 479 trans.).

Certainly, we do not immediately see the effects of this food of immortality already acting in us; we will even have to pass through death. But the participation in the "Liturgy of the sacraments" renders this eschatological reality already present—in the actual economy of the faith in "figures and symbols"—in *tupos*:

"Because we are not, up to the present, in possession of this heavenly gift, it is by faith that we carry on to the time when we shall ascend to heaven and go to meet our Lord; and then it will no longer be as in a mirror or obscurely that we shall see him, but face to face. Since we are waiting to receive that effectively by the resurrection, in the time fixed by God . . . we have an order to realize in this world the figures (*tupos*) and the symbols of these gifts to come; in order that the people, who in figure and through the "Liturgy" of the sacraments enter into the enjoyment of the heavenly gifts, we already have the possession and the sure hope of these awaited gifts. Therefore, in the same way that the true new birth is that which by the resurrection we await, whereas it is a new birth in figure (*tupos*) and in symbol that we accomplish in Baptism, thus the true food of immortality is that which we hope to eat, that by a gift of the Holy Spirit we shall then truly enjoy, whereas now it is in figure (*tupos*) that we are fed with immortal nourishment that we have either in figure, or thanks to figures (*tupos*) by the grace of the Holy Spirit" (*ibid.*, 18; p. 493).

This is an important affirmation, and it is necessary to understand it without diminishing its force. For Theodore, the veritable new birth which makes us enter definitively into the kingdom of God will take place only at the resurrection of the flesh; in the same way the veritable food of immortality will be offered only in heaven. For then, and then only, we shall enjoy it in fullness, as then, and then only, we shall see God face to face. However, the same as in faith we already know something of God (even though in a mirror, in enigma), in the same way in Baptism and the Eucharist we already possess something of this new birth and of this bread of immortality; in "*arrhes*," * not in fullness; under signs, "types." Therefore, we are in a state of tension toward the definitive and veritable realization (no longer under signs or symbols) of what is already really present (under signs or symbols). And this future plenary enjoyment will be in fact only the growth of the reality already sown in us by the body and blood of the Lord's table:

"He placed the two before us: the bread and the wine; and it is his body and his blood by which we eat the food of immortality, and by which the grace of the Holy Spirit flows toward us and nourishes us in view of making us immortal and incorruptible in hope; by them (the bread and the cup), in an unspeakable manner, he leads us to partake of the gifts to come. Then purely, by the grace of the Holy Spirit, without sacraments or signs, we shall be nourished and shall become perfectly immortal, incorruptible and steadfast by nature" (*Hom. Cat.*, XVI, 2nd on the Mass, 25; p. 575, trans.).

Christian hope is then ceaselessly renewed and deepened by the Eucharist: "We take the immortal and spiritual food which is the body and blood of our Lord . . . all of us who believe in Christ, and successively make commemoration of the death of our Lord Christ, and by that receive an unspeakable food whence we have a hope capable of drawing to us the communion of the gifts to come" (*ibid.*, 10; p. 551). Theodore comes back ceaselessly on this certainty which he situates at the heart of the Christian experience: "(The bishop) begins to break the bread as is fitting, so that henceforth by this bread it is our Lord Christ whom we must represent in our heart since in each of the small pieces he approaches him who receives it. He greets us and reveals his resurrection, and he gives us the first-fruits of the gifts to come, because of which we also approach this holy mystery; this is the way that we are nourished by the gift of immortality, by an immortal food" (*ibid.*, 20; p. 563). Commenting on the rite of communion he explains: "By communion with him it is the resurrection that he announces to us all. Although he comes to us all in giving himself, he is whole and complete in each part and near to all of us; he delivers himself to each one of us in order that we might grasp him and embrace him with all our might and that we might show our love toward him according to each of our desires. It is thus truly that the body and the blood of our Lord nourish us and make us wait to be transformed into an immortal and incorruptible nature" (*ibid.*, 26; p. 577, trans.). And this hope must radiate into the daily life of the faithful:

"These sublime gifts with which we have been favored you must henceforth use in a fitting spirit. In a manner suitable to the grandeur of such a gift you will esteem what you were and that to which we have passed: we who were mortal by nature wait to receive immortality; corruptible we become incorruptible,

from passive to impassive, from changing to absolutely steadfast; from the earth and terrestrial evils we pass into heaven
and enjoy all these gifts and refinements of heaven. And this
hope we have received of the Economy realized by Christ our
Lord, who was taken up from among us; the first Christ received
this transformation by divine nature and it is thus that he has
become for us him who procures communion with such gifts.
That is why we force ourselves to partake of the mysteries
because by means of these sorts of figures (*tupos*), in signs too
high for speech, we believe we possess already these very realities,
having even received in this communion with the mysteries the
first-fruits of the Holy Spirit (Rom. 8, 23), that in receiving
Baptism we take a new birth, and that in receiving the Sacrament [41] we have the faith to receive the food and subsistance
of our life. Those are the dispositions and like ones, which we
must have each day and all our life and apply to ourselves to
make us, as much as possiblie, worthy of these mysteries. . . .
We shall receive mercy and the gifts which have been prepared
by God from the beginning only if we force ourselves according
to our power to be merciful to our neighbor. We will, therefore,
be worthy of this awesome sacrament if we have the dispositions
which have already been commanded: having, according to
our power, our heart above earthly things, searching for heavenly
gifts, and considering always that it is in the hope of obtaining
them that we have received this sacrament" (*ibid.*, 30-31; pp.
583-585, trans.).

For the celebration of the mystery reveals its meaning only if
we situate it in this climate of hope: "Having ordered our life,
recognizing the grandeur of the mysteries and of the infinite gift
to which we have been called and which we need for our life,
having taken care to amend our faults as is suitable, we shall be
seen worthy of the hope to come. It is because of that that
we have obtained from divine grace the privilege to celebrate
this mystery now, to enjoy the kingdom of heaven and all these

---

41. Note the expression, by comparison with Baptism the Eucharist
is "The Sacrament" for Theodore.

ineffable gifts which will last forever, gifts that we are all going to receive by the grace of our Lord Jesus Christ" (Ibid., 44; pp. 603-605).

Let us not forget, however, that if the hope of the believer is renewed in this fashion, at the moment when sin is pardoned and the soul strengthened against the assaults of evil ("rendered unmoveable, inaccessible to all sin," ibid., 29; p. 581), that goes hand in hand with the reassertion of the bond of love uniting brothers among themselves. At the same time that our tension towards the benefits to come becomes more alive by the actual participation in the risen and immortal body of the Lord, in virtue of this same participation, our fraternal communion is increased:

"It is a holy and immortal food, too sublime for words, which we receive from the awesome altar. . . . There is not any difference in the food itself since it is one bread which has been presented, which by the sole coming of the Holy Spirit receives such a transformation and of which all of us take in equal shares because all of us are the one body of Christ our Lord, and it is of the same body and the same blood that we are all nourished. . . . By the one food of the holy mysteries with which the grace of the Holy Spirit feeds us, we all enter into the one communion with Christ our Lord. . . . When, therefore, it is of the same body of our Lord that we all are fed, and it is communion with him that we take by means of this food, it is the whole body of Christ that we all become; and it is communion and joining with him as with our head that we receive thereby. . . . Thus this gift of communion in the mysteries is given to all of us in a general way because all of us need it equally, since we believe that in this gift the enjoyment of eternal life is proposed to us (ibid., 24-25; pp. 560-573, trans.).

The Eucharist comes as the end of the baptismal work: "As by the new birth they have been perfected in one body, may they now be strengthened as in one body by the communion with the body of our Lord, and in concord, peace and application to good may they be made one. . . . Thus we will be united in the communion of the Holy Mysteries, and thereby we will be joined to our head, Christ our Lord, of whom we believe we are the body and by whom we obtain communion with divine nature" (*ibid.*, 13; p. 555, trans.).[42]

In this theology everything is perfectly balanced: the Eucharistic bread appears truly as the spiritual food adapted to the present condition of the Christian, already passed into Christ but, however, still in hope, already entered into the sanctity of God but, nonetheless, still a sinner, already united to all his brothers in the one ecclesial body but still worked on by the law of egoism and hatred. It is the bread of the economy of the faith.

John Chrysostom shows us that this theology of Theodore is a common good of the Antiochian tradition. For he also recalls to his faithful that the Eucharist gives them the risen body of the Kurios * to introduce them into immortality and the new life; and that they must find there the spring for a greater fraternal love, a life worthy of this hope:

"For we all partake of the one bread." Now if we are all nourished of the same and all become the same, why do we

---

42. "Certainly, by Baptism we have received a new birth, all of us are one since it is by this in a single natural joining that we are united; and it is the same food that we all take, where we take the same body and the same blood, we who in the baptismal joining have been herded together as Blessed Paul said: 'Indeed, all of us partake of a single bread because it is a single bread that we are, we numerous bodies.' It is necessary, therefore, before approaching the mysteries and the liturgy, to fulfill the command of "giving the peace" by which we all utter a profession of union and love toward one another. It would certainly not be fitting for those who form a single ecclesiastical body to judge some brother in the faith odious, who by the same birth as ours has come to form a single body with us, and of whom we believe that he is equally a member of our Lord Christ himself, and that he is nourished also by the same food taken from the spiritual table" (ibid., 40, p. 523. This text situates magnificently the ecclesial effect of the Eucharist, so strongly affirmed by Theodore in its relation with the baptismal effect. For baptism plunges the new member of Christ into the Church, therefore into fraternal unity with Christ and the other members.

not also show forth the same love, and become also in this respect one?... And Christ indeed made thee, so far remote, one with himself: but thou dost not deign to be united even to thy brother with due exactness, but separatest thyself, having had the privilege of so great love and life from the Lord. For he gave not simply even His own body; but because the former nature of the flesh which was framed out of earth, had first become deadened by sin and destitute of life; He brought in, as one may say, another sort of dough and leaven, His own flesh, by nature indeed the same, but free from sin and full of life; and gave to all to partake thereof, that being nourished by this and laying aside the old dead material, we might be blended together unto that which is living and eternal, by means of this table.... For Christ came not forth again by the mouth of death, but having burst asunder and ripped up in the very midst, the belly of the dragon, thus from His secret chambers right gloriously He issued forth and flung abroad His beams not to this heaven alone, but to the very throne most high. For even thither did He carry it up. This Body hath He given to us both to hold and to eat; a thing appropriate to intense love.... For as the approaching at random is dangerous, so the not communicating in those mystical suppers is famine and death. For this Table is the sinews of our soul, the bond of our mind, the foundation of our confidence, our hope, our salvation, our light, our life. When with this sacrifice we depart into the outer world, with much confidence we shall tread the sacred threshold, fenced round on every side as with a kind of golden armor. And why speak I of the world to come? Since here this mystery makes earth become to thee a heaven. Open only for once the gates of heaven and look in; nay, rather not of heaven, but of the heaven of heavens; then thou wilt behold what I have been speaking of. For what is there most precious of all, this will I show thee lying upon the earth. For as in royal palaces, what is most glorious of all... in heaven (but) the Body of the King. But this, thou art now permitted to see upon earth.... Perceivest thou how that which is more precious than all things is seen by thee on earth; and

not seen only, but also touched; and not only touched, but
likewise eaten? (*Jn 1 Cor., hom.* 24; *NPN,* 1st series, vol. xii,
pp. 138-143).

This eating makes "us to become with Christ a single
and same body, a single flesh" (*Jn Mat.,* 82; *P.G.,* 58, 743).

The Liturgies of the Eastern Churches

The Fathers of the East are then in accord on this point,
whatever be their fundamental Christological option. Their
affirmations, moreover, only reflect the common faith which
is expressed in the various Liturgies which we know.

The Liturgy of Saint James, belonging to the liturgical
group of Antioch, is a magnificent example of it. In the communion prayers it expresses itself thus: "Let us pray to the
Lord that this communion with holy things be to us the
avoidance of any evil deed, the *viaticum* of eternal life, the
koinonia * and gift of the Holy Spirit" (Mercier-P. O., 26, p.
238; Brightman, pp. 65-66); "God who hast made us worthy
to partake of this heavenly table, do not condemn us, we
sinners, in the communion with your immaculate mysteries,
but save us in sanctification that having become worthy of
your most Holy Spirit we might find a share and a heritage
with all the saints who through the ages have pleased you, in
the light of your face, thanks to the mercies of your only-
begotten Son, our *Kurios,** and our God and our Savior Jesus
Christ" (Mercier, p. 238; Brightman, pp. 65-66); "Lord, you
have given us sanctification in partaking of the most holy
body and of the precious blood of your only-begotten Son,
our *Kurios* * and our God and our Savior Jesus Christ; give
us also the grace of your Spirit of goodness, and keep us
irreprehensible in the faith, and lead us to the perfect adoption,
redemption, eternal happiness which we await; for you are our
sanctification and our illumination" (Mercier, p. 240; Brightman, p. 68).

The *anamnesis* * of the same Liturgy had, in the very
heart of the *Anaphora,** made memory "of the second glorious

and awesome coming of the Lord when he shall come in his glory to judge the living and the dead, to give to each one according to his works" and made clear that in the very moment when it offered the paschal sacrifice of the Son to the Father, the Church prayed the Father to pardon its sins and to concede to it "the heavenly and eternal gifts that the eye has not seen, that the ear has not heard, which have not entered into the heart of man, all that you have prepared for those that love you" (Mercier, p. 204; Brightman, pp. 52-53). The *epiclesis*,* in asking the coming of the Spirit on the bread and wine, had thus explained the desire of the Church: "In order that they might procure to those who partake of them the remission of sins and eternal life, the sanctification of souls and bodies, the production of the fruits of good works, the strengthening of your holy Catholic Church" (Mercier, p. 206; Brightman, p. 54). And the formula of distribution of the consecrated bread only repeats the same idea again (Mercier, p. 236).[43]

The same insistences pierce into the Nestorian Liturgy. The text of the *epiclesis* * asks: "O Lord, may your Holy Spirit come and repose on this offering of your servants, may he bless and sanctify it in order, O Lord, that it be for us the pardon of offenses and remission of sins and powerful hope

---

43. The *Liturgie syriaque de saint Jaques* ought to be studied here also. See A. Raes, *Anaphorae syriacae, quotquot in codicibus adhuc repertae sunt,* vol. II, fasc. 2, Rome, 1953. See also "The Modern Liturgy of Saint James," easily accessible in the *Petit Paroissien des Liturgies orientales,* Harissa, 1941, pp. 17-266. Of this letter let us cite the prayer accompanying the communion of the celebrant of the precious blood: "By your living and life-giving blood shed on the Cross, may my sins be forgiven, and my faults pardoned, O Jesus Word of God, who are come to save us and who shall come for our resurrection, O our Lord and our God in eternity" (*Petit Paroissien,* p. 257); that which preceeds the communion of the faithful: "May your pardon descend on your servants, O Son of God, who are come to save us and who shall come to raise us up and renew the human race" (*ibid.,* p. 257); the final salutation to the altar: "May the Lord accord me to see you in the assembly of the first-born which is in the heavens, in this covenant I put my confidence" (p. 265).

in the resurrection of the dead and in the new life in the Kingdom of heaven with all those who knew how to please you" (Brightman, p. 287). The rite of the fraction-consignation bears the Johannine text: "You are the living and life-giving bread which has come down from heaven, which gives life to the whole world; those who eat it do not die, those who take it are saved and pardoned in him and living in him for eternity" (Brightman, p. 290), and it is finished by this magnificent prayer: "These glorious, holy, life-giving, divine mysteries have been separated, consecrated, consumed, brought to perfection united, blended, bound, marked one by the other in the adorable and glorious Name of the glorious Trinity, Father and Son and Holy Spirit, in order that they be for us, O Lord, the sign of the pardon of offenses and of the remission of sins, and the great hope in the resurrection of the dead and in the new life in the Kingdom of heaven, for us and for all the holy Church of Christ our Lord, here, in every place, now and forever in the world without end" (p. 292).

Here the Liturgy sings the great ecclesial hope, nourished by the participation in the body and blood of Christ. This the rite of communion will recall: "Let us receive then with an overflowing love and a full will of humility the gift of eternal life" (p. 294); "May these Holy Mysteries be to us the pledge of the resurrection of our bodies and the salvation of our souls and of life without end" (p. 294); "Brothers, receive the body of the Son, says the Church, and drink his cup with faith in his Kingdom" (p. 298); "The precious blood is given to ... for the pardon of offenses, for the spiritual feast and eternal life" (p. 298); "May these *arrhes* that we have received and that we receive procure for us the pardon of offenses, the remission of sins and the great hope of the resurrection from the dead and of the new life in the Kingdom of heaven with all those who have pleased you, because of your grace and your mercies forever" (p. 302); "He who has blessed us with all the spiritual blessings of heaven in Jesus Christ our Lord, who has invited us to his Kingdom and has called us and has led us close to such desired gifts which do not pass and do not cease and are not destroyed, as he has promised us and assured us in his life-giving Gospel, saying to the blessed assembly of disciples: 'Truly, truly, I tell you that he who eats my flesh and drinks my blood dwells in me and I in him, and I shall raise him up at the last day and he shall not enter into judgment for he has passed from death to eternal life,' may he bless our assembly, keep our Church, make our people glorious, since they have come and are gladdened in the power of his glorious and holy and life-giving and divine Mysteries" (pp. 303-304).[44]

The Byzantine Liturgies in their turn emphasize this dimension of the Eucharistic mystery. The *Anaphora of Saint Basil* includes in its epiclesis this prayer: "May all of us who partake of a single bread and of a single cup be united in the communion of a single Holy Spirit and may he have no one of us partake of the holy body and of the holy blood of your Christ for his judgment or his condemnation, but may we find pity and grace with all the saints who in the ages have pleased you, the Fathers, the Patriarchs, the Prophets, the Apostles, the preachers, the martyrs, the evangelists, the confessors, the masters and every righteous spirit who has died in the faith" (Mercenier-Paris, t. I, p. 262; Brightman, p. 330 for the text of the IX century, p. 406 for the modern text): the hope of the assembly meets the whole glorious Church, at the very moment when they ask the Lord to reassert the unity of the fraternal community. The prayer of preparation for communion comes back on this theme: "Grant up to our last

---

44. Of the modern rite let us cite the following phrases: "Finally, united with the body and blood of our Christ (may we deserve) to shine with all your saints in the day of the great and triumphant epiphany" (*ibid.*, p. 418); "Grant us all, on the day of your *apotheosis*, to go forth with assurance to meet you and in company with the heavenly hosts to sing to you the hymn of glory" (p. 427); "May he place us at his right hand in the heavenly Jerusalem by his grace and mercy" (p. 430); We will note in all these contemporary texts the accent on the Parousia: the ecclesial hope nourished by the Eucharistic bread is truly finalized quite completely by this event, itself profoundly ecclesial. The Western Liturgy will be less marked by this historical dimension of hope; it will see the accomplishment of this more as a state than as an event.

sight that we receive worthily our share of your holy things, as a *viaticum* (*ephodion*) of eternal life and an efficacious defense at the awesome tribunal of your Christ, in order that with all the saints who have pleased you for centuries we be partakers of your eternal gifts that you have prepared for those who love you, Lord" (Mercenier-Paris, p. 266; Brightman, pp. 338-339, 410). The Liturgy of John Chrysostom also recalls ceaselessly that one participates in the "Mysteries of the holy and spiritual table" for "the remission of sins, the pardon of faults, the communion of the Holy Spirit, the heritage of the celestial Kingdom" (Mercenier-Paris, p. 244; Brightman, pp. 338, 390), a formula which abbreviated comes back as a refrain during the whole rite of communion (Mercenier-Paris, pp. 247-249; Brightman, pp. 394-396). This achieved, during the purification of the communion plate the priest renders thanks to God that "in this day, you have judged us worthy of your celestial and immortal mysteries" (Mercenier-Paris, p. 250).[45]

Let us emphasize finally the prayers of the Byzantine office of Holy Communion, of which certain ones take up these formulas again (thus Mercenier-Paris, pp. 298, 299) often in a very beautiful language: "May the glowing embers of your most holy body and your venerable blood ... be for me a token of your divine grace and of my admission into your Kingdom ... allow me to sit at your right hand with all your saints" (p. 300); "May I partake of your venerable and most pure Mysteries with a pure heart, my intelligence enlivened by your fear and my soul broken: whoever indeed eats and drinks with a weak heart is enlivened and divinized" (p. 303); "You who by your glorious ascension have divinized the flesh which you assumed and have honored it with a seat at the right hand of your Father, make me worthy by this participation in your holy Mysteries to take my place at your right hand among

---

45. Mercenier-Paris insert here a very significant paschal *tropaire*: "Great and holy Pasch, O Christ, O Wisdom and Word and Power of God. Grant admission to your communion in a still more intimate manner in the endless day of your Kingdom" (*op. cit.*, p. 249).

the elect. . . . You who shall come one day to judge the universe in all justice, permit me also to come before you with hosts of your saints" (pp. 304-305); "Make your holy gifts . . . to sanctify my soul and body, to be for me a token of eternal life in the Kingdom; it is good for me to be attached to God and to place the hope of my salvation in the Lord" (p. 307). And it finally gives out with this magnificent prayer of thanksgiving: "May these Mysteries increase in me your divine grace and 'nake me to dwell in your Kingdom. Thus saved by them in your sanctification, I shall always remember your grace and, henceforth, I shall no longer live for myself but for you, our Lord and our benefactor. When I have passed my life in the hope of eternal life, I shall arrive one day at the rest without end, where the concert of feasts and the enjoyment without limit of those who contemplate the beauty of your face never ends, for you are truly him towards whom we aspire and the unspeakable joy of those who love you, Christ our God, and all creation will sing of you until the end of time, Amen" (p. 308); "Lord Jesus Christ, may your holy body procure for me eternal life and may your divine blood erase my sins" (p. 309).

The *epiclesis* * of the first *Anaphora* * *of the Twelve Apostles*, without doubt dependent on the Byzantine Liturgy, is on this point very rich theologically: "Send your Holy Spirit on these offerings and show us that this bread is the venerable body of our Lord Jesus Christ, this chalice the blood of our Lord Jesus Christ, in order that for all those who partake of it they might be profitable for life and resurrection and remission of sins and health of soul and body and illumination of the spirit and defense before the awesome tribunal of your Christ; may no one of your people, Lord, be lost, but make us all worthy, serving you without trouble and living in your service for all our life, to enjoy your heavenly and immortal and life-giving Mysteries by your grace and mercy and love, now and forever unto the end of the ages" (A. Raes, *Anaphorae Syriacae*, vol. I, fasc. 2, Rome, 1940, pp. 218-221). That of the *Anaphora of Timothy of Alexandria* emphasizes: "That they be to us for the reception of incorruption and the partaking of thy Holy Spirit" (Rucker, *ib.*, vol. I, fasc. 1, Rome, 1939, p.25).

The *Syrian Anaphora*, said to be of Saint Cyril, asks that the coming of the Holy Spirit, in transforming the bread and wine "make us by this divine communion pure and holy in your eternal Kingdom in your blessed company in the mansions of your splendor in glowing contemplation in the joy of those who have accomplished your will in this enjoyment which is at your right hand in order that by all and in all and for all we give to you glory and exaltation as to your only-begotten Son and to your living and holy Spirit" (A. Raes, *ibid.*, vol. I, fasc. 3, pp. 345-347). The communion prayers of the first *Anaphora of James of Sarug* are not expressed otherwise: "May the body and blood of your only-begotten Son be for us a ferment of life and the token of the life in the day of judgment and already now and forever unto the end of time" (Codrington, *ibid.*, vol. II, fasc. 1, p. 37); "May this blessed and life-giving banquet be to us propitiation for our offenses, remission of our sins and the *viaticum* of eternal life" (p. 37); "Make us arrive at the blessed end and at the enjoyment of the Kingdom in order that with all your saints we render to you on high the glory and confess to you, Lord God, with your Father and your Holy Spirit" (p. 39), and, after communion, the *Anaphora of John Sabae* implores the Lord "may the bodies and souls of all be sanctified by this communion with the Mysteries in order that they be the *viaticum* of our life and our eternal Salvation" (Raes, *ibid.*, vol. II, fasc. 1, p. 103).

The *Alexandrine Liturgy of Saint Mark* develops its *epiclesis* thus: "May (this bread and wine) become for us who partake of it the means of faith, of sobriety, of moderation, of sanctification, of renewal of body and spirit, of a share in the happiness of eternal life and of immortality, of praise of your most holy Name, of pardon of sins" (Brightman, p. 134). And in the prayer of thanksgiving it comes back on this idea, qualifying the "communion of the holy body of the only-begotten Son and of his venerable blood" of *"viaticum"* (*ephodion*) of eternal life (p. 141).

Let us cite finally the present *Maronite Liturgy*, which in formulas, where are present in amplified fashion the great affirmations of the second *Anaphora of the Twelve Apostles*, speaks thus to Christ: "Remembering your Economy, Lord who love men so much, we pray you to have pity on those who are prostrate before you and to save those who are your heritage the day when you will appear at the end of time to judge each man according to his works and according to your divine justice. To this intention your Church implores you and, by you and with you, implores your Father saying: ... Have pity on us, Lord, and send us your Holy Spirit from heaven, the author of life, in order that he brood over this sacrifice and make it a life-giving blood for the pardon of our sins, for our purification and our sanctification" (*Petit paroissien*, pp. 315-317; compare with Raes, *op. cit.*, vol. I, fasc. 2, p. 247). During the fraction of the bread the priest says to Christ: "Blessed are you, Lord Jesus Christ, bread of life come down from heaven in order to be for those who receive you life for all eternity. May each of the faithful who has taken part with us in this Eucharist participate in your heavenly kingdom from now to the end of time. At the day of judgment, Lord, may your body and blood be not for our condemnation to eternal pain. Grant me, Lord Jesus, to present myself before you with a serene face when you appear with your angels in the majesty of your glory at the end of time" (*Petit paroissien*, pp. 333-334). After the communion, this hope is expressed in a marvelous formula: "Your body and blood which we have received will be for us the way where without fear we shall pass from dark to light. Joy for the inhabitants of heaven, holy hope for the people of earth in the host which the living offer for their dead" (p. 340).

These texts (and we have cited only the most typical) do not permit us to doubt any longer the essential place that the dimension of eschatological hope holds in the Eucharistic celebration of the Eastern Churches. The pardon of sins, of which we have said in the preceding chapter that it was the first salvific effect of the Lord's table, snatches man from the influence of evil. But at the same moment man thus purified receives in him the seed, "the *arrhes*," of a new life, called to blossom in all its beauty in the day of the *Parousia*.* This certainty supports his daily trek toward this Kingdom, which is already no longer strange to him.

The Western Liturgy

The Western Liturgy flows together on this point with this Eastern liturgical tradition, although its insistence is less on the Parousial coming and more on the state of glory of the elect. It suffices to survey either, in the ancient sacramentaries or in the present *Missale Romanum*, the list of post-communions and secrets to state that here again we find ourselves faced with a constant: the Latin Liturgy attributes, as an effect, to the Eucharist the gift of immortality (and the increase of hope) as often as it makes of it the sacrament of purification and of ecclesial unity. To cite all these instances would be fastidious. It seems to us, however, necessary to show well the multiple expressions of this truth in the following texts:

"We who are filled with food for the spirit ask you to teach us, who share in this mystery, to reject things earthly and to love things heavenly" (2nd Sunday of Advent); "We have been fed on the holy Sacraments. May your power make us ready to win what they pledge (*ad eorum promissa capienda*)" (2nd Sunday After the Epiphany); "We ask you that we may receive the effect of that Salvation of which we have received the pledge in these mysteries (*ut illius salutaris capiamus effectum cujus per haec mysteria pignus accepimus*)" (5th Sunday After the Epiphany); "may your faithful people be made strong by your gifts. By receiving them may they desire them. And by desiring them, may they always receive them" (Septuagesima); "we have been nourished by the gift of heavenly life. We ask you that this same gift which is a mystery in our present life may become a help to bring us to life everlasting (*ut quod est nobis in praesenti vita mysterium fiat aeternitatis auxilium*)" (Saturday after Ash Wednesday); "may the receiving of your holy Sacrament revive us. May it cleanse us of our former evil ways and enable us to take part in the fellowship of your saving mysteries" (1st Sunday of Lent); "May this Communion cleanse us from sin. May it also make all of us sharers in a heavenly remedy (*et caelestis remedii faciat esse consortes*)" (Monday after the 2nd Sunday of Lent); "by this Sacrament kindly give us your holiness. May it cleanse us from our earthly vices and bring us to heavenly gifts (*ad caelestia dona perducat*)" (Tuesday after the 2nd Sunday of Lent, secret); "we ask you to grant that we who have received the pledge of life everlasting may yearn for it and so be able to attain it (*sic tendere congruenter ut ad eam pervenire possimus*)" (Friday after the 2nd Sunday of Lent); "may the heavenly meal which we have eaten make us holy. May it cleanse us from all error and make us worthy of your heavenly promises (*supernis promissionibus reddat acceptos*)" (Wednesday afer the 3rd Sunday of Lent); "may the receiving of this Sacrament cleanse us from sin and show us to the kingdom of heaven" (Friday after the 3rd Sunday of Lent); "grant us that the gifts now offered in the sight of your majesty may win for us the grace of true zeal and the reward of a happy eternity (*effectum beatae perennitatis acquirat*)" (Palm Sunday, secret); "Strengthened by this life-giving food, we pray you that what we seek in this age of our mortality we may attain by the gift of your immortality (*ut quod tempore nostrae mortalitatis exsequimur, immortalitatis quae munere consequamur*)" (Holy Thursday); "Accept the prayers of your people with the offering of this sacrifice. May what we have begun in these Easter mysteries obtain for us by your power an everlasting remedy (*ut Paschalibus initiata mysteriis ad aeternitatis nobis medelam, te operante, proficiant*)" (Easter, secret); "we who have had our oldness cleansed away ask that the holy reception of your sacrament may transform us into a new creature (*in novam transferat creaturam*)" (Easter Wednesday); "May this holy sacrament of our redemption bring us help in this life and assure us of eternal joy (*ut redemptionis nostrae sacrosancta commercia et vitae nobis conferant praesentis auxilium et gaudia sempiterna concilient)*" (Easter Thursday); "We pray you to accept the gifts of your exulting Church. Let her, to whom you have given cause for such great gladness, reap a harvest of everlasting joy *(ut causam tanti gaudii praestitisti, perpetuae fructum concede laetitae)*" (Low Sunday, secret); "accept the prayers of the faithful with the offering of sacrifice. While we pay you our duty of loving devotion, may we gain the glory of heaven *(ad caelestem gloriam transeamus)*" (5th Sunday afer Easter, secret); "we ask your mercy in receiving this heavenly sacrament, that what we receive as a temporal gift, we may enjoy for all eternity *(ut quod temporaliter gerimus aeternis gaudiis consequamur)*" (Ember Wednesday after Pentecost); "Grant us to be filled with the power of your everlasting divinity. This is prefigured here in time by our reception of your precious Body and Blood *(divinitatis tuae sempiterna fruitione repleri quam pretiosi corporis et sanguinis tui temporalis perceptio praefigurat)*" (Corpus Christi); "may we experience the partaking of your sacrament as a healing of mind and body so that both being saved, we may glory in the fulness of divine healing *(ut in utroque salvati, caelestis remedii plenitudine gloriemur)*" (11th Sunday after Pentecost); "we ask you that the heavenly sacraments which we have received may increase in us the fruits of eternal redemption *(ad redemptionis aeternae proficiamus augmentum)*" (13th Sunday after Pentecost); "may your sacraments always cleanse and guard us. May they guide us to the attainment of eternal salvation *(ad perpetuae ducant salvationis effectum)*" (14th Sunday after Pentecost); "we pray that your sacraments bring about in us what they contain. May we inwardly obtain what is now signified in outward signs *(perficiant tua sacramenta quod continent ut quae nunc specie gerimus, rerum veritate capiamus)*" (Ember Saturday in September); "We who have obtained the pledge of immortality ask you that we may cherish with a pure mind that which has passed our lips *(immortalitatis alimoniam consecuti)*" (21st Sunday after Pentecost); "we have been admitted to the holy table. We have drawn water with joy from the fountains of the Savior. We pray that his Blood may be a fountain of water springing up to eternal life (*sanguis ejus fiat nobis fons aquae in vitam aeternam salientis*)" (Feast of the Precious Blood); "God who has accorded to blessed Louis . . . to desire with all his heart the true happiness of the eternal Kingdom, grant us the love of this same happiness of which we have received the token in this sacrament (*cujus in hoc sacramento pignus accipimus*) (Feast of Saint Louis).

For the majority, these various translations of the same faith are found already in the prayers of the ancient sacramentaries,[46] which increases their value as witnesses: in them

---

46. As more marked examples, let us cite: From the Gelasien (we cite after the edition L. C. Mohlberg, *Liber Sacramentorum Romanae Ecclesiae Ordinis anni circuli*, Rome, 1960): "*Da nobis Domine quaesumus ipsius recensita nativitate vegetare, cujus caelesti mysterio et pascimur et potamur, Jesu Christi Domini nostri filii tui*" (*Postc. in natale Domini in die*, p. 10); "*Sit nobis quaesumus Domine cibus sacer potusque salutaris, qui et temporalem vitam muniat et praestet aeternum*" (*Postc. in Sexagesima*, p. 17); "*Perpetuo Domine favore prosequere quos reficis divino mysterio, et quos inbuisti caelestibus institutis salutaribus comitare solatiis*" (*Postc. fer. sept. in quadr.*, p. 23); "*Refecti Domine pane caelesti ad vitam, quaesumus, nutriamur aeternum*" (*Postc. sec. dom. in quard.*, p. 29); "*Percipientes Domine gloriosa mysteria referimus gratias, quod in terris positus iam caelestium praestas esse participes*" (*Postc. fer. tret. hebd. tert.*, p. 35); "*Sumpto Domine sacramento suppliciter depraecamur ut intercedentibus beatis apostolis quod temporaliter gerimus ad vitam capiamus aeternam*" (*Postc. vig omnium Apost.*, p. 147); "*Pignus aeternae vitae capientes humiliter imploramus ut apostolicis fulti patrociniis, quod imaginem contingimus sacramenti manifesta percepcione summamus*" (*In oct. Apost. pridie nonas julias*, p. 148); "*Caelesti munere saciati quaesumus omnipotens Deus, tua nos protectione custodi ut castimoniae pacem mentibus nostris atque corporibus intercedente sancta Maria propiciatus indulge, et veniente sponso filio tui unigenito accensis lampadibus ejus digni praestulemur occursum*" (*Postc. in adsumptione sanctae Mariae*, p. 154); "*Praesta Domine quaesumus ut terraenis affectibus expiatis ad superni plenitudinem sacramenti cujus libavimus sancta tendamus*" (*Postc. in tribulatione*, p. 198); "*Exaudi nos Domine salutaris noster ut per haec sacrosancta commercia in totius Ecclesiae confidemus corpore faciendum quod ejus praecessit in capite*" (*Super oblata in vig. Asc.*, p. 265).

From the *Leonien de Verone* (edit. L. C. Mohlberg, *Sacramentarium Veronese*, Rome, 1965) and which is more ancient: "*Praesta Domine quaesu-*

is read the traditional expression of the faith of the Western Church. It would be necessary to add certain communion antiphons, in particular those of the Thursdays of Lent (going back doubtless to the VIIIth century).

Moreover, this perspective of hope traverses the whole

---

mus ut sicut populus christianus martyrum tuorum temporali sollemnitate congaudet ita perfruatur aeterna; et quod votis celebrant compraehendant effectu" (*In natale sanct. quat. cor.,* p. 147); *"Da quaesumus Domine populo tuo inviolabilem fidei firmitatem; ut qui unigenitum tuum in tua tecum gloria sempiternum in veritate nostri corporis natum de matre virgine confitentur, et a praesentibus liberentur adversis, et mansuris gaudiis inserantur"* (*In nat. Domini,* p. 160); *"Praesta misericors Deus, ut natus hodie salvator mundi, sicut divinae nobis generationis est auctor, ita et immortalitatis sit ipse largitor"* (*In nat. Domini,* p. 162); *Ecclesiam tuam Domine benignus inlustra, ut apostolicis beati Johannis evangelistae inluminata doctrinis ad dona perveniat quae de tua fidelibus retributione promisit"* (*In natali sancti Joh, Evang.,* p. 164); *"Tribue quaesumus Domine ut illuc tendat christianae nostrae devotionis affectus quo tecum est nostra substantia"* (*In Asc. Dom.* p. 24); *"Da quaesumus Domine Deus noster, ut sicut tuorum commemoratione sanctorum temporali gratulamur officio, ita perpetuo laetemur aspectu"* (*In nat. Sanct. Joh. et Pauli.* p. 37); *"Sumpto Domine sacramento beatis Apostolis intervenientibus depraecamur ut quod temporaliter gerimus, capiamus aeternum"* (*Conj. oblat. virg. sacr.,* p. 46); *"Supplices te rogamus Domine Deus noster, ut qui percepimus caelestis mensae substantiam ad vitam pertineamus aeternam"* (p. 62); *"Quaesumus Domine Deus noster ut quod nobis ad immortalitatis pignus esse voluisti ad salutis aeternae tribuas provenire suffragium"* (p. 64); *"Satiati munere salutari, tuam Domine misericordiam depraecamur ut hoc eodem sacramento quo nos temporaliter vegetas efficias perpetuae vitae participes"* (p. 67); *"Haec nos communio purget a crimine et caelestis gaudii tribuat esse consortes"* (p. 111); *"Deus qui bona cuncta et incoas benignus et perficis, da nobis sicut de initiis tuae gratiae gloriamur, ita de perfectione guadere"* (*In natale episc.,* p. 129); *"Mentes nostras et corpora Domine quaesumus operatio tuae virtutis infundat; ut quod participatione sumpsimus, plena redemptione capiamus"* (p. 142).

From the *Missale Gallicanum Vetus* (edit. L.C. Mohlberg, Rome, 1958): *"Impleatur in nobis quaesumus Domine sacramenti paschalis sancta libatio, nosque de terrenis affectibus ad caelestem transferat institutum"* (*In vig. pasch.,* p. 43); *"Animae nostrae quaesumus omnipotens Deus, hoc potientur desiderio ut a tuo spiritu inflammentur, ut sicut lampadas divino munere saciati ante conspectum venientis Christi Filii tui velut clara lumina*

Roman canon. It appears in several places. Thus in the *Hanc Igitur*: "Establish our days in your peace, save us from everlasting doom, and count us among your chosen ones." The *Unde et memores* speaks of "the sacred bread of life eternal" —"the cup which gives salvation forever." Which the *Supplices te rogamus* expresses thus: "so that whoever shares in receiving the most holy Body and Blood of your Son from this altar here below may be filled with every blessing and grace from heaven above." Finally the *Nobis quoque peccatoribus* expresses this hope in all its ecclesial context: "Please give us part and fellowship with your holy apostles and martyrs . . . and all your saints. We pray you, let us share their company not in view of our merits but because of your mercy." The prayers of communion in their turn lean on this point: "May this mingling and consecration of the Body and Blood of our Lord Jesus Christ give everlasting life to us who receive it." (*Haec commixtio*); "Grant . . . that from a temporal gift it may become for us an eternal remedy" (*Quod ore sumpsimus*).[47]

The Latin Fathers

It is this certitude, which gives all its dynamism to the liturgical celebration of the Eucharist, that the Latin Fathers explain in their cathecheses or their treatises.

A text of Cyprian, in his commentary on the Our Father, carries us back to the third century and shows us that spontaneously "the daily bread" evokes for the Christian of this time the bread which sanctifies for eternal life:

"For Christ is the bread of life; and this bread does not belong to all men, but it is ours. And according as we say, "Our Father," because He is the Father of those who understand

---

fulgeamus" (*De adv. Dom. nostri*, p. 12). We will note how (on the part of the prayers of Advent) the goal of hope is here a state and less the glorious coming of Jesus in its reality as the ultimate event of Salvation. That seems to us moreover characteristic of all the Western thought. We cannot develop it in this work, but this point would bring us much light.

47. We cite according to the *Saint Andrew Bible Missal*, New York, 1962.

and believe; so also we call it "our bread," because Christ is
the bread of those who are in union with His body. And we
ask that this bread should be given to us daily, that we who
are in Christ, and daily receive the Eucharist for the food of
salvation, may not, by the interposition of some heinous sin,
by being prevented, as withheld and not communicating, from
partaking of the heavenly bread, be separated from Christ's
body, as He Himself predicts, and warns, "I am the bread of
life which came down from heaven. If any man eat of my bread,
he shall live for ever: and the bread which I will give is my
flesh, for the life of the world." When, therefore, He says,
that whoever shall eat of His bread shall live for ever; as it is
manifest that those who partake of His body and receive the
Eucharist by the right of communion are living, so, on the
other hand, we must fear and pray lest any one who, being
withheld from communion, is separate from Christ's body should
remain at a distance from salvation; as He Himself threatens,
and says, "Unless ye eat the flesh of the Son of man, and
drink His blood, ye shall have no life in you." And, therefore,
we ask that our bread—that is, Christ—may be given to us daily,
that we who abide and live in Christ may not depart from
His sanctification and body" (*De Dom. Or.,* 18; *AN,* vol. V,
p. 452).

We would not be able to insist better on the necessary
bond between the reception of the body of the Lord and the
possession of eternal life: to be deprived of communion amounts
to being condemned to die to the new Life, as to be deprived
of material bread amounts to being condemned to die of
hunger.

We have already, in studying the role of Eucharist on sin,
brought in the witness of Ambrose of Milan. But this bishop
shows equally the marvelous efficacy of the body of the
Lord for the gift of immortality. Commenting on the Gospel
according to Luke he notes: "As to the righteous man, he is
in the image of God if, to reproduce the resemblance of divine
life, he scorns this world in order to know God and disdains
earthly enjoyments to receive the Word who is the food of our

life: which is why we eat the body of Christ, in order to be able to partake of eternal life" (*In Luc.* 10, 49; trans.). The *De Mysteriis* is more evocative:

"In very truth it is a marvelous thing that God rained manna on the fathers, and fed them with daily food from heaven; so that it is said, "So man did eat angels' food." But yet all those who ate that food died in the wilderness, but that food which you receive, that living Bread which came down from heaven, furnishes the substance of eternal life; and whosoever shall eat of this Bread shall never die, and it is the Body of Christ. Now consider whether the bread of angels be more excellent or the Flesh of Christ, which is indeed the body of life. That manna came from heaven, this is above the heavens; that was of heaven, this is of the Lord of the heavens; that was liable to corruption, if kept a second day, this is far from all corruption, for whosoever shall taste it holily shall not be able to feel corruption" (*De Myst.* 47-48; *NPN*, 2nd series, vol. X, p. 323).

In fact, by the word of Christ ("Who could make of nothing what was not") (*ibid.*, 52; p. 187) the bread becomes "the true flesh of Christ who was crucified, who was buried" (*ibid.*, 53: p. 189). This divinized flesh is a "spiritual" food, for "The body of Christ is the body of the divine Spirit, because Christ is Spirit" (*ibid.*, 58: p. 191). Then, the *De Sacramentis* can express itself with more density:

" 'I am the living bread,' He says, 'which came down from heaven.' But flesh did not come down from heaven, that is, He took on flesh on earth from a virgin. How, then, did bread come down from heaven and living bread? Because our same Lord Jesus Christ is a sharer of both divinity and body, and you who receive the flesh participate in that nourishment of His divine substance" (*De Sacr.* VI, 1, 4; *CF*, vol. 44, p. 320).

And that, after having compared this food to the manna of Exodus: "What is greater, manna from heaven or the body of Christ? Surely the body of Christ, who is the Author of heaven. Then, he who ate the manna died; he who has eaten this body will effect for himself remission of sins and 'shall not die forever.'" *(Ibid.* IV, 5, 24; vol. 44, p. 305; see also V, 2, 24).

But on this point Augustine is again to Latin tradition what Cyril of Alexandria is to the Alexandrine tradition and Theodore of Mopsuestia to the Antiochan tradition. With him, especially in the *Tractatus 26 on John* (well known for the difficulties which its interpretation poses), this faith is explained and finds its maximum emphasis in connection with the other aspects of the Eucharistic mystery, very especially with the progressive construction of the ecclesial Body of the Lord in love, of which he is equally the great cantor among the Latins. These pages will not be surpassed; each attempt at commentary risks weakening them. Then we must be content with citing here the passages which appear to concern directly the Eucharistic bread and not faith only (although it is difficult to separate the two aspects):

"The bread that I will give," saith He, "is my flesh, for the life of the world." Believers know the body of Christ, if they neglect not to be the body of Christ. Let them become the body of Christ, if they wish to live by the Spirit of Christ. None lives by the Spirit of Christ but the body of Christ. . . . Wouldst thou then also live by the Spirit of Christ? Be in the body of Christ. For surely my body does not live by thy spirit. My body lives by my spirit, and thy body by thy spirit. The body of Christ cannot live but by the Spirit of Christ. It is for this that the Apostle Paul, expounding this bread, says: 'One bread,' saith he, 'we being many are one body.' O mystery of piety! O sign of unity! O bond of charity! He that would live has where to live, has whence to live. Let him draw near, let him believe; let him be embodied, that he may be made to live. Let him not shrink from the compact of members; let him not be a rotten member that deserves to be cut off; let him not be a deformed member whereof to be ashamed; let him be a fair, fit, and sound member; let him cleave to the body, live for God by God: now let him labor on earth, that hereafter he may reign in heaven. . . . 'Who so

eateth my flesh, and drinketh my blood, hath eternal life.'
Wherefore, he that eateth not this bread, nor drinketh this
blood, hath not this life; for men can have temporal life without that, but they can noways have eternal life. He then that
eateth not His flesh, nor drinketh His blood, hath no life in
him; and he that eateth His flesh, and drinketh His blood, hath
life. This epithet, eternal, which He used, answers to both. . .
For he who will not take it shall not live, nor yet shall he who
will take it live. For very many, even who have taken it, die;
it may be by old age, or by disease, or by some other causality
But in this food and drink, that is, in the body and blood of
the Lord, it is not so. For both he that doth not take it hath
no life, and he that doth take it hath life, and that indeed
eternal life. And thus He would have this meat and drink to
be understood as meaning the fellowship of His own body and
members, which is the holy Church in his predestined, and
called, and justified, and glorified saints and believers. Of these,
the first is already effected, namely, predestination; the second
and third, that is, vocation and justification, have taken
place, are taking place, and will take place; but the fourth,
namely, the glorifying, is at present in hope, but a thing future
in realization. The sacrament of this thing, namely, of the unity
of the body and blood of Christ, is prepared on the Lord's
table . . . and from the Lord's table it is taken, by some to life,
by some to destruction: but the thing itself, of which it is the
sacrament, is for every man to life, for no man to destruction,
whosoever shall have been a partaker thereof. . . . When He
had said, 'He that eateth my flesh, and drinketh my blood, hath
eternal life,' He forthwith subjoined, 'and I will raise him up
on the last day.' That meanwhile, according to the Spirit, he
may have eternal life in that rest into which the spirits of the
saints are received; but as to the body, he shall not be defrauded
of its eternal life, but, on the contrary, he shall have it in the
resurrection of the dead at the last day. 'For my flesh,' saith
He, 'is meat indeed, and my blood is drink indeed.' For whilst
by meat and drink men seek to attain to this, except this meat

and drink, which doth render them by whom it is taken immortal and incorruptible; that is, the very fellowship of the saints, where will be peace and unity, full and perfect. Therefore, indeed, it is, even as men of God understood this before us, that our Lord Jesus Christ has pointed our minds to His body and blood in those things, which from being many are reduced to some one thing. For a unity is formed by many grains forming together; and another unity is effected by the clustering together of many berries.... This it is, therefore, for a man to eat that meat and to drink that drink, to dwell in Christ, and to have Christ dwelling in him ... just as we are made better by participation of the Son, through the unity of His body and blood, which thing that eating and drinking signifies. We live then by Him, by eating Him; that is, by receiving Himself as the eternal life, which we did not have from ourselves. Himself, however, lives by the Father, being sent by Him, because 'He emptied Himself, being made obedient even unto the death of the cross! ... but that any should live by me is effected by that participation in which he eats me. Therefore, I being humbled, do live by the Father, man being raised up, liveth by me....'This is the bread that cometh down from heaven;' that by eating it we may live, since we cannot have eternal life from ourselves. 'Not,' saith He, 'as your fathers did eat manna, and are dead: he that eateth this bread shall live forever.' That those fathers are dead, He would have to be understood as meaning, that they do not live forever. For even they who eat Christ shall certainly die temporally; but they live forever, because Christ is eternal life." (*Jn Joan, Evang.*, tr. XXVI; *NPN*, 1st series, vol. vii, pp. 172-174).

We will be excused for this long citation which dispenses us with commentary. The Eucharist nourishes us with the seed of immortality, and, therefore, increases our hope in making us meet in the personal body of Christ, the whole Christ, the ecclesial Body. We are nourished with eternal life at the moment when, purified of our sin, we nourish our fraternal union.

The theological reflexion of Thomas Aquinas

All the witnesses here assembled,[48] concerning the relation between the Eucharist and the eschatological glory, are unanimous. It is, without any possible doubt, a traditional truth. It is not necessary then to be astonished to see medieval Scholasticism integrate it into its synthesis in the wake of Augustine.

Although less explicitly put to light than the aspect of love, this eschatological aspect of the Eucharist is often affirmed by Saint Thomas Aquinas, the most illustrious representative of the Middle Ages. And that as much in the plan of the simple sacramental signification (the *"sacramentum tantum"* *) as in

---

48. We would have to be able to lengthen the list. We must at least make mention here of Cyril of Jerusalem; "Therefore, with a complete assurance let us partake of the body and the blood of Christ. For in the figure of the bread is given you his body and in the figure of the wine his blood; in order that by this share of the body and blood of Christ you become concorporal and consanguine with him. For we welcome lovers of Christ by the fact that his body and blood is diffused in our members and thus, according to blessed Peter, we become partakers of divine nature" (*Cat. Myst.*, 4, 3: J. Quasten, Monuments Euch. [*Flor. Patrist.* 6], pars 2, p. 94).

"Reassure your heart, partake of this bread as of something spiritual and illumine the face of your soul. Having thus reclothed it with a pure conscience you can contemplate as in a mirror the glory of God and grow from glory to glory in Christ Jesus our Lord" (*ibid.*, 4, 9: pp. 96-97).

A very interesting witness is the *Homélie pascale inspirée du traité sur la Pâque d'Hippolyte*, edited by Nautin, *Sources chrét.*, 1950. Nautin thinks that this homily which is not of Hippolytus although it is inspired by him, would date from the IVth century. Let us cite these passages: "In order that we be completely nourished by the Word, fed, not with earthly food, but with heavenly food, let us also eat of the Pasch of the Word with spiritual desire with which the Lord himself has desired to eat it with us" (p. 122); "This is what the food of the sacred feast is for us, this is our spiritual banquet, this is our immortal food and this is our immortal delight. Fed with the bread of heaven and nourished with the cup of happiness, the glowing and boiling cup, the blood marked from on high by the warmth of the Spirit . . . ." pp. 132-134); "the spiritual body of Christ is glowing" (p. 152, see Introd., pp. 79-81). These passages are clarified by pages 164-174 where the author gives his concept of the incarnation.

the plan of the effect accomplished in the faithful ("*res tantum*" *).

We speak of "sacramental signification." Each sacrament in its very structure as a sign bears a triple dimension: it recalls the Mystery of Jesus the source of the new Life given to me, it designates the actual gift of the *agape* * of the Father, attaining *hic et nunc* the faithful, it heralds the future glory toward which this gift itself is in tension (III, 60, 3).[49] The sacrament has then the value of a memorial of an actual event of grace and of an eschatological announcement. Not in a juxtaposition or a simple addition of significations, but in the ontological unity of a single sign, because the sign used by the Church is (by its use in the history of Salvation) bound to the whole unfolding of the design of God.[50] As each sacrament, the Eucharist, in the complex of its symbolism, just as it signifies the effect actually produced in the faithful, is opened on a dimension of hope: in this banquet which it is and of which it produces the effects, it heralds the messianic banquet of the end of time, where God will give himself to his own in the glory of the face to face vision and of the resurrection of the flesh. Saint Thomas will say: "(the Eucharist) has a third signification, that which looks at the future, in so far as it prefigures the fruition of God which we shall enjoy in the Fatherland; therefore, one calls it *viaticum*" (III, 73, 4). We have insisted on this symbol of the "Eucharistic meal" in presenting the sense and the nature of the paschal meal, we do not want to come back on it any more.

Moreover, this sacramental signification is directed entirely towards the "res", the realities caused in the faithful of which faith is put in wakefulness and instructed and provoked by this "revealing and dynamic word" of God in his Church. Then, for Saint Thomas, the Eucharist is not content with signifying

49. See our study: *La triple dimension du signe sacramentel* in *N.R. Théol.*, 1961, pp. 225-254.

50. See our study *Principes pour une catechèse sacramentaire vraie*, in *N.R. Théol.*, 1962, pp. 1053-1061, and *Le sacrement, événement de salut*, collection *Les études religieuses*, Paris-Bruxelles, 1964.

the future glory, by recalling to faith that toward which the Christian life of here below marches; it nourishes our hope in the same fashion that it causes love, in posing in the believer a "reality" ("res") which, actually truly possessed, already gives him the "arrhes" * of what he awaits and thus strengthens him in his march toward the end. What it signifies of the future, it causes already in a certain fashion, "efficit hoc quod figurat." What St. Thomas says of the value of love can be applied analogically to this value of hope: "This sacrament is at once quasi figurative and effective" (III, 78, 3 and 6), sign and cause. Besides, just as love given by this sacrament is ecclesial, and welds further together the Christian with the Father and with his brothers, in Jesus the Lord, the hope which is deepened there must lead the individual to a surpassing of himself and of his personal hopes, to meet the whole Church in its awaiting for the return of the Lord. The theology of Saint Thomas seems to us to go to this depth. We must show it.

The treatise on the Eucharist in the Summa Theologica contains numerous allusions to eschatology * envisaged however most often in a strictly individual plan. Thus, when it is a question of justifying the sense of the word "viaticum" (III, 73, 4) "way to arrive at the fruition of God," or to give the sense of the drop of water added to the wine "in accord with the ultimate effect of this sacrament, the entrance into eternal life" (III, 80, 2, ad 1), or finally to show the fitness of the real presence: "He has not deprived us of his corporal presence during our wandering; on the contrary, by the truth of his body and blood, he has united us to him in this sacrament according to the word of John 6, 57; therefore, this sacrament is the sign of the most intense love and the basis of our hope (nostrae spei sublevamentum) on account of so companionable a joining of Christ to us" ((III, 75, 1).

When he arrives at the explicit study of the effects of the Eucharist, Saint Thomas Aquinas poses to himself the question: "Is entrance into glory the effect of this sacrament?" (III, 79, 2). This obliges him to expose his thought with greater fullness.

He writes this then: "The spiritual meal and the unity signified by the species of bread and wine are certainly realized in the present life, but imperfectly; they are realized perfectly in the state of glory. From this it happens that Augustine thus comments on John 6, 56: 'Men take nourishment and drink only to appease their hunger and thirst; such an effect is produced truly only by this food and this drink where those who partake draw out immortality and incorruptibility, and that in the society of the saints where peace and a full and perfect unity will reign' (III, 79, 2). The *ad* 1 emphasizes that 'this sacrament does not introduce us immediately into glory' but that moreover 'it gives us what is necessary to get there.' "

One would have expected a more explicit response; however, in spite of its laconicism, this article has an important dogmatic content: the dimension of hope not only is projected there onto the ecclesial plan, but is bound in fact to the whole ecclesial mystery. The *"res"* of the Eucharist, its ultimate effect, is called the Church, "mystical Body of Christ, society of the saints" (III, 80, 4), communion of men with the Father and among themselves in Christ the Head by the bond of love; and Saint Thomas does not hesitate to write: "Whoever eats this sacrament signifies by the very fact his union with Christ and his incorporation into its members" (ibid.). But the Church thus aimed at is the perfect Church, in its state of fullness: Christ gives his body and his blood for the upbuilding, in the bosom of humanity and in the rhythm of human generations which succeed, of the glorious Church of which Paul has revealed the place in the great salvific design of the Father. This triumphant Church which Saint Thomas describes as "the true Church, our Mother toward which we tend, exemplar of our militant Church" (*In Ephes.*, cap. 3, lect. 3, n° 161). The ultimate effect of the Eucharist, its *"res perfecta,"* is nothing less than the parousial Church. In the divine plan of Salvation this will appear only at the end of time, and the intimate structure of the "communion of Life of men with the Father and among themselves" cannot be realized fully in the pilgrim stage of the Church: Christians remain sinners. Then, it is one of the gifts of the Promise that we still expect, although already we possess its *"arrhes."* * Nevertheless, the Eucharist, at the moment when it ties together fraternal unity and purifies from sin, impresses on the Christian life a dynamism which brings nearer this ideal and thus nourishes hope: "full and perfect" unity, characteristic of the eschatological "society of the saints," makes a step in each "true" celebration. Thus in this one *"res"* which is the Church, are perfectly united the three traditionally affirmed effects of the sacrament of the Lord's Table.

The commentary on the sixth chapter of John brings us more light on this thomistic concept of the eschatological* role of the Eucharist. For the affirmations of the Gospel will ask him to clarify the connection between the eating of the body of the Lord and the resurrection of the flesh. He will do it in being inspired by the *Tractatus* of Augustine, and again we shall find ourselves face to face with very rich texts, inspired by a profound intuition, but unfortunately not very explicit, leaving us in suspense.

The first realistic affirmation to underline is that of the "grandiose and universal usefulness of this sacrament." In fact, what depth does the efficacy of the Eucharist attain in us? The very depth of the efficacy of the whole mystery of Christ the Savior: "It causes in us now the spiritual life, later eternal . . . since its efficient capacity coincides with that of the passion of the Lord which it applies to us. As it was not fitting that Christ always dwell visibly present among us, he wanted to remedy it by this sacrament. Then, the destruction of death that Christ effected in his death, and the reparation of Life which he accomplished in his resurrection are manifestly the effect of this sacrament" (*In Joan.*, cap. 6, lect. 6; ed. CAI, n° 963). And that in a universal fashion "since the Life that he gives is not only the life of a man, but (*quantum in se est*) that of the whole world, for which the death of Christ suffices" (n° 964). The Eucharist is then "the sacrament of the resurrection." Commenting on John 6, 55, ("he who eats my flesh and drinks my blood has eternal life, and I will raise him up at the last day") Saint Thomas is going to explain his thought in an unequivocal fashion. Let us distinguish a double *"res"* of the sacrament: "one contained and signified, Christ in his integrity, contained under the species of bread and wine; the other signified and not contained, the mystical body of Christ present in the predestined, called and justified." He who eats the body of the Lord not only "sacramentally" but also "spiritually" [51] perceives in fullness the first *"res:"* united to Christ by faith and love, he is transformed in him "and becomes his member" (since this food, in the inverse of others, changes into it him who eats it). Since Christ is God and eternal life, he who eats it thus possesses already eternal life (cap. 6, lect. 7: n° 972). But, at the same time, united to Christ, he becomes a "participant in the ecclesial unity" (*particeps unitatis ecclesiasticae*) and, therefore, perceives the second *"res"* of the sacrament.[52] All this can only pose in him a new certainty of resurrection: "Necessarily, if he perseveres he will obtain eternal life, for the unity of the Church comes from the Holy Spirit who constitutes the *arrhes* of our heritage (according to Eph. 4, 4; 1, 14); the utility of this food which gives eternal life to the soul then appears great to us, great since it gives this eternal life even to the body" (*ibid.*). Here again, the effect of the Eucharist on the resurrection is indissolubly bound to its first effect of the upbuilding of the ecclesial Body of the Lord in connection with the proper work of the Holy Spirit. Saint Thomas goes on to explain himself immediately:

"Therefore, Jesus adds:

" 'I shall raise him up at the last day.' As we have just said, he who eats and drinks spiritually becomes a partaker of the Holy Spirit by whom we are united to Christ in the union of faith and love, and by whom we become members of the Church. The Holy Spirit gives the resurrection (*resurrectionem autem facit mereri Spiritus Sanctus*) its worth, according to Rom. 4, 24: 'He who raised Jesus Christ our Lord up from the dead will raise up also our mortal bodies

---

51. "[*Virtus sanguinis effusi in Passione*] *ad tria ordinatur. Primo et principaliter ad adipiscendam aeternam haereditatem.*"

52. See chap. II, p. 99, note 38.

because of his Spirit who dwells in us.' Therefore, the Lord can say that he who eats and drinks will rise up for glory and not for condemnation, for this resurgence (*resuscitatio*) would then be useless. It is very fitting to attribute this effect to the sacrament of the Eucharist since, according to the word of Augustine, the Word raises up souls, but the Word makes flesh give life to flesh. In this sacrament the Word is present not only according to his divinity but also in the whole reality of his flesh. Therefore, it is not solely the cause of the resurrection of souls but even of the resurrection of bodies; according to I Cor. 15, 21: 'by a man came death, by a man will come the resurrection from the dead.' We see clearly then the utility of this process of eating" (n° 973).

The Eucharist has then the value of the "sacrament of the resurrection." The same ideas will reappear farther on in the *Commentary*: "He eats *spiritualiter*, having had regard to the reality as simply signified, who, by the union of faith and love, is incorporated into the mystical body, for love renders God present in man, and vice versa . . . that, the Holy Spirit accomplishes" (n° 976); "Whoever eats this bread dwells in me and I in him; I am eternal life, then he who eats this bread as he should will live for eternity" (n° 981).

In the second chapter we tried to investigate the precise role the Holy Spirit played for Saint Thomas in this gift of resurrection which we see him appropriate to it. Certain indices permitted us to conclude that our Doctor belongs to the great line traced by the Alexandrian tradition in its cross-connections with the Latin Fathers, the accent being always put more on the presence of the *Logos* (breathing the Spirit) in the flesh of Jesus than on the personal and "communicative" glorification of the Lord Christ at the end of his paschal mystery. This permits us to synthesize the contents of these texts in some propositions. He who eats *"sacramentaliter et spiritualiter"* the Eucharistic body of Christ receives the "reality signified but not contained" of this sacrament (*"res signata et non contenta"*), the "communion" in the beautiful Patristic sense of union with the Father and with the brothers in Jesus, the nucleus of the mystery of the Church. This "ecclesial unity" ("*unitas eccle-siastica*") is the work of the Holy Spirit. But, because this one is at once the bond of the Church and the "*arrhes* of our heritage," in the Eucharist the believer receives in this very deepening of his insertion into the Church the source of the resurrection both of his soul and of his body; resurrection which does not come from the Spirit alone, but of the Spirit insofar as joined (by the divinity of the Word) to the flesh of Christ from the first instant of the hypostatic union. Therefore, the Eucharist has as its effect the resurrection of the whole man, body and soul.

Thus the living Tradition of the Church conceives the marvelous efficacy of the Eucharistic bread and wine at the moment when, with the triumph of Scholastic theology, it tries to situate in a view of wisdom the diverse elements of its faith. Saint Thomas Aquinas not only presents the Eucharist as the food of the resurrection, nourishing hope in rendering its object nearer; but especially he shows how it produces this effect only in making the faithful inscribed more deeply in the mystery of the Church after having been purified of his sin in the same act. It is truly a question of an ecclesial effect, of an ecclesial hope. This confident march toward the Parousia* of the Lord is accomplished then only in the Church, and the personal hope of the Christian is increased only proportionally to his most living participation in the mystery of the Mystical Body. One sacrament realizes at once this increase of unity and fraternal communion, this snatching away from sin, this projection into the universe of the resurrection, quite simply because it has the effect of constructing, with the men of earth, the eternal Church.

It is what the 13th session of the Council of Trent will express very briefly when, after having recalled the purifying effect of the Eucharist, it will say: "Our Savior finally willed that this sacrament be the token of our future glory and of our eternal happiness, as the symbol of this one Body of which he is the Head and to which he wills that we, its members, be closely attached by close bonds of faith, of hope, and of love" (Denz., 875).

The first moment of Salvation of the Church appeared to us, above, as intimately bound to the first moment of the paschal mystery of Jesus the Servant * of God. And at the end of our reflection we could write that in the faith of living Tradition the Eucharist built up the Church, the "communion of Life," in ceaselessly purifying the members of their sin, the radical source of all separation from God and from their brothers, for it gives them the body and blood offered in a sacrifice of expiation and of redemption. We see now how this view must be completed. Then even as the ecclesial unity is thus welded by breaking with the world of evil, in the positive face of the same act, in the same "event of Salvation," it is deepened by plunging into the second moment of the Pasch of Jesus, his glorification as Lord * by his resurrection from death. It is a passage from sin not only to a recovered purity but to a marvelous world where, under the power of the *agape* * of the Father, the universe of the first Adam is transformed. This is what the Eucharist effects, which is why we call it here the "Salvation of the Church."

But if it is thus the "Salvation of the Church," it is more simply because its end is the "upbuilding of the Church" in the present stage of the economy of Salvation; and now this Church is in the state of Salvation. For as all the sacraments, the Eucharist belongs to the Church on earth, the Church being edified in leading little by little all human generations into this "communion of Life" which defines it. Living center of the sacramental organism, sacrament *par excellence* (III, 73, 4, ad 2), the Eucharist must build up the Church Pilgrim, the Church of the faith and not yet of the "face to face vision"; then it must be homogeneous with it. Here again resides the precise point which permits us to situate at once its definitive effect of love and its intermediary effect of hope.

The Church on Earth, the Church en marche

At the risk of repeating ourselves, let us try to translate the status of this wandering Church. We can do it only in taking up the terms, the expressions used in speaking of the Eucharist. It is already, and essentially, community of love, communion of Life. Already its members enjoy the divine goods of the Promise; they know God, live in union with him by love, possess by grace a participation in his intimate life. When, in the liturgical assembly which expresses it perfectly, it is reunited, it blesses the same Father as the saints in heaven around the same immolated and risen lamb, for the same "marvels" which stir up its admiration and its thanksgiving. One cannot, in the strict sense, call it the Church in gestation, for it is already the Church of God. It is already the People of the saved. It is the Spouse of Christ. It is the Body of the Lord. It is the new humanity. And on this plan, nothing more is awaited. Nevertheless, the present state of the Church is one of tension. Not simply, because its members stil bear within themselves the heavy call of sin, but even on the level of these positive values considered in all their richness as the "divine gift." For it is the Church of the faith, in all the Biblical implications of this term of faith. Certainly, its faithful know the same God as the saints of heaven, but in the obscurity of faith, in awaiting the vision. They love the same God as the saints of heaven, in a love which meets God himself; however, their love could not always be actual (II-II, 24, 8). They possess the divine gifts but in a state of seed, since sanctifying grace itself must flourish in glory (*"gratia nihil est aliud quam quaedam inchoatio gloriae in nobis"*: II-II, 24, 3, ad 2). Moreover (and they have this in common with the saints of heaven till the Parousia) they will have to pass through death and find their body only after a long wait. In the liturgical assembly the Church truly possesses the Lord of heaven, but under the signs of which faith alone can pierce the secret, which cannot satisfy it fully.

The same expression as in the preceding chapter is imposed on us if we want to characterize this state of the earthly Church: the Pasch, the Exodus. No longer, this time, under the aspect of snatching away from the slavery of evil, but under the aspect of a march forward to a not totally unknown earth, of deepening, of blooming of one reality already acquired which has not yet attained all its fullness. It is then a question of a "state of hope" based on the possession of a certain foundation. Faith and hope cannot be separated because one knows in the clear yet obscure light of faith, one loves; but because the object loved is not yet possessed in fullness one tends (with assurance) toward the total and definitive possession of which the word of God gives the guarantee. Perhaps current theology does not insist enough on this quasi identification between the wandering and the hoping Church. In heaven the love that we have on earth will remain, our faith will be surpassed in the vision ("*fides est habitus mentis qua inchoatur vita aeterna in nobis:*" II-II, 4, 1), hope will vanish. It constitutes a theological dimension exclusively proper to the march of the People of God on this earth, and characterizes this stage of the realization of the mystery of the Church of God. The wandering Church can then be defined as the communion of Life of men with the Father and among themselves in Jesus the Lord, already realized, but, however, still in a status of hope, of tension toward the definitive enjoyment of the good possessed now in the modalities of a not total bloom, of a simple seed, proper to the Christian condition in the stage of faith.

The Proper Effect of the Eucharistic Food

There, in this well characterized tension, is situated the "*res tantum*" * of the Eucharist. Essentially and primarily, this "*res*" consists of love, conceived not in an individualistic sense but as the truer and more profound entrance into the love of the Father and of one's brothers. The participation in the consecrated bread and wine makes us enter into the totality of love which culminates in the Pasch of Jesus, the infinite love of the Father giving his Son to men, and giving him all his goods, the immense love of the incarnate Son giving himself without reticence to the Father for the salvation of his brothers and the accomplishment of the will of this Father. It enroots then all the baptized, participating in this unique mystery of *agape*, * into the "communion of Life," into the Church.

However, because destined to man *"in via,"* it thus nourishes love in function of the present economy. In making us deepen the communion,* it is then into the pilgrim Church in Exodus that it integrates us further, but under its precise formality of "marching forward," in a tension toward the heavenly Jerusalem. Let us say that it makes then the great glow of the hope of the Church traverse us and uphold us, when, in the risen body of the *Kurios*,* it gives to us (under the veil of the "signs of faith") the *"arrhes"* * of heavenly life. It unifies, and, therefore, perfects the Church, but in training it toward the eschatological future, toward the diffusion in all the members of the glory of Christ made Lord by his resurrection from the dead, and Head of the new humanity.

That leads us back to the presence in this sacrament of the risen body of the *Kurios*.* For if it can realize this edification of the Church Pilgrim in all the realism and the "situation" of its existential condition, that can have its source only in the mysterious reality which it bears. We said above that the body of the risen Jesus was the initial cell of the definitive universe toward which converges all human hope. The love of the Father for men, his great design of Life and Salvation, are realized concretely in the Lord Jesus Christ who bears the goods of the Promise in their maximal realization since he bears them as the new Adam, the new starting point. In the sacramental signs of the Eucharistic meal, the Father gives Jesus to men in this very being of glory, not simply that they possess him statically (in the fashion of which one possesses a precious object) but above all that he transforms them little by little into what he is. His glorified flesh blends with their flesh and already (under an invisible mode, since we are in the realm of faith) impregnates them.

There rooted and in all its realism and its depth, is the ecclesial hope: in the common partaking of the meal of the *Kurios* (note this Pauline expression which is not fortuitous). It is no longer question of a hope leaning only on the promise of a distant future; but on the contrary of a hope enrooting itself in a promise which has already begun to be realized, therefore, in an acquired basis, an experience. The aim has already met us, man has already overleaped (in all the complex of what one calls Christian initiation) the definitive step leading him into the universe of glory, in him the work of transformation has begun. It can no longer, too, be a question of a strictly personal hope, aspiring to the acquisition of a blessedness in the measure of each one and looking at other men only laterally. For it appears in us from the active presence of him whom the Father predestined as Head for all the redeemed. This seed of new Life transforms us insofar as it builds the mystical Body, then insofar as we are a very strict member, being able to define his vocation and his destiny only in function of the whole Body, Head and members. Because the "spiritual" body given in nourishment is also the "sacramental" body, given in faith and under the signs of faith, the entrance into what he bears has not yet the evidence and the definitive status of vision. Of this very fact, the tension of the Church toward the advent of this ultimate stage of its mystery is intensified, finds a new vigor. In the paschal Christ the community of believers has accomplished one stage of its passage from the condition of the flesh to that of the Spirit.

In short, in strict theology, the unique effect of the Eucharist is the edification of the Church, the communion of Life. Not however a vague Church, abstract, outside the existential context of Christian experience, but the Church still on this earth in its state of Exodus, still (although already essentially "communion of Life") very definitely tending toward the plenary possession of the divine gifts. In other terms, the Eucharist constructs the paschal Church in its state of *transitus ex hoc mundo ad Patrem* in Christ who, as precursor (Heb. 6, 20), has preceded it into the glory of heaven, and who does not cease to attract all of it to him till the day when he shall appear a second time to give it the totality of Salvation (Heb. 9, 28), in the flashing glory of the resurrection of the flesh. But this definitive event will not have the value of absolute newness, it will be only the marvelous flourishing of the gift ceaselessly repeated in the salvific Eucharist. Such is, it seems to us, the strong and pregnant sense which it is necessary to give to the traditional expression: "The Eucharist builds the Church." Thus are harmonized in unity the three effects that the whole Tradition attributes to the sacrament of the Lord's Supper: love in union with the Father and with the brothers in Jesus the Head, pardon from sins, increase of hope. The Eucharist plunges the community of the baptized into the very dynamism of the mystery of Salvation. It is the "Salvation of the Church."

The Eucharist and the Engagement of the Faithful in Salvation

We have to be even clearer yet. The Sacramental grace exercises its efficient capacity beyond the event of Salvation which it signifies and makes present: it must be fruitful already in this earthly life, in the daily acts of human existence, which permit the redeemed faithful to live truly in redemption. The sacramental gifts are not to be confounded, let us remember, with values that can be amassed, a quantitative whole to increase and to treasure; they are ordained above all to a certain quality of life to attain. Here again the law of the priority of the *actus secundus* on the *habitus* is verified: the latter exists only in function of the former. In the case of the Eucharist, it will be necessary that the eschatological tension which we have described be prolonged in this earthly life, once the Lord's meal is finished and the liturgical assembly dissolved.

This radiating of the Sacramental Eucharistic event into the current events of the Christian life is so radical that it gives to this whole life a new energy. Of what, in fact, does that which we call the moral effort of the Christian consist? Fundamentally in his response to a gift. Contrarily to all philosophical ethics, even the most sublime, its starting point does not reside in a febrile effort of man trying to attain the sole object capable of supplying his deepest aspirations. God makes the first step; in his *agape* * he comes to open the dialogue. We know how, in his treatises on justification and on Penance, Saint Thomas has strongly emphasized this point: *"Primum principium est Dei operatio convertentis cor"* (III, 85, 5). God reveals himself in his Word and the historic work realized under his leadership. Then he enters into the life of man. If by faith man accepts him, he gives him in the baptismal event the gifts of his intimacy.

However, all cannot stop there. The God of Jesus Christ does not want to consider man as a mere beggar who could only open his hand and receive. In the delicacy of his love he respects human liberty and its responsibilities: he gives himself, but in making covenant, in binding the faithful in the new Covenant realized in Jesus. This demands a human engagement, a response of rightness, engaging all the human values informed by love. Quite as Jesus, because he was true man, assumed in him all human values, making of them the instrument of his salvific work in submitting them lovingly to the design of the Father, the Christian must, with all his life respond to the divine initiative. This response to the gift or grace of God is Christian morality, as demanding as the natural morality, since it crossconnects its elements, nevertheless no longer anxious, because it does not lean on poor human efforts, always limited and always fallible, but on the initial and permanent gift of divine grace. A morality of hope. . . .

One can guess the key-role that Eucharistic grace, defined, as we have just shown, as the "grace of insertion into the mystery of the pilgrim Church," is going to play in this human response to the new Covenant. For the Eucharist, in the sign of transformed bread, offers to the faithful, in all its realism, the foundation, the keystone of Christian dynamism. If, in fact, this latter consists in passing more and more into the risen Christ, here Christ is offered really (although sacramentally), precisely in his glorious body, the bearer of all the communional gifts in which is realized in all its fullness the supreme gift of the Father, and in order to transform the communicant into it. This one will no longer search to be united with an exterior reality (as the beatifying object of natural morality): he will tend on the contrary to penetrate further into a mystery which he is already. Therefore, he will be sanctified essentially as one already participating the communion of Life with the Father and with his brothers in the Lord Jesus, as already a member of the Church. To this depth, personal effort in holiness and ecclesial hope meet. In granting us to communicate with the goods of the *Kurios*, in all their truth and realism, the Eucharist ceaselessly revives the point of origin of all Christian moral effort and on the other hand sets this point in its ecclesial framework.

And, since it is a question of a "morality" of Covenant, the daily effort of the faithful becomes a simple response, generous and free, a simple cooperation with the call of the Lord asking his Church to transform our world into a world of resurrection: this call, according to his pedagogy, in Salvation history, God addresses through the salvific event, the marvelous intervention of his *hesed we emet* (mercy and faithfulness *) which is for the Church Pilgrim the Eucharistic celebration. For God reveals his designs, in posing acts, the dynamism of whom orients man towards a future which will not be realized without the faithful collaboration of the first beneficiary.

The Christian finds himself then, through the Eucharist, more lively associated with the effort of the pilgrim Church toward the realization of God's eschatological design for it. Sanctity which it draws from the Lord's Table is nothing like a closed, egocentric sanctity, and Eucharistic grace is in the strict sense a grace of the "communion of the saints," in the richest sense of the traditional expression.[53] Not simply a "communion with holy things" (this sense has always been secondary and has come to the fore only relatively lately), but especially a "community of destiny with all the saints," those of past generations who, since Abraham, have made living Tradition, those who, in our days, leaning on this deposit received from the past, assure the presence of the Church in the contemporary world, those who, in the future, will carry on till the Parousia.[54]

Onto this community of destiny is grafted a community of mission, for the Covenant, whether it be a question of the Old or the New, always implies mission.[55] For inserted further into

---

53. This point has been very finely studied by J.N.D. Kelly, *Early Christian Creeds*, London, 1952, pp. 388-397. See J.P. Kirsch, *Die Lehre von des Gemeinschaft der Heiligen im Christlichen Altertum*, Mayence, 1900; H.B. Swete, *The Holy Catholic Church, the Communion of Saints*, London, 1916, pp. 145-262 (which remains a classic study); J. M. R. Tillard, *La Communion des Saints*, Vie Spir., 1965, pp. 249-274.

54. We borrow from J.N.D. Kelly, *op. cit.*, p. 391 and from H.B. Swete, *op. cit.*, p. 160, this text of Nicetas: "What is the Church if not the assembly of all the saints? Since the beginning of the world, the patriarchs, the prophets, the apostles, the martyrs, all the other righteous who have lived or who live now or will live, are united in the Church since they have been sanctified by one faith and one mode of living and marked with a seal by the one Spirit, and thus made one sole Body of which Christ is the Head, as the Scripture says . . . . You believe that in this Church you shall participate in the communion of saints, know that this one catholic Church is implanted throughout the whole world and that it is your duty to attach yourself firmly to its communion." We think that Nicetas of Remesiana Bishop of Dacia (toward the end of the IVth century, beginning of the Vth century) would be the first serious witness of the presence of the clause relative to the "communion of saints" in the Credo (Kelly, *op. cit.*, pp. 388-389).

55. On this point see E. Jacob, *Théologie de l'Ancien Testament*, Neuchâtel-Paris, 1955, pp. 176-181; Y. Raguin, *Théologie missionnaire de L'Ancien Testament*, Paris, 1947; R. Martin-Achard, *Israël et les nations*, Neuchâtel-Paris, 1959; A. Gelin, *L'idée missionnaire dans la Bible*, in *Ami du Clergé*, 1956, pp. 411-418; *L'âme d'Israël dans le Livre*, Paris. 1957 pp. 84-96.

the "communion," at this pilgrim stage of the Church of God, the faithful must enter generously into the realization of the mission of the Church in this world. Mission of personal sanctity of its members, certainly. But also mission of expansion. To each "generation of the baptized" God confides the task of announcing the Good News of Salvation to "the whole contemporary generation." Then the adult confirmed Christian finds in the partaking of the Eucharistic bread the food of his vocation of witness to Christ in union with all his brothers. And let us recall that this partaking of the sacramental body of Jesus takes place at the end of the sacrificial movement, in which, with the whole Church, he offered to the Father the sacrifice of all humanity, therefore, of all men and of all times.

In the event of the Parousia the grace of the Eucharist of the earth will flourish marvelously in all men; they will arise. But this resurrection will follow the great law which ruled the sacramental economy. Men will not arise one after the other, they will surge from the earth "ecclesially." In the strict sense, the whole Church will pass from the pilgrim state to the state of glory, and, in it, the members. The elect of the first generations of the Church, pioneers of the penetration of the Gospel of Salvation into the world, will enjoy the fruit of their fidelity only in the instant when their brothers of the latter centuries will also enjoy it. For in this glory it will be less a question of individual fidelity than of the fidelity of the whole Body of Christ. As the Eucharist had nourished and deepened the ecclesial hope, it will find its ultimate fruit in an ecclesial resurrection. As it had nourished and strengthened ecclesial love, it will realize its final effect in an ecclesial communion of all to the good of each and of each to the good of all. From the *res tantum** of the Eucharist to the eschatological Church, there is only then the passage from the semi-obscure to full light, from the economy of the faith to that of the vision, from the *"arrhes"** to the totality of the heritage. The second moment of the Pasch of the Church into the Kingdom is already accomplished (but under the veil of faith) in each true celebration of the memorial of the Supper of the Lord.

Eucharistic Grace and Baptismal Grace

One will wonder perhaps if, in this insistence on the Eucharist, we are not minimizing to the extreme the role of Baptismal grace. For the effect of baptism must be prolonged throughout life.[56] It also admits two moments, lived in the two moments of the Pasch of Christ, and which remain as the two great pulsations of the new life in the justified, making him live his Christian experience literally in the death and resurrection of Jesus.

This initial act, in fact, puts into the Christian (as the initial act of physical life in the newborn) all the dynamism leading him to the glory of the Parousia. And, from this inaugural instant, this dynamism has its two moments, which will remain inseparable as long as the faithful will find himself in the pilgrim stage of the Church: a moment of death in Jesus the servant of Yahweh, a moment of projection into Jesus the Lord. The first will be completed in the physical death of the Christian and what follows it, the second will run out into the bursting light of the final resurrection. From the baptismal event till the day of the Parousia Baptism will remain thereby for the faithful a present deed.

It goes the same for the grace of chrism. It operates in the baptized a passage from the new Life to the adult age, and by that turns him toward others as a "witness" of Christ, actively engaged in the ecclesial work of the Salvation of the world. And this effect lasts also till death, given "once for all" in this sacrament which, like baptism, cannot be repeated, which implies a real perennity of its influence. Moreover, how could a life admit backward steps? Once attained, the adult age cannot vanish: each vital stage is definitive.

Does not the Eucharist, presented in perspectives that we have developed here, take the place of these two sacraments? Does not its perfection and its amplitude of field erase

---

56. We permit ourselves to refer again to a quick study that we have made on this point, *Le baptême, entrée dans la mort-résurrection de Jésus,* in *Liturgie et Vie chrétienne,* 1962, pp. 113-120.

their own efficacity? No. Let us remark first how much it is necessary to avoid contrasting radically between the diverse sacramental graces, especially when it is a question of Christian initiation. This, in fact, forms a homogeneous whole dominated by three characterized summits, but at the base cross-connections are operative. The proof of that is the delicate historical problem of the appearance of chrismation as a rite dissociated from baptism. But that does not suffice to answer the question.

In a splendid article of the *Summa theologica* (III, 73, 3), Saint Thomas furnishes us with the principle of solution. In fact, all sacramental grace comes from the Eucharist because of the very facts that we have explained up to here.

But one can perceive in two ways the *res* of a sacrament: in effectively receiving it, in desiring it with a true desire. In each sacrament is found objectively inscribed, by the very nature of the sacramental organism, an avowal, a desire for the Eucharist. Saint Thomas can write in a categorical fashion "no one has grace before having received, at least in desire, this sacrament" (III, 79, 1, ad 1).

He explains himself. In his pedagogy towards man, God models the gift of new Life on the initial and fundamental gift of natural life: not only does the "supernature" far from destroying nature, perfect it but it is founded on it and often uses its laws. The mystery of life, as humans experience it, follows a certain evolution: the living being receives life in the initial event of his birth, then it increases with him and leads him to the adult stage. But the maintenance of life quite as well as its increase demands food without which the living being perishes, wastes away, dies. In all this evolution it is the question of only one life. It goes like this for supernatural life. The Christian is born in the baptismal event, arrives at his adult status by the growth in him of chrismal grace, and is nourished by the Eucharist. This reveals to us a primary relation between the Eucharist and the two other sacraments of initiation: it maintains and prolongs their effect, assures the permanence of their grace in the way in which food conserves life.

It happens here that, by its mysterical content, the food not only bears within itself a power capable of acting on this life, but that it is in fact the fullness of the new Life, its source itself, since under the species of consecrated bread is truly found Jesus the Lord, the unique principle of the grace, the Head of the whole Body. The baptismal bath and the chrismal unction depended then, in their very efficacy, on the content of the Eucharist. On the other hand, since they are instituted to lead the faithful to the most perfect identification possible with Jesus Christ, these rites are ordained to the "consumation," and the "maximal communion" which alone can permit the sacramental eating of this food which (and here the analogy with natural life becomes sterile), instead of being transformed into the substance of him who receives it, changes little by little this one into its own content (III, 73, 3, ad, 2, citing Augustine, *Confess.*, 7, 10). In his love, God preserves and develops the new Life by plunging it into the Principle which possesses it in fullness, and putting it in real contact with the efficient capacity of the end to which (by its very nature) it tends to be assimilated. Therefore, we must say that in each sacrament, in the deepest area which renders account of its nature and its finality, exists an objective orientation toward the Eucharist. And we can immediately emphasize that when *Mater Ecclesia*, in whom the intention of Christ is realized, gives birth, in the water and the Spirit, and the breath of new Life to a new member of Christ, it wants him to arrive one day at the Lord's meal in which this life will be deepened and will find its fullness. It is even in function of this desire, "in this desire," that it engendres. For God plants the seed of Life only to see it blossom and attain maturity; in this supernatural creation as in the natural creation his intention is never minimal. By this objective *votum*, if not always of the faithful, at least always of Mother Church, the *res* of the Eucharist already reaches the faithful and makes him live: "No one has grace before having received this sacrament, at least in a certain desire, whether it be a question of personal desire, as in the case of an adult or of the desire of

the Church as it happens for little children" (III, 79, 1, ad 1).
It will be possible (as in certain Churches, not possessing
a perfect Eucharist) that this life will remain there, lack
real contact with the risen body of the Lord; however, in this
minimum, the Eucharist will already have acted, in reason of
the objective orientation towards it of the baptismal rite. One
guesses the importance of this point for a theology of ecumenism:
already all the baptized find themselves, after a certain fashion,
united (by the "truth" of their baptism) in the bread of unity,
of pardon, and of hope. In short, not only does the Eucharist
render more vivacious and more profound the effect of the
two other sacraments of initiation, but it is already operative in
their celebration: they can produce their proper grace only by
reference to it.

Must we conclude that the proper effect of the Eucharist is
to be confounded with theirs? Certainly not. Here again, it is
necessary to return to the principle of sacramental theology that
we have ceaselessly put to work up to here: the signification of
the rite reveals to us its efficacy since *"efficit hoc quod figurat."*

The baptismal bath, by the symbolism of the water as
assumed by Scripture, signifies the plunge into death to sin and
the return to the light of Life. It regenerates. Therefore, the
proper modality of its grace is that of the newness of Life
blossomed from the paschal work of Jesus. For eternity, the
new Life of the baptized will remain precisely new (with all
the pregnancy of this term in soteriology) and new in reason
of the event by which the son of the first Adam, a
sinner, has been transformed into a member of Christ and, by
that, into an adopted son of the Father. The Eucharistic eating
itself demands this prior event: the Church offers it only to
those who already live by Christ, born anew in water and the
Holy Spirit. In fact, as we have shown, because it is the meal
of the Lord, it presupposes as already constituted the "family
of the Lord." But it tightens progressively the bonds of love
in this family and enflames their hope. That does not render
the baptismal effect useless or bypassed since the members
of this family receive thereby *hic et nunc* their reality as members

of Christ." Then, when the proper modality of the baptismal grace makes the Christian reborn as a member of Christ, the Eucharist enroots him further and deepens his union to the Lord and to his brothers which results from it. We grasp the nuance.[57]

Confirmation arms the baptized for an adult life as a witness of the Gospel of Salvation, whether this witnessing be made through his word, his engagement in human structures, or the simple example of his action in conformity to the demands of the Gospel. It infuses in him the power necessary for an act of opening to others, of missionary radiation of Salvation upheld by love in the line of the "public ministry" of Jesus during the earthly stage of his Mystery.[58] The Eucharist, by the eating of the glorious body, intensifies hope and on the other hand the insertion into the tension of the pilgrim Church, without which the Christian apostolate loses its glow. It situates then the proper effect of the chrism in its ecclesial milieu, brings to it the mold in which it must normally take its shape; and all this without dissolving it as a too violent light might absorb a weaker one; in other words, without taking away from it that which is characteristic of it. It does not confer on the faithful the grace and the power of apostolic engagement; it presupposes them. But, because of all that it produces in the subject it assures them of being rooted in an authentically ecclesial "Christian being," authentically traversed by the dynamism which pushes the mystical Body of Christ toward the dimensions which the Father, in his design, willed that it attain.

How, in finishing this chapter, can we neglect to cite the great text of the Epistle to the Ephesians where Saint Paul evokes in grandiose terms this Mystery of the Salvation of the Church of which the Eucharist has just appeared to us as the Sacrament:

Blessed be that God, that Father of our Lord Jesus Christ,

---

57. See III, 73, 3, ad 3.

58. We follow here the reasoning of L.S. Thornton, *Confirmation, its Place in the Baptismal Mystery*, Westminster, 1954.

who has blessed us, in Christ, with every spiritual blessing, higher than heaven itself.

"He has chosen us out, in Christ, before the foundation of the world, to be saints, to be blameless in his sight, for love of him; marking us out beforehand (so his will decreed) to be his adopted children through Jesus Christ.

"Thus he would manifest splendor of that grace by which he has taken us into his favor in the person of his beloved Son.

"It is in him and through his blood that we enjoy redemption, for forgiveness of our sins. So rich is God's grace, that it has overflowed upon us in a full stream of wisdom and discernment, to make known to us the hidden purpose of his will. It was his living design, centered in Christ, to give history its fulfillment by resuming everything in him, all that is in heaven, all that is on earth, summed up in him.

"In him it was our lot to be called, singled out beforehand to suit his purpose (for it is he who is at work everywhere, carrying out the designs of his will); we were to manifest his glory, we who were the first to set our hope in Christ;

"In him you too were called, when you listened to the preaching of the truth that gospel which is your salvation. In him you too learned to believe, and had the seal set on your faith by the promised gift of the Holy Spirit; a pledge of the inheritance which is ours, to redeem it for us and bring us into possession of it, and so manifest God's glory (Eph. 1, 3-14)."

All that we have said can be easily situated on this vast horizon. That the Eucharist have its place there, is it not the sign *par excellence* of the primordial role which it plays in the Salvation of the Church?

CONCLUSION

We have questioned Scripture and the living tradition of the Church, asking them to teach us what relation they see between the celebration of the Lord's Meal and the Mystery of the Church of God. They have revealed to us the closeness of this bond, to the point that the Eucharist appeared to us as the sacramental sign of the qualitative growth, of the continual renewal, of the forward march of the ecclesial Body of the Lord.

The conclusion which is imposed no longer has anything new for us, and already we have outlined it in the course of this study. If the *res tantum*,* the ultimate effect of the Eucharist, is, according to purest tradition, the unity of the mystical Body (*unitas Corporis mystici*), it is not possible, however, to isolate the Church so constituted from all its existential content. The Eucharist which, like all the sacraments, belongs to the economy of the faith, perfects the Church Pilgrim in all the complexity of its situation, which is essentially a situation of Salvation. For this Church "of the faith" bears already in it the eschatological gifts of the glorious Church; it has already set foot on the shore of the promised Land. And, however, it still belongs to this world of sin. Like a People in exodus it marches, often heavily, often with backward movements, often exhausted with fatigue, towards the marvelous end of the Parousia, sure of arriving there (since the Word of God has promised it and in the Lord * Jesus it has already begun to be) but, also, conscious of its poverty. A People already saved, and yet to be saved: there is the paradox of the Church in its pilgrim stage, and there is the precise point where the grace of the Eucharist comes to be effective.

For this sacrament does not perfect the Church in giving it its members. It presupposes an assembly, able to offer to the Father, in truth, the paschal sacrifice of the Son in a movement of blessing and of praise for all the divine goods which it experiences already. But, from this community of Life, it will progressively erase sin (source of disunion, therefore, of properly ecclesial disintegration) in plunging each of its participants into all the realism of the redemptive death of Jesus, which will eliminate the attachment to the world of the old Adam and will lighten the mounting of the whole organism toward the Parousia. Besides, it will permit the entire assembly to partake fraternally of the glorious body of the Lord, the bearer of the totality of the Parousial gifts, and thus will accent the entrance into the eschatological world of glory. In each Eucharist, the Church frees one stage of its Pasch. It is snatched a little more from slavery and passes a little more into the gifts of the Promise.

The Eucharist then assures the increase of the Church, more qualitatively than quantitatively, more dynamically than statically. In the earthly Church it makes the Church of glory transpire more and more. From the first communion to the last *viaticum* it develops the seed of new life, deposed in each Christian by Baptism, till the ultimate point of maturation, so that after the long winter of the corporal death it will flourish marvelously with all the others in the radiant morning of the Parousia.

"Now how it is that we are in Him through the sacrament of the flesh and blood bestowed upon us, He Himself testifies, saying, And the world will no longer see Me, but ye shall see Me; because I live ye shall live also; because I am in My Father, and ye in Me, and I in you. If He wished to indicate a mere unity of will, why did He set forth a kind of gradation and sequence in the completion of the unity, unless it were that, since He was in the Father through the nature of Deity, and we on the contrary in Him through His birth in the body, He would have us believe that He is in us through the mystery of the sacraments? And thus there might be taught a perfect unity through a Mediator, whilst, we abiding in Him, He abode in the Father, and as abiding in the Father abode also in us; and so we might arrive at unity with the Father, since in Him who dwells naturally (*naturaliter*) in the Father by birth, we also dwell naturally, while He Himself abides naturally in us also. Again, how natural this unity is in us He has Himself testified on this wise—He who eateth My flesh and drinketh My blood abideth in Me, and I in him. For no man shall dwell in Him, save him in whom He dwells Himself, for the only flesh which He has taken to Himself is the flesh of those who have taken His. Now He had already taught before the sacrament of this perfect unity, saying, As the living Father sent Me, and I live through the Father, so he that eateth My flesh shall himself also live through Me" (Hilary of Poitiers, *De Trin.*, 8, 15-16; *NPN*, 2nd series, vol. ix, pp. 141-142).

AGAPE. This term, in fact untranslatable, is the simple transcription of the Greek word *agape* (the verb *agapan* often translates the Hebrew *ahab*). We have sometimes translated it here by love, but we must emphasize how much precision this translation lacks. For *agape* designates divine love, charity in all its dimensions: the love that God manifests with regard to man, but also the love that man must exercise toward God and toward his brothers. On God's side it is a question of a radically free love, not motivated by any exterior reason, prevenient, generous, exceeding itself in mercy and faithfulness (see these words). The best definition of this term is found in I John 4, 7-10; see also Rom. 5, 7-8; 8, 32.

ANAMNESIS. The Liturgical term designating the prayer in which the Church commemorates her Lord and his redemptive acts.

ANAPHORA. A term of liturgical language, the transcription of the Greek *anaphora* which designates the action of bearing on high or of offering the sacrifice. It is used especially to designate the liturgical text which accompanies and expresses this offering of the sacrifice of the Church to the Father. The anaphora is therefore the essential portion of the Eucharistic Liturgy.

ANAW and ANAWIM. See Poor, Suffering Servant, *Ebed.*

ARRHES. This translates the Greek *arrabon.* In this current language the word designates the sum given as a guarantee in the market, the portion received now of a whole which will be given later (for the Biblical usage see Gen. 38, 17-20). But Paul gives this term a very rich theological sense: by Baptism the faithful receives the active and transforming presence of the Holy Spirit who is already acting in him by depositing in him the token, the *arrhes,* of the plenary and definitive transformation which will attain its perfection only at the day of the Parousia (see this word) of the Lord. See II Cor. 1, 18-22; Eph. 1, 14. Sometimes in the same sense, Paul uses the word first-fruits (from the Greek *aparche*); thus Rom. 8, 23.

BACHAR. See Election.

BERIT. See Covenant.

BREATH. See Spirit.

COMMUNION. Thus we translate the Greek *koinonía.* We are concerned here with one of the key words of the theology of the Church, of Salvation, and of grace. By the Covenant (see this word), and especially by the New Covenant concluded "in the Lord Jesus," God enters into communion with man. We are concerned with a communio in love, in *agape* (see this word), but one which ends up in a sharing of the same life. "In the Lord Jesus" men commune with the gifts of the Father (vertical communion), but they commune also among themselves in the sharing of the same grace which comes from the same Breath of Life (see this word) (horizontal communion). The fruit of this communion is the Church.

COVENANT. Translation of the Hebrew *berit,* and of the Greek *diathéke.* For the execution of his plan of Salvation, God made Covenant with Israel; in Jesus he concluded the new and definitive Covenant. The Covenant is a pact which creates a bond between the two contractors. God takes the initiative in great liberality, and it is the fundamental gift which he makes to his People. God is engaged in a certain way by the Promises which are completely oriented toward a marvelous future; the People are engaged in observing certain clauses of the whole Law. The history of the People will be the history of this Covenant which is led on God's part by mercy and faithfulness (see these words), and on man's part by obedience to the demands of Yahweh. The most frequent Greek translation of the Hebrew term, *diathéke* (testament) in place of *synthéke* (treaty), emphasizes magnificently the absolute priority of the divine initiative. In the risen Jesus, the bond of communion (see this word) between the Father and men attains a fullness and a depth where bursts the transcendence of the *agape* (see this word) of God. See Ex. 24, 1-11; Deut. 26, 16-19; Jer. 31, 31-34; Heb. 8, 6-13.

DIATHEKE. See Covenant.

DWELL. We translate thus the Greek verb *menein.* It signifies stable and permanent residence in a lasting place. In Biblical language it becomes a key expression to translate at once the lasting quality of God and his works, and the experience of grace. It is in this latter sense that we use it here. The Christian dwells in Jesus and thereby in the Father; here is where henceforth his life will unfold in a stable fashion and in a state of communion (see this word) with the Father.

EBED. See Suffering Servant.

ECCLESIAL BODY OF CHRIST. By this expression we designate what is currently called the mystical Body of Christ. We know that the word mystical is not from Paul and that the expression Mystical Body first referred to the Eucharistic Body of Jesus and expanded (after the XIIth century) to take the significance which is now current; to say the Mystical Body is to say the Church. In this work Ecclesial Body always signifies the Church, in order to distinguish from the natural body of Jesus and his Eucharistic Body.

ELECTION. Translates the Hebrew *bachar*. A fundamental notion is in question here, one which is radically inseparable from that of Covenant (see this word). Election designates the absolutely gratuitous and free choice that God made of Salvation for the People (Deut. 7, 6-8; Ez. 16, 1-63). Rooted simply in *agape* (see this word), it is sealed in Covenant (Deut. 7, 9) and makes the People the People of God. The Church is in Jesus the Elect People of God. The Greek Bible translates this by *ekloge* (election) and *eklegesthai* (elect).

ELEVATION. In Greek the corresponding verb is *upsoun*. We use it here in the Johannine sense where the elevation of Jesus designates at once his elevation above the earth on the cross and his exaltation to the right hand of the Father. See John 3, 14; 8, 28; 12, 32, 34. The acts of the Apostles uses this verb only in the sense of exalt or glorify (Acts 2, 33; 5, 31).

'EMET. See Faithfulness.

EPICLESIS. Term of the liturgical vocabulary (from the Greek *epiklesis*, invocation), designating an invocation beseeching the descent of the Holy Spirit on the bread and wine that he transform them into the body and blood of Christ, and also that they produce their effects in the participants in the Eucharist.

ESCHATOLOGICAL. From the Greek eschaton the last thing, the end. This term concerns all that relates to the final ages of Salvation History (see this word), to the end toward which it marches and which finalizes it in giving it its meaning.

EULOGIA. Term in liturgical language, benediction. The span of uses of this word is rather broad. It seems that it designated primitively the breads offered by the faithful and which had not been consecrated (they are not the body of Christ, however, they are a holy thing; it is no longer ordinary bread, Augustine says of them). From there, especially at Alexandria and under the influence of I Cor. 10, 16, *Eulogia* comes to designate the consecrated bread: it is in this restrained sense that we use the term here. Then its use grows to designate the gifts which they take or drink, indeed all blessed objects.

EXPIATION. We render by this word the Hebrew *kipper*, atonement, sacrifice of expiation. See Lev. 16, 1-34. The People is pardoned in a state of Covenant by the annual bloody sacrifice in which it asks and obtains remission of its sins. To expiate (*kipper*), is to destroy one's sin in order to render oneself pleasing to God, to obtain his efficacious pardon. The Greek translates by *hilaskesthai*. Jesus accomplished expiation by a single sacrifice, offered "once for all." See Heb. 9, 6-14, 24-28.

FAITHFULNESS. Thus we translate the Hebrew *'emet* which the Greek often renders by *aletheia*. Bound to *hesed* (mercy; see this word) *'emet* is the proper characteristic of the God of the Covenant (see this word). It evokes the essential solidity of a being, which allows one to trust in it and be sure of it. God is solid (true) in his words and in his promises — he doesn't lie; we can rely on him in all confidence and find in him all security. He is the "rock of Israel" (Deut. 32, 4).

FIRST-FRUITS. See *Arrhes*.

FORM. To translate *morphe*. See Image.

HEILSGESCHICHTE. See Salvation History.

HESED. See Mercy.

IMAGE. Translates the Greek *eikon*, which itself is used to translate the Hebrew terms *selem* (which designates the very concrete representation of reality, a status) and *demut* (which designates a ressemblance in a more abstract fashion) (see Gen. 1, 26-27; 5, 1, 3; 9, 6). *Eikon* is oriented especially toward the sense of a simple copy and implies a reproductive force, a derivation. Another Greek word, *morphe* (which we have translated by form) underlines the value of participation in remaking the image according to the model.

KIPPER. See Expiation.

KOINONIA. See Communion.

KURIOS. See Lord.

LOGOS. Greek translation of the Hebrew *debar* which designates the word. We use it here in the sense of *debar* Yahweh, *logos tou Theou*, Word of God. The Word of God is at once revealing and dynamic in Biblical thought; it reveals through action — what it reveals it does. We would distinguish the more charismatic word; the words (*debarim*) of the Law, and — with the New Testament — the Person of the Word (Word) of God. The words of the Liturgy, eminently those which are integrated into the sacramental sign itself, are the words of God. This explains their efficacy.

LORD. Current translation of the Greek *Kurios*, answering to the Hebrew *Adonai*. We are concerned here with a divine name which has become a proper name for God, replacing even the name Yahweh in liturgical reading (at least from the first century before Jesus). It evokes the absolute sovereignty of God, his universal dominion, his "lordship." In his Resurrection Jesus is made Lord (Rom. 10, 9; I Cor. 12, 3; Phil. 2, 11; Acts 2, 36; etc.). His divinity bursts then, and in response to his obedience and his humiliation as the Servant (see this word), the Father gives him universal sovereignty over the Church, all mankind, indeed over the whole universe.

LOVE. See *Agape, Hesed,* Mercy.

MARANATHA. This is the liturgical cry which comes from the two Aramaic words which we can group in two ways: either *maron atha* (the Lord comes), or *marana tha* (come, Lord!). It is the cry of hope for the return of the Lord at the Parousia (see this word). One either proclaims the imminence of this event or beseeches the Lord to hasten his return. See I Cor. 16, 22; Apoc. 22, 20.

MEMORIAL. Thus we translate the Hebrew *zikkaron* which the Greek translates by *anamnesis.* The Memorial is a recalling, a remembrance, in all the aspects of the two terms. One either thinks about a reality of the past, or relives in his own spirit certain obligations or certain situations which demand that he assume a certain attitude, or remembers something in favor of someone or against someone, or recalls something to someone. Here we use the term in its liturgical sense. The liturgical memorial is an act of worship in which we recall an event of Salvation in the past but relive *hic et nunc* its grace in thanksgiving and blessing. It revives hope in the definitive completion of this Salvation at the very moment when we recall to God his Promise by beseeching him to execute it. The most typical case of this is the Passover Meal of the Old Covenant.

MERCY. We have chosen this very imperfect translation of the Hebrew term *hesed* because of the Greek term *eleos* by which it is most often rendered in the LXX and in the New Testament. But *hesed* says much more than mercy, as current language understands it. It designates the fundamental attitude of the God of the Covenant (see this word), especially in connection with '*emet* (faithfulness; see this word). It concerns the mutual attachment between two persons whom a special bond of relationship, of love, of justice, unites. It implies a duty of love, a faithfulness in this love, a permanence, a certain compassion for the other, an inclination to pardon him ceaselessly. Very often it should be translated by goodness or by conscious goodness expressed by acts; for one does not feel *hesed* one makes *hesed.*" See Ps. 103, 8-12; Ps. 136.

ONLY-BEGOTTEN. From the Greek *monogenes,* only. It is a Johannine expression to designate the transcendence of the sonship of Jesus: he is the only Son of the Father (John 1, 14, 18; 3, 16, 18; I John 4, 9).

PARACLETE. From the Greek *parakletos,* he who is called to the aid of another in order to counsel him, to stand him up, to defend him, to succor him; therefore, a defense advocate. It is a Johannine term to designate both Jesus (I Jean 2, 1; John 14, 16) and the Person of the

Holy Spirit. But living Tradition has reserved it to characterize the Holy Spirit; it is this use which we find in the liturgical texts mentioned in this work.

PAROUSIA. From the Greek *parousia,* presence, coming. The profane use designates the official visit of the king. In Christian language the Parousia is the glorious return of Christ the Lord (see this word) at the end of time, in the great Day of the Son of man. It is toward this end that all Salvation History (see this expression) marches.

PEOPLE. Thus we translate the Hebrew *qahal;* in Greek, *ekklesia.* We must not confuse it with *'am;* in Greek, *laos.* For the *qahal* designates very precisely the assembly convoked by the Word of God. The *qahal* Yahweh is, at the time of the Exodus, the community of the desert (Deut. 23, 1-9; 31, 30) in its assembly. Then after the Exile, the worshipping assembly gathered around the Temple (Neh. 8, 2). The *qahal* announces and prepares for the *Ekklesia* of all who will hear the call of the Father in Jesus and will gather around him, indeed "in him", in a communion (see this word). Thus he will make them the definitive Holy People.

PNEUMA. See Spirit.

POOR. Translates the Hebrew plural *anawim* (*anaw,* singular). The term designates originally the indigent, the afflicted. But, on the basis of this experience of poverty, it comes around to expressing one of the fundamental dispositions of the soul of the believer. The poor one is he who, in humility, patience, sweetness, lives in a state of transparentness before the will of God, of openness and abandon to God, of reserve for God and for other men.

QAHAL. See People.

RES TANTUM, RES ET SACRAMENTUM. Technical expressions of Scholastic terminology to designate the levels of depth of the sacramental action. In each sacrament we distinguish: a) the *sacramentum tantum*: this is the exterior sign, the visible rite accomplished by the Church which symbolizes the work which God wants to accomplish by it (thus the ablution for Baptism, the meal for the Eucharist, the imposition of hands for Orders). It contains at once words (called *form*), and a gesture with some matter or a step by the faithful in order to exteriorize his interior attitude (*matter*); b) the *res et sacramentum*: the intermediary reality produced by the *sacramentum tantum,* but which is not ultimate because it is ordained to a deeper effect (the Baptismal character); c) the *res tantum*: this is the spiritual and saving reality produced by the sacrament: grace.

RUAH. See Spirit.

SACRAMENTUM TANTUM. See *Res tantum.*

SALVATION. Thus we translate the Greek *soteria,* which is used in the New Testament to express the intervention of God by which he snatches man out of the clutch of sin and death in order to lead him into communion (see this word) with his own Life.

SALVATION HISTORY. Translation of the German expression *Heilsgeschichte.* It is a question of a story aimed at a specific end, of a progressive story whose diverse stages are not simply successive but also organically bound up among themselves: the ultimate stage "accomplishes," realizes in fullness, what the preceding stages were preparing for and announcing. The limit, the end, of it is Salvation (see this word).

SAVIOR. Fundamentally *soter* designates God (who saves us in Jesus; see Jud. 25), but more immediately Jesus, Christ and Lord, by whom is accomplished concretely the salvific plan of the Father (Luke 2, 11; John 4, 42; Acts 5, 31; 13, 23; Eph. 5, 23; II Pet. 1, 1, 11; I John 4; 14; etc.).

SOTER, SOTERIA. See Savior, Salvation.

SPIRIT. Thus we translate the Hebrew *ruah* and the Greek *pneuma.* In Biblical thought spirit appears essentially as the breath of life (see Gen. 6, 3; Job 34, 14-15; Ez. 37). It arrives at designating God's own Breath of Life, who, with the New Testament, reveals himself as a Divine Person. Jesus, glorified by his Pasch delivers this Spirit to men in order that he might create new life in them. See John 20, 22; Acts 2, 32-33.

SUFFERING SERVANT or SERVANT OF YAHWEH. We understand this as designating the prophetic figure realized in Jesus of the *Ebed Yahweh.* This figure dominates the Songs of the Servant which are inserted in the Book of Isaias (Is. 42, 1-9; 49, 1-6; 50, 4-11; 52, 13-53, 12). We are concerned here with one of the poor (see this word) whose martyrdom effects the justification of the many. The messianic hope of Israel will be expressed through this figure. Jesus, in his sorrowful death, accomplished in humble and total submission to the will of the Father, will be this poor Messias, the Suffering Servant.

TRUTH. See Faithfulness. This term often renders the Hebrew *'emet'.* However, the New Testament uses *aletheia,* which signifies truth. It is not a question of abstract truth which is purely speculative, but of the certainty of a person, of his authenticity (as when we say: "He is a true friend."). Each time the New Testament means the more Hellenistic sense of truth where it is conceived as a manifestation of reality, of the essence of a thing as it is.

ZIKKARON. See Memorial.

SHORT INDEX OF THE PRINCIPAL THEOLOGICAL NOTIONS

In order to guide the reader who is only slightly initiated into the language of theological reflection, we give here a short index of the principal theological notions to which we often refer, together with a brief analysis of the notion in question.

ACCOMPLISHMENT, REALIZATION. This term, when we use it in its theological sense, intends to signify that the mystery of Jesus, especially his Pasch (see this word), is by correspondence to all that preceded it the definitive realization of his announcements, of his promises. Jesus is truly "he who is to come" and he whose whole life is inscribed in the wake of the hope of the People of God. His work is not then a starting point, but a point of arrival, as the fruit is the point of arrival of the long process of germination, growth, flowering and finally maturation. In a marvelous little book (*According to the Scriptures*, London, 1961), C. H. Dodd has shown the profound sense of the expression "according to the Scriptures," which appears so often in the writings of the New Testament. In Jesus all Scriptures and all the History of Israel, of which Scripture is the expression, finally find their definitive realization. In this realization the hope of the People of the Covenant is culminated: the accomplishment surpasses all that one could expect. In the light of the event of the Pasch of Jesus, one can now reread Salvation History and there disclose the "approaches," the "preparations" for the Jesus-event.

ALEXANDRIAN and ANTIOCHAN SCHOOLS. These are the two great theological schools whose oppositions dominate the history of the first centuries of Christian thought in its Greek expression and which find their summit in the great dogmatic quarrels of the fourth and fifth centuries. But they are also those which, parallel with Latin tradition, bring to the evolution of theological reflection its most positive elements. One can characterize them thus:

a) *Alexandrian School*: It is born in a milieu already marked by the Judeo-Hellenistic theological tradition. Its philosophy is Platonic. In exegesis, it professes allegorism: under the literal sense of Scripture lies a more profound spiritual sense which alone is the true sense willed by God. The Old Testament is molded from prefigurations. In Christology, it tends to absorb all the humanity of Jesus into the divinity, to the point of taking from him his proper consistency; certain of its members will fall into Monophysitism (in Jesus there is a single nature, the divine nature) or Monotheletism (in Jesus there is only one will, the divine will, therefore no human liberty). Among its most celebrated members, let us cite Clement of Alexandria, Origin, Denys of Alexandria, Athanasius, Didymus the Blind, Cyril of Alexandria. The Cappadocian Fathers (Basil, Gregory

Nazianzen, Gregory of Nyssa) are in its orbit. Eutyches will also be Alexandrian.

b) *Antiochan School*: It is in opposition to the allegorical method as practiced at Alexandria. Its theology is founded on a literal and grammatical exegesis of Scripture. The mystery of Jesus is prepared for by all Scripture, and moreover, it is not always prefigured. In philosophy, Antioch undergoes the influence of Aristotle, which leads it to insist on the proper consistency of the natures. In Christology, Antiochan theology will tend to accentuate too much the duality of the natures in Jesus, and not to insist enough on the unbreakable personal unity of the incarnate Son; Nestorius is of this school. Among its more illustrious representatives, let us cite Lucian of Samosata (its founder), Arius, Diodorus of Tarsus, John Chrysostom, Theodore of Mopsuestia and Theodoret.

CHRISTIAN INITIATION. By this term Christian Tradition designates the original rite of Baptism — Confirmation (or Chrismation) — Eucharist, which is separated today in the Western Liturgies. Initiation is not to be taken here in its current sense of a "first introduction," of first contact with the rudiments of a science (as one speaks of an "initiation into philosophy or into Biblical archeology"). We must take it in the strong sense of admission to full participation in the Mystery of Christ. At the end of his Christian initiation, the faithful becomes an active and authentic member of the Church; he becomes perfectly capable of living fully the life of Christ in his rank in the ecclesial body (see this term in the lexicon).

We will be permitted to refer to our study: J. M. R. Tillard, *Principes pour une catéchèse sacramentaire vraie*, N. R. Théol., 1962, pp. 1048-1051.
CHURCH as "COMMUNION OF LIFE" and "MEANS OF SALVATION."
These are the two areas of the mystery of the Church. In its essential and eternal reality, it is "the communion of Life of all the believers with the Father and among themselves in Christ the Lord." God admits men into his friendship and infuses a new life into them. This new life blossoms in the risen Christ and renders them participants in a certain way in his own Mystery. We call this the life of sanctifying grace. The Church is, and will remain so for eternity, the *"societas sanctorum,"* the assembly of all those who bear in them this participation in the one divine life. And this fundamental communion opens up in the climate of ecclesial love (see this word) which we have already described.

But the Church is also a institution, the means of Salvation. This is its transitory aspect which will disappear at the moment when Salvation History has attained its end. Christ desired that it should be provided with powerful means which would render it capable of constructing itself as the "communion of Life;" it is a prophetic (or "magisterial") institution which continues to announce to men the Gospel of Salvation and to explain its content, a sacerdotal (or "sacramental") institution which can give to men the gifts of the Pasch (eminently by the Eucharist), a royal institution which can promulgate lawful regulations for its own life as a visible society, but always in view of the "communion of Life."

CONTRITION. We understand this word here in the very strong sense which Saint Thomas has given to it. It concerns an interior act of sadness in the face of committed sin. This sadness arises from love although we are still dwelling under the clutches of our sin. We can define it as a voluntary regret of the fault insofar as it has offended God: this regret inspires a firm promise never again to commit such a fault and a strong desire to make reparation for the past according to the decision of the Church's power of the keys. It is not inspired simply by the fear of pain, of the punishment incurred, or by shame which is the deception caused in the heart by the setback of sin. The fundamental work on this point remains H. Dondaine, *L'attrition suffisante*, Paris, 1943.

EASTERN AND WESTERN LITURGIES. The Christian Liturgy, which centers around the celebration of the Eucharist, is expressed differently according to the diverse mentalities, customs, temperaments, and religious aspirations of the peoples converted to the Gospel. From this has resulted a rather complex collection of liturgies wherein, under very different forms and expressions, a single and unique nucleus is found. This is a marvelous sign of both the unity and the catholicity of the Church. We still find a lucid exposition of the various liturgies in I. H. Dalmais *Les liturgies d'Orient*, Paris (Je sais, je crois), 1959. Here we give a brief table of the great liturgical families:

GROUP OF THE PATRIARCHATE OF ANTIOCH

(Syrian Group)

The Eastern Syrian Group.

Marked by the influence of the Church of Edessa. Rather closed milieu which escapes the influence of Antioch and conserves several Semitic traits of the exiled Jewish communities. Syrian language; passes into Nestorianism. Limited to the Tigris-Euphrates basin (Mesopotamia).

NESTORIAN RITE.

— Anaphora of the Apostles Adaeus and Maris (very ancient);

— Anaphora of Theodore of Mopsuestia (imported from Antioch but adapted);

— Anaphora of Nestorius (imported from Antioch, adapted).

CHALDEAN RITE.

— Adaptation of the Nestorian Liturgy after the return of the Chaldeans to Rome (conserves the traditional Anaphoras).

SYRO-MALABAR RITE.

Maladroit Latinization of the Nestorian Rite of the Church of Malabar by the Portuguese. Only remains the Anaphora of the Aposles Adaeus and Maris.

The Western Syrian Group.

Marked by the influence of Antioch, of Jerusalem, and later of Byzantium.

ARMENIAN RITE.

Synthesis of Syrian and Cappadocian elements. One single Anaphora, said to be of St. Athanasius, but an adaptation of the old Anaphora of St. Basil.

BYZANTINE RITE.

Composite rite which groups elements from Antioch, others from Cappadocia, and elaborated at Constantinople. Considerable influence from Jerusalem. Anaphora of St. Basil and Anaphora of St. John Chrysostom. Originally in Greek, but translated into Syrian, Slavonic, Arabic, Georgian, etc..

SYRIAN RITE OF ANTIOCH.

Greek by origin, then introduction of Syrian and Arabian. It is the rite of the Monophysite Jacobites, conserved by the Syrians of Antioch who are allied to Rome. Anaphora of St. James and seventy others, later.

MARONITE RITE.

Variant of the Syrian Rite of Antioch in the Churches of Libanus. Has only seven Anaphoras of which one is of old structure, said to be St. Peter Sarar.
Very Latinized.

Attached here:

RUTHENIAN RITE,

MELKITE RITE.

GROUP OF THE PATRIARCHATE OF ALEXANDRIA

(Egyptian Group)

THE COPTIC RITE.

Originally in Greek, at least at Alexandria and in Lower-Egypt, then in Copt.

In Greek, the Anaphora of St. Mark which, translated into Copt and adapted, becomes the Anaphora of St. Cyril (very long and difficult to sing).

Two Anaphoras of the Syrian type are also in use:

    The Anaphora of St. Basil,

    The Anaphora of St. Gregory.

THE ETHIOPIAN RITE.

Comes from the Coptic Liturgy, but many Syrian borrowings. Has seventeen Anaphoras.

The Roman Anaphora of Hippolytus is known and translated.

The Anaphora, said to be of our Lord, is a rearrangement of the Testament of our Lord, itself from Apostolic Tradition.

GROUP OF WESTERN LITURGIES

THE ROMAN RITE.

Liturgy of the city of Rome. originally in Greek, then in Latin. From Rome it gains Italy, then Ireland and Gaul (where it supplants the local Liturgies). Imposed on Spain in the XIth century. With a single Canon (Anaphora), but admits variants according to the solemnities, in the *Preface*, the *Communicantes*, the *Hanc Igitur*. Its origins are knows to us especially by the Saccramentaries:

Leonine (of Verona)
Old Galesian
(doesn't carry the Papal Liturgy, but that of a Roman presbyterial title of the middle of the VIIth century)

Gregorian (the Pope's Use)
In its expansion, has known several lines of evolution, rather autonomous even at Rome (in the various basilicas). There remain witnesses of these proper lines:

THE AMBROSIAN RITE.

Liturgy of the Roman type with many proper elements. A little different Canon from the Roman Canon.

THE RITE OF LYON.

THE RITE OF BRAGA.

THE DOMINICAN RITE.

THE CHARTREUSE RITE.

THE RITE OF THE PREMONTRES.

THE MOZARABIC RITE.

Liturgy of Spain organized in the Visigoth epoch. Strong Eastern influences. No fixed Canon, but a collection of moveable pieces grouped around the Narrative of the Institution:

Illatio (Preface)
Vere Sanctus (between the Sanctus and the Institution)
Post pridie (following the consecration)

Many prayers addressed directly to Christ. Influenced strongly the Gallican Liturgies. Is celebrated still in the Cathedral of Toledo and, three days each year, in the Cathedral of Salamanca.

THE GALLICAN RITES.

Were stifled by the reform of Charlemagne. Of like structure to that of the Mozarabic Liturgy, here again no fixed Canon. Strong Eastern influences.

Influenced on several points the Roman Liturgy since its expansion.

ECCLESIAL HOPE. For the New Testament, hope is not simply individual (each man's expectation of his own beatific vision); above all, it is ecclesial. Let us understand by that that it is the expectation of the definitive event of the Parousia in which God's plan will finally attain its end, and which will coincide with the entrance of the whole Church into the glory of the resurrection. The faithful works not only for the acquisition of his own personal salvation, but for the realization in the world of the mystery of the Church; and the end which enlivens his efforts is precisely this marvelous glorification of the whole ecclesial body (see this term in the lexicon) of the Lord at the glorious day of return of Christ.

ECCLESIAL LOVE. This expression, which we use here expressly is to be situated in the vast climate which we evoke in another part of this index under "Church as communion Life and means of Salvation." If the Church is a communion, it is so first on the level of love, in all the dimensions of the mystery of Christian love. First in its descendant dimension: in it, the *agape* (see this word in the lexicon) of the Father, manifested "in Jesus", meets men, and it is fundamentally in this divine love that they are united. Then in its ascendant dimension, and this time on two levels. On the vertical level, the faithful baptized "in the death of Jesus" must live on only for the Father under the efficacious motion of a love which trains them toward him. But this love for the Father stretches out in some way horizontally into a love of all our brothers, a fraternal love grafted on the very love of Jesus for all men in his Pasch. The encounter of these diverse dynamic lines of love is the Church. And this encounter is made "in Jesus;" he is the perfect gift of the love of the Father for men (John 3, 16), the perfect response of human love for the Father (John 6, 38), the perfect gift of fraternal love (John 15, 13).

ECONOMY OF THE FAITH. We designate by this expression the characteristic climate of the Church in its terrestrial stage. We said above (see Ecclesial love) that the Church was essentially a community of love. But love, conceived as a friendship, demands first (at least in logical priority) a certain knowledge, a certain reception of the friend: this reception is faith. And thus the whole Church is founded on faith in the two dimensions of theological faith. On the one hand, the Father is revealed in Jesus, and we possess the truth. But on the other hand, we do not possess it yet in evidence of the vision: we believe in what he told us by Jesus; we accept it on word. The terrestrial Church, the community of those who have "received the Word" and believed in God, lives then its experience essentially in faith and not yet in the clarity of the face-to-face vision. It is the Church of Faith.

EUCHARIST, SACRAMENT OF SACRIFICE. Catholic theology has often separated in a radical fashion in the Eucharist its "sacramental" and its "sacrificial" aspects (sacramental: real presence and communion with the body of Christ; sacrificial: the Mass). The renewal of sacramental theology has shown how this dichotomy has not been acceptable. See Dom Vonier, *La clef de la Doctrine eucharistique,* trans. Roguet, Paris, 1941. The Eucharist is situated entirely at the core of the sacramental universe. It is the sacrament of the sacrificial act of Christ. The communion with the consecrated bread has for its goal only to render us participants in the sacrifice of the Pasch of Jesus; the bread and wine are consecrated to render sacramentally present this paschal sacrifice.

ECCLESIAL TENSION. This is the expression of the quality proper to the expectation of the Church, relative to the end of Salvation History. The Church does not await the Parousia in a cold, resigned fashion. It waits in ardent desire, and that is because of its present experience of Salvation. For already it has the *arrhes* (see this word in the lexicon) of the future glory; it wants then ardently to see them be exceeded in the full, entire and definitive possession of the gifts of the Promise. This has been clarified by O. Cullmann, *Christ et le temps,* Neuchâtel-Paris, 1957.

GOD'S PLAN (THE PLAN OF THE FATHER, THE PLAN OF SALVATION). The great plan of God, which we have revealed in all its light in the Pasch of Jesus, is in fact the Salvation of all men in Christ Jesus. The central texts here are Eph. 1, 3-14; 3, 1-13; Col. 1, 24-29; Rom. 16, 25-27. Paul calls it the Mystery. The whole Christian concept of history is dominated by this faith in the great plan of Salvation, present from all eternity in the thought of the Father. Creation, and the history which it inaugurated, has its origins in the knowing and free act of love of a personal God. He wants to lead his creation into a sharing of his own glory, he wants to diffuse his goodness and his perfection. After sin this plan of God can be realized only by means of a Salvation of man in which will burst the power of divine love. This Salvation, realized historically in the event of the death and resurrection of Jesus, is announced and prepared for in the Old Covenant, and it is diffused into all humanity by the Church until the ultimate event of the Parousia. This will be the end of history, the precise point where the Father's Plan will have finally acquired its perfect realization. Then the Son will hand over the Kingdom to his Father (I Cor. 15, 23-28). And, says Paul, "this will be the end." The Church will be consumated in the perfect "communion of Life" with the Father, in Jesus.

LITURGICAL ASSEMBLY. The liturgical assembly is not a simple meeting of Christians. It is the gathering, around its president, of a community of the faithful to live an ecclesial act "in Christ." And by that it is as a sign, a manifestation, an "epiphany" of the Church, but always in a mysterious, sacramental fashion. In fact, he who convokes it and presides over it (the bishop in the ideal case or the priest in the second instance) is the bearer of a sacerdotal character which configures him, mysteriously but really, into Christ the Head of the Church. He is thus the sacramental presence of Christ himself. The faithful, by their Baptism, have become members of the ecclesial body of the Lord Jesus. Then, the gathering of the members around the Head expresses, in realizing it sacramentally, all the mystery of the Church. The liturgical assembly has moreover its power point in the common celebration of the Eucharist, the sacrament of the new Covenant which makes all men, by the blood of Christ, bearers of the same life from the Father in the one body of the Lord. This assembly can lift up to the Father, in the Lord Jesus and by the Lord Jesus, the great thanksgiving of the People of the redeemed at the very moment when it receives from the Father the gifts of Salvation. We will be able to read A. G. Martimort, *L'assemblée liturgique*, M. D., 20, 1949, pp. 153-175; *L'assemblée liturgique, mystère du Christ*, M. D., 40, 1954, pp. 5-29; *Précisions sur l'assemblée*, M. D., 60, 1959, pp. 7-34.

MEAL. The Eucharist is a meal. In the Bible, the meal is rich with a whole sacramental signification. It is, even in the simple human level, a sign and a factor of communion: invited by the benevolence of a unique host, the convivials share a unique food. Taken to the temple of a god, the sacred meal confirms or seals a unity between the god and the faithful (see Ex. 24, 11; Lev. 3, 1-17, a part of the victim is given to the divinity, the other is eaten by the offerers; it is the sacrifice of communion. The prophets use this experience to illustrate the hope of Israel: the final happiness to which God invites his People will be as a great festival meal, taken in his company (Is. 25, 6; 55, 1-3). Jesus announces that in him this hope is finally going to be realized (Mat. 8, 11; Luke 13, 28-29; 12, 37). It will be the great feast of the Kingdom (Luke 22, 14-18; Apoc. 3, 20).

MYSTERY. See God's Plan.

PASCH. By the expression Pasch of Christ, we designate here the Paschal Mystery of Jesus, his passage from this world to the world of the Father, realized historically by the events of his death and of his resurrection and ascension. This traditional designation recovers a theological foundation which is more than ample. The Pasch of Jesus, realized at the moment when the Jewish People celebrated the memorial (see this word in the lexicon) of its passage from the slavery of Egypt to the liberty of the Promised Land, accomplishes (see this word) what was only preparation and prefiguration of his own Mystery. In this passage he trains the whole Church after him.

PILGRIM (PEREGRINE) CHURCH and GLORIOUS CHURCH. We are concerned here with the two great stages of the Mystery of the Church. By Pilgrim (Peregrine) Church we mean the Church in its stage of progressive edification, of march forward, generation by generation, toward the final event of the Parousia. By Glorious Church we mean the Church finally arrived at its end: the general resurrection at the Day of the Son of man. Our distinction does not recover exactly then the more current distinction between the Church Militant (those whore are *hic et nunc* on earth) and the Church Triumphant (those who are already arrived in the house of the Father).

SACRAMENT, SIGN and CAUSE. This formula takes up all the complexity of the sacrament. St. Thomas sees it first and essentially as a sign, the sign of the sacred realities in an act *hic et nunc* in the faithful in order to sanctify him. But the elements, the gestures, the words which constitute the sacrament do not have simply this function of signification. Christ assumes them as instruments to cause this sanctification of the faithful. Then, they cause what they signify, and they signify what they cause.

SACRAMENTAL GRACE. From Christ the Head, filled with the fulness of grace (called capital grace), grace derives toward men in order to make them pass into Jesus and thus to introduce them into the communion of Life. This derivation is made (in the normal economy of things) by the mediation of the sacraments. Each of them assimilates the faithful to one of the aspects, one of the modalities of the fullness of the grace of Christ the Head in function of the situation of this Christian in the Church or of his degree of evolution in the new Life. The grace of Christ thus modalized, particularized, is what we call sacramental grace.

SACRAMENTARY. Among all the liturgical books, the sacramentary is the one which contains the parts of the sacramental celebration said or sung by the celebrant. When we speak of the "ancient Western sacramentaries" we are alluding to the *Leonine Sacramentary* (or that of *Verona*) to the *Gelasian Sacramentary* and to the *Gregorian Sacramentary*. They are, with the *Ordines Romani* (descriptions of the ceremonies), our most precious sources for the history of the origins of the Western Liturgy.

SACRAMENTS OF THE FAITH. The Sacraments are not magic rites; they are the radiation of faith. On the one hand, in all their richness of signification, they announce and reveal the very precise design of God on such an individual in the Church; and thus they provoke in the faithful a subjective response of faith. On the other hand, they will produce in him their effect of grace only if he opens himself to divine action in a free reception of the benevolence of the Father in Jesus, a reception which is essentially rooted in his faith. See J. M. R. Tillard, *Principes pour une catéchèse sacramentaire vraie*, N. R. Théol., 1962, pp. 1053-1061.

SPIRITUAL BODY. It is the human body of Jesus insofar as, in the mystery of his exaltation, he receives in him the power of the Holy Spirit (The *Pneuma tou Theou*) which transforms him. Let us recall here one of our major insistences. In his personal spiritual humanity, the Lord Jesus becomes the starting point of the new humanity, the new Adam. By Baptism, which is a second birth, entrance into a new universe (the universe of Salvation), the faithful receives from the new Adam, in the water and faith of *Mater Ecclesia*, the breath, the vital respiration, of this new humanity. He receives its gifts also. From the first Adam he received in his first birth the breath of natural life, which since sin ends up in death. The whole Christian mystery will be the progressive victory, by means of the active and generous collaboration of man, of the second Adam over the first, the whole ends up in the great ecclesial resurrection of the Parousia in which the Lord Jesus will deliver definitively to his Church his own body of glorious spiritual quality. Reread I Cor. 15, 21-22, 45-49; Rom. 5, 12-21.

TRANSUBSTANTIATION. This term, confirmed by the Council of Trent (Denz., 877, 884), designates the change according to which what was bread and wine becomes the body and blood of the Lord. It is a replacement of the first substance, in its totality (bread and wine), by another, in its totality. It is a unique and transcendent case of substantial change. The body of Christ is not displaced to come "under the appearances of bread;" the substance of the bread is changed into that of Christ. See J. De Bacciochi, *Présence eucharistique et transsubstantiation*, in *Irenikon*, 1959, pp. 139-160.

TYPOLOGY, TYPES. The historical realization of the plan of God (see this expression) is marked by the law of unity. God does not proceed by successive additions, but he begins by planting a seed which will blossom progressively. The events and the rites of the Old Covenant prepare for and already prefigure those of the New Covenant which will accomplish (see this word) them. We call types (from the Greek *tupos*, trace, figure) these realities of the Old Testament considered in their connection with those of the New Covenant. Typology is the science of the correspondences between the two Covenants. We should read on this point J. Coppens, *Les harmonies des deux Testaments*, Tournai, 1949; J. Danielou, *Bible et Liturgie*, Paris, 1951.